WOMEN AND POWER

WOMEN AND POWER

Rosalind Miles

Macdonald

For
Susan J. Fletcher
a woman of power

A Macdonald Book

Copyright © Rosalind Miles 1985

First published in Great Britain in 1985
by Macdonald & Co (Publishers) Ltd
London & Sydney

British Library Cataloguing in Publication Data

Miles, Rosalind
　Women and power.
　1. Women　2. Power (Social sciences)
　I. Title
　305.4′2　　　HQ1233

ISBN 0-356-10645-4

Photoset in North Wales by
Derek Doyle & Associates, Mold, Clwyd
Reproduced, printed and bound in Great Britain by
Hazell Watson & Viney Limited,
Member of the BPCC Group,
Aylesbury, Bucks

Macdonald & Co (Publishers) Ltd
Maxwell House
74 Worship Street
London EC2A 2EN
A BPCC plc Company

CONTENTS

I want to do it because I want to do it. Women must try to do things that men have tried. If they fail, their failure must be but a challenge to others.

Amelia Earhart

FOREWORD

Until very recently, the idea of women and power was a contradiction in terms. The corridors of statecraft, business and industry were reserved for men, and the rare woman who penetrated them did so through fulfilling some function for one of the male power holders as wife, mistress, servant or surrogate. But now, throughout the world, women are coming to power in numbers too great to ignore. Their rise makes necessary not only an account of their own success against all odds, but a revaluation of every cherished myth of power and of womanhood itself.

For women have in the past been held back not only by external factors like the denial of education and access, but also by fears that the price of power for a woman is the loss of womanhood. The negative associations of powerful women have been strong, and strongly fostered by males who preferred to keep power a club for men only. Another damaging myth is the widespread assumption that only the exceptional woman ever makes it to the top. Now there are so many 'exceptions' as to encourage all women to dismiss this out-dated 'rule'.

This book analyses the recent phenomenon of women's successes in penetrating male bastions in a wide range of areas, and makes the case for women in power. Not all schoolgirls have their eye on the Presidency of the United States. But those who have ambitions should be able to go forward in the knowledge that the top jobs are now accessible to women, and that power is a good place for women to be.

Personal power is in itself an under-researched subject, with a dark and taboo side in a democratic age. Social scientists have applied themselves safely to community and organisational power structures, while psychologists have followed Freud in concentrating on the neurotic damage caused to victims by others' power, rather than analysing the power people themselves. But power is a fact of life, and men have monopolised it. Now that women are discovering this unknown territory, some urgent questions arise. Can I make it? Should I? How did other women? Will it be good? How does it change your life? What does it mean for men? These and other demands are being made by women on all sides.

Women and Power tackles the question of what power means for women and gives answers to the specific areas of difficulty that women experience. It is based on in-depth interviews with over 40 top women in Britain and the USA, who are acknowledged in full at the end of the book. To all I extend my grateful thanks, and especially to the few very highly placed women who felt that they could give more freely if their contribution remained anonymous. These women, and many, many more have made it – latest figures from the Registrar-General's census show that in Britain alone the number of top women has *doubled* in the last ten years. So could you. This book is based on the assumption that all women can become more powerful. It is written by a woman, for women, and takes a woman's perspective throughout. But it should also be of interest to men. For women are strengthening and growing into positions in which they not only hold power, but will change the nature of power itself.

Today's top women are pioneering in power for a whole sex. Today's bright and ambitious young women are only just beginning. The future will be dazzling – and it's for you, if you want it. On your way, then, and happy travelling!

Rosalind Miles

CHAPTER 1

The Female Face of Power

No more phallic imperialism! Women have moved forward from demanding equal opportunity and now demand equal power.
Andrea Dworkin

There are two cultures, the powerful and the powerless. Traditionally these have been men and women. As more women ascend the ladders of state, and move to positions of leverage in society, the time has come to look again at the whole idea of power. All the clichés of power are masculine. How do they relate to today's women of high achievement?

A study of powerful women tells us as much about the nature of power as it does about the abilities and potential of women. It reveals some main weaknesses in our conceptual armoury. So much of what is written about power, these women make nonsense of. So much of what we take for granted as power behaviour is shown up as the petty manoeuvring and paranoid self-aggrandisement of little men. Powerful women throw some of our cherished notions not into the melting pot, but into the garbage can. And they do it with style, grace and humour. Before breakfast, every day.

All power fascinates – it must, if it is to work. Absolute power fascinates absolutely, as Lord Acton might have said. What distinguishes the power-seeker? What are the qualities necessary in a power-holder? What is the attraction of certain people towards power – and what is the attraction for the rest of us not simply in watching but in legitimating them?

These old riddles take on a fresh and tantalising slant when

9

the power-holder is not of the historically dominant sex, but a woman. How did she break out? How did she get there? How does she hold it down? And the question underlying all these – is a woman of power the rare exception, an anomaly – or is she only doing what millions of other women would be doing, given even a whisker of a chance? The hundreds and thousands of women now taking power in politics, government, business and industry provide the answers to all these questions.

When Sirimavo Bandaranaike became the world's first woman Prime Minister in 1960, it did not look like much of a portent. Her country Sri Lanka was both small and distant from the centres that the 'advanced' countries call power. Moreover, she only achieved greatness in, if not at, the wake of her Prime Minister husband, offering herself as his successor after his assassination in a highly emotional nationwide tour. Like Nancy Reagan, she was a woman uncritically invested in a two-person political career, and much given to wifely pronouncements like 'Mr Bandaranaike would never have been a happy husband if I had not thrown myself in politics.'

Next in historical line, Indira Gandhi never claimed that she was only doing it for spouse Feroze. But initially at least she was involved in power politics by and for her father Pandit Nehru as his hostess, aide-de-camp, and delegate. As India's first Prime Minister, Nehru founded his country's closest approximation to an all-India royal line. Fate visited him with the ultimate tragedy of the patriarch – he fathered only girl-children. What would have been Indira's story if Nehru had had a son to succeed him? Or even an able son-in-law, since the less-than-adequate Feroze was certainly tried out as a Crown Prince?

Even Golda Meir was not originally perceived as a woman moving by and for herself. She had retired from her post as Secretary-General of the Israeli Labour Party when in March 1969 the Knesset, caught on the hop by the death of Prime Minister Eshkol, made her a stop-gap Premier. She was supposed to keep the seat warm while the rightful heirs to the throne sorted themselves out. Golda Meir immediately demonstrated her grasp of one of the fundamentals of power – if it comes your way, grab it. At the subsequent October election she went on to pulverise the opposition and to rule both parliament and people with a blend of toughness and warmth that made her into an international stateswoman. But the circumstances of her rise to power still allowed it to be explained away – Israel was a new country, Golda a mother-figure, an interim measure, a one-off. 'And let's face it,' says a senior Conservative politician, 'looking like that, she must have been a man anyway.'

'My Government and I'

Margaret Thatcher changed all that. Coming out of a nowhere called Grantham to become the first woman Prime Minister in two thousand years of British history made her internationally famous – but far more remarkable was her previous feat on which the Premiership turned, winning the election for the leadership of the Conservative Party. Until the very moment of her victory hardly anyone, from the princes of the party to its potboys, had thought it possible. As a woman, she was so far out of sight and mind that many only saw her properly for the first time as she streaked past the winning post. The shock waves went all the way down to the grass roots. As ancient Tories turned truly blue, frenziedly demanding what the Party, the world, and womankind was coming to, they comforted themselves with the thought that something so unnatural as a woman's rule would prove to have a short and defective life. It took a member of the Labour Party to put them right. 'That woman is the bees' knees,' he said. 'She is the most remarkable woman alive; and she is the best man there is.'

As these comments of male politicians show, any connection of a woman with power produces a gender jumble in the general consciousness. Margaret Thatcher has been repeatedly hailed as 'the best man in the Tory Party', and praised for 'having a mind like a man's'. Yet she has also been equally consistently subjected to attacks of vicious sexism for being a woman – her womanhood is an irresistibly handy insult for every male non-thinker from the architects of the Labour Party's 'Ditch the Bitch' campaign to the *Guardian*'s political correspondent Peter Jenkins, who offers 'her head has grown too big for her hairdo' as his insight into Thatcher power politics. But as Margaret Thatcher has sailed (many would say majestically) down the

11

decade since her election as leader, such things have reflected less upon her than upon the political and intellectual poverty of her opponents.

For Margaret Thatcher's career has amply fulfilled a phrase of Sophocles that she is fond of quoting: 'once a woman is made equal to a man, she becomes his superior.' She dominates her party like a colossus, not only head and shoulders above her colleagues in the private councils of government, but in the country too. She fought for her power in ways now forgotten; from 1951 to 1959 searching in vain for a parliamentary seat, short-listed and defeated on various occasions, on others, amazing as it seems in retrospect, not even considered. She weathered a serious professional disappointment when an eminent barrister let her down after her pupillage and she was denied a tenancy in Chambers. She had the galling experience of fighting one constituency so successfully that she increased the Conservative vote by 50 per cent at the general election – and still lost. She did not even get into parliament till she was thirty-four. She finally made it, by herself, for herself. Understandably she has now settled down to enjoy herself.

And the way that she enjoys herself is by the practice of power. As Harold Wilson observes in *The Governance of Britain*, during this century 'the Prime Minister in each decade has exercised, or has been able to exercise, more power than his predecessor'. Margaret Thatcher has inherited much, and accreted more. Through her legendary tirelessness, and her phenomenal ability to digest documents in great numbers, she burns off even her own people and so runs a uniquely personal style of government. 'Can't we call it a day and go to bed, Prime Minister?' is a plaintive bleat not unheard in 10 Downing Street. 'You go, you go,' is the reported response. 'But you know me; I'll just finish these papers.'

Margaret Thatcher has also built her power with the people in a way unprecedented in modern times. Her shrewd populism is a gift to the media, who daily deliver to her a massive constituency of stunned and bedazzled consumers primed for the next helping of Thatcherism. 'She talks to the press too much,' says Harold Wilson. 'But then, it's a Tory press.' Margaret Thatcher's power base with the Fourth Estate goes back to the dawn of her parliamentary career. The first private member's bill she introduced was to give the press access to council meetings, previously forbidden to them. This attracted a lot of very favourable coverage, and Margaret Thatcher has never put a foot wrong since. From tabloid and quality papers alike, she can count on almost daily readings from the bible of Thatcherism.

This much-canvassed entity of Thatcherism is in fact less of a political philosophy than a series of media and ideological victories. Her Falklands venture, no matter how many Britons dissented and despaired, no matter how history will judge this British bulldog/gunboat caper, was an enormous popular success. The British work-force unquestioningly kisses the rod of unemployment and expresses its appreciation of the Thatcher policies by returning their architect to Number 10 with the unassailable power mandate of a hugely increased majority. Thatcherism Smatcherism. It's all power. She wields it and it works.

It works so well that any real opposition has effectively been blown away. There is at present no serious check or challenge to Margaret Thatcher, other than the sheer weight of the age-old democratic processes, within either parliament or her own party. It works to keep her up on thin ice, on slippery slopes, and on the countless banana skins littering the roads of political life. It works on the greatest power-holder in the greatest country of the world. 'Dear Margaret,' wrote President Reagan to Mrs Thatcher following her visit to America in September 1983:

> World affairs today demand the boldness and integrity of a Churchill. In his absence I know he would want us to look to you as the legendary Britannia – a special lady, the greatest defender of the realm.
>> Sincerely,
>> Ron.

Primus Inter Pares

As this shows, Margaret Thatcher has succeeded in turning her greatest drawback, her womanhood, into a trump card of power play – would President Reagan have written in that vein to Harold Wilson? To Edward Heath? Even before she married Dennis Thatcher in true blue velvet and Gainsborough ostrich

13

plumes, Margaret Thatcher was thoroughly wised up on the political capital to be made out of her womanhood. Not for her the stout brogues and tweeds of the surrogate male. To this day she answers seriously questions about her favourite colour (turquoise), her hair ('honey-blonde', in the lyrical press phraseology), her clothes. She has been seen, as well as photographed, doing her own shopping and being with her children, especially when they were younger – she was the only parliamentary candidate before or since to be photographed with new-born twins (her own!), one on each arm. Margaret Thatcher has shown that it is perfectly acceptable for a woman to want power, to win it, and to hold it down within her own definition of femininity.

In this she has been aided and echoed by a number of other powerful women throughout the world. The decade of Margaret Thatcher's flowering also gave birth to a wealth of female talent, placing women at the forefront in various different areas on a quite unprecedented scale. Once there, they wasted no time deploying their womanhood as a hitherto untapped resource of power politics, and in tackling head-on the obstacles to women that still lay across the route to the top. In France Simone Veil, the only woman to reach full ministerial rank in the Fifth Republic, succeeded single-handed in reversing French law and custom when she got through the National Assembly a bill making contraception freely available. She worked a similar miracle in her strongly Catholic country with a law which permitted abortion for the first time in France. All this was achieved in the teeth of the hostility of the Premier Jacques Chirac, who undermined President Giscard d'Estaing by various assaults on the power of Giscard's female appointees. Dr Hélène Dorhlac, for instance, Secretary of State at the Ministry of Justice, found herself relegated to an office well away from her ministry building. She met this by standing outside her ministry in all weathers, then addressing the National Assembly in her sodden raincoat. She got her office. 'These women mean business,' Chirac acknowledged.

In January 1975, because rather than in spite of her involvement as a woman with the most personal and controversial of women's issues, Simone Veil topped the Figaro-Sofres poll as the person whom the French nation believed to be most capable of the highest responsibilities, well ahead of the President and all his Ministers of State. As elected President of the first directly elected European Parliament in 1979, she consolidated her reputation for courage and political agility. In the mid-eighties she retains her standing as what *The Times* calls 'the best card in the French political pack with a popularity rating that far outstrips any of the dominant leaders'. And just let any political backwoodsman try telling the French that their beloved 'Veil' must be a man, really.

Recent years have also seen women reaching for the top in statecraft as well as government. Both Britain and the USA have appointed women ambassadors. America's ambassador Jeane Kirkpatrick became the first female permanent representative to head the mission of any European civilisation to the United Nations, something which she merrily describes as 'a real role-buster in this close men's club'. Role-busting is something that Jeane Kirkpatrick has made a habit of, from her days as the first woman resident scholar at the high-prestige think-tank, the American Enterprise Institute for Public Policy Research. She was the first woman on the Rank Committee at Georgetown University ('Now that *was* the holy of holies,' she comments drily). She was the only woman in the Cabinet for the first two and a half years of the Reagan administration, where she occupied a higher post than any American woman had ever done previously in the US Foreign Policy Department.

In her private life Ambassador Kirkpatrick is married to a fellow-intellectual and political scientist, and they have three sons. She strongly defends these 'life experiences' for women, and in more general terms urges women not to undervalue the skills and capabilities that they develop as mothers, attributing her own grounding in problem-solving and the art of diplomatic resolution to the eight years she spent at home with her boys. To meet she is extremely attractive, a luminous presence, grave and womanly. Just as Margaret Thatcher does in private discussion, Jeane Kirkpatrick combines a quick vitality of response with an ability to concentrate all her forces upon the person she is talking to and the matter in hand. Like Margaret Thatcher, too, she speaks of 'the advantages of our sex': 'Being a woman has indubitably enhanced my visibility,' she says.

Britain's only woman ambassador, Dame Anne Warburton,

agrees with Ambassador Kirkpatrick. 'I have often thought that women have some advantages,' is her comment. 'You stand out more and have rarity value. In a committee room essentially staffed by men, people quickly know who you are.' This advantage does not only apply at the very top, but on the way up too. 'It is easier for women to talk with everybody. Diplomatic life can be a little hierarchical; you are conscious of the difference between a second secretary and an ambassador. As a woman second secretary, you can have a rapport more easily with an ambassador than most male second secretaries could have.' As the only woman ambassador out of over a hundred at the United Nations headquarters in Switzerland, 'our man in Geneva' is frequently called upon to demonstrate that 'there is nothing like a dame'.

This affirmation has sounded in a number of countries, large and small, in the last few years. From the Mediterranean to the Arctic Circle women are taking up reins of power that their mothers never dreamed would pass out of the hands of men. Agatha Barbara has become the first woman President of the Republic of Malta, as she was the first woman to be elected to Malta's parliament back in 1947. In Iceland, Vigdis Finnbogadottir became the world's first democratically elected woman head of state in 1980 after fighting women's issues by every means, including what she describes as 'our great Women's Strike in 1975'. As she recalls it,

> This was one of the greatest days of my life! The main square in Reykjavik was filled with thousands of women and children. We paralysed society for a day and proved how much society depends on women. Shops, offices, the banks, many schools, newspapers, TV, telephones, restaurants shut their doors – everything.

To a country like Britain, where many high-achieving women still feel compelled to protest that they are 'not women's libbers', such a precursor to supreme office, even of a formal rather than executive nature, would seem unthinkable. But Vigdis Finnbogatir is adamant that it was a critical factor in her success when she ran for President. 'The atmosphere created by the strike certainly helped me to be elected,' she says. 'It gave

16

people the idea that a woman as leader would be a valuable thing.'

A Valuable Thing

Ever-growing numbers of women now endorse this view wholeheartedly, and the men who disagree have (mostly) learned not to say so out loud. 'Women are no longer afraid of power,' says Lesley Abdela, founder of the influential 300 Group set up to get more women into parliament.

> They're learning to pick up the ball and run with it, run with it *hard*. Some women are prepared to go the route where power is, even though it's male-constructed. There's no future in throwing up the flagstones – we need to get enough into positions of power to be able to change the system to one more suited to women.

One of the women newcomers to Parliament in the last election, the controversial Conservative Edwina Currie, wholeheartedly endorses this view: 'It comes round to yourself in the end. And if you want to see more women in parliament, it's no good looking for other people to do it!' Edwina Currie's own career amply demonstrates a woman's ability to dovetail the political and the personal. Of her time on Birmingham City Council she states:

> I'd usually have a baby tucked under one arm, or be pregnant or something, but all the senior councillors would say was, 'OK. On you go.' I was four months' pregnant in 1977 when I was asked to take on Social Services with a budget of £15 million.

Both Edwina Currie and another recent incomer, Anna McCurley, manifest an unselfconscious commitment to power and a robust toleration of the inevitable knocks. As Anna McCurley describes her first election:

> I got 707 votes, a lost deposit, and it was very salutary, I tell you. But I could only go up thereafter. There was no other place to go but up. I'd reached rock-bottom by then. It was three weeks of sheer hell, but we came out of it laughing. You've just got to be hell-bent on it. I worked my passage in this way;

17

whenever there was an election, a by-election, anything doing, I was there. They used to say there was no show without Punch!

The new wave of bright, tough young women in British politics has yet to break with its maximum force over the Palace of Westminster. The most exciting single new development in the contemporary history of women's access to power was the selection of a female running-mate by Walter Mondale, Democratic candidate for the US Presidential election in 1984. Up to the moment of the announcement many observers felt that the choice of a woman was too daring for the man whose supposed solidity and dullness has led to his nickname of 'Fritz'. Richard Nixon in his new role of political pundit opined that Mondale was just stringing all the female possibles along, and Ambassador Kirkpatrick said, 'If I had to bet on it, I'd guess he wouldn't.'

One of the reasons he did must have been the confidence of congresswoman Geraldine Ferraro that he would be right to do so. Like Golda Meir, when the chance of power came her way, she reached out her hand for it. 'What are the qualifications a Vice-President needs?' she was asked on nationwide television. Her response, crisp and cool, without a hint of bombast, helped to clinch her selection: 'The qualifications a Vice-President needs? Integrity, intelligence, strength. Do I have those type of qualities? Yeah.'

Geraldine Farraro works woman-style; 'I have a brain and a uterus and I use both,' she says, quoting her fellow-Democrat congresswoman Patricia Schroeder. Her status as 'good-Catholic-wife-and-mother-of-three' was a main plank of her image and acceptability. But she is on record with the statement that she brings her whole life as a woman into Congress, and her voting record supports this claim. In one instance, she went against the tenor of her New York constituency, and even more courageously against the powerful Speaker of the House and her personal mentor 'Tip' O'Neill, when she refused to endorse legislation extending the stay of US marines in Lebanon. Her reason was, 'I'm a *mother*, and I saw those kids over there. I just *can't*.' It is not easy to imagine Ronald Reagan, say, playing his fatherhood card with such confidence. Ferraro's action suggests that a distinction made by American writer John Wheeler could usefully be applied to political styles and the use of power: 'Masculinity expresses the idea that there are things worth dying for. Femininity expresses the idea that there are things worth living for.'

But Ferraro is far from the soft-hearted sentimentalist that this one act implies. She is a committed feminist who according to US political correspondent Sheila Caudle 'has fought for the Ediths and the Glorias on abortion rights, the ERA, women's economic equity, peace, and funding for social programmes'. She has done so with shrewdness and a ferocious tenacity. 'She's got political smarts,' says Representative Leon Panetta, who sits with her on the Budget Committee, 'and she just *will* not let go.' A fine tribute came her way when she used her power to threaten a million-dollar project important to O'Neill himself. So far from being angry, O'Neill congratulated her on her skill at 'hardball politicking'. 'You did a good job,' he said. A wholesome-looking woman with an edge like a hatchet, Geraldine Ferraro sounds the bells of woman-power all the way from Mrs Miniver to Ma Baker.

Adverse criticism centred on the idea of any woman carrying sufficient clout for the post of Vice-President. American psychologist Susan Reverby argued that 'a woman can't psychologically reassure you that she is in control. Mommy isn't a father figure.' There was the predictable spate of vulgar anti-feminist rubbish along the lines of 'What would happen if a woman were negotiating with Chernenko and she got the hot flushes?' Lance Marrow quoted Roosevelt's VP in his declaration that the office itself 'isn't worth a pitcher of warm piss', a view implicitly endorsed by Patricia Schroeder who feels that women should not campaign for the Vice-Presidency: 'They should campaign for President.' Meanwhile, Theodore White, long-time scrutineer of Presidential campaigns, weighed in with the pronouncement that the only woman who could make any difference to Walter Mondale's chances would be Florence Nightingale or Joan of Arc.

Specific censure focused on Geraldine Ferraro's relative lack of experience, the narrowness of her power base in Queen's, New York, and the fact that as she herself said, 'I would not be considered for Vice-President if my name were *Gerald* Ferraro.' President Reagan clumsily attempted to make political capital

19

out of all this by comparing Geraldine Ferraro adversely with his admired Margaret Thatcher who, he argued, had been adopted by the Tories on her own high merits: 'There was no tokenism or symbolism in what they did.' This betrays not only Reagan's deep ignorance of British power politics, but also his lack of the quality that Harold Wilson singled out as essential for a Premier, a sense of history. Everything being said about Geraldine Ferraro in the summer of 1984 was said about Margaret Thatcher before she became the British leader: the inexperience (Margaret Thatcher's highest post had been the lowly 'soft' Education ministry); the shortage of legislative achievement; the ignorance of foreign affairs; with the knee-jerk response to a woman, and 'a blonde' to boot, 'all fluff and no substance'. In Margaret Thatcher's case, it was no time at all before Finchley housewife became Iron Lady. Similarly Ferraro, although as a woman she can never totally escape the 'little bit of knitting' stereotype, has shown that the wool she is made of is steel.

The achievement of Geraldine Ferraro to date encapsulates an instructive paradox. She made it to her place on the Democratic ticket as a woman, and partly at least because of her womanhood. Yet she also asserted the fundamental truth that power is ultimately gender-free. In the event the Ferraro factor was not enough to put life into Mondale's lack-lustre Presidential campaign, or to turn the rising tide of Reaganite conservatism. Ferraro herself was not helped by revelations of her husband's business irregularities, questions of unpaid tax, and allegations of hidden links with the Mafia. None of this, however, had any connection with her being a woman. She was universally agreed to have outperformed not only her rival for the Vice-Presidency, George Bush, but also her leader Mondale during the long and gruelling campaign.

Geraldine Ferraro's sex may not have provided the hoped-for electoral advantage in bridging the 'gender gap'. Her candidature did not bring an entirely new constituency of female voters into the Democratic camp. But neither did it prove to be the *disadvantage* that had been feared. Geraldine Ferraro's real achievement in 1984 was to have shown that the sex of a politician is not the live issue that it has been taken for.

John A. Meyers, publisher of *Time* magazine, summed it up:

'Ferraro proved that the ingredients of leadership are the same for men and women.' Finally, then, the individual woman Geraldine Ferraro is irrelevant, a fact that she has drawn attention to herself. 'Once you open up a job as significant as Vice-President of the United States to a woman,' she says, *no job could ever be closed to us again.*' And as a very senior Conservative woman politician commented on Mrs Thatcher, 'You may hate her policies – or her guts. But no one can ever say again that women *can't do it.*' Women are knocking at the door of the White House. The Oval Office is just down the corridor – one small step for a woman, one giant leap for womankind. In 1988.

> I'd like to quote you from *Proverbs* on woman: 'Strength and dignity are her clothing and she smiles at the future. She opens her mouth in wisdom, and the teaching of kindness is on her tongue.' Women have been a civilising influence. You are kind of the superior people.
>
> President Ronald Reagan

'I Want to Talk about Women and Power'

So said Katharine Graham, chairman of the board of the Washington Post Company, speaking at a lunch to honour the winners of the New York Women in Communications Matrix Awards, adding, 'How to acquire it and how to use it.' The women in the audience, most of whom were hardly power virgins, were keen to listen. But the focus of the speech was not on politics. Katharine Graham addressed what she called 'real power', outlining the power routes for women into positions of authority, influence, financial control, and economic and social initiative. As this shows, women's top-level political achievement provides a useful way in to a consideration of women and power. But as a focus it is far too narrow to encompass the range and brilliance of today's women of power.

In addition, the spectacular success of women like Margaret Thatcher and Indira Gandhi serves to illuminate rather than to obscure the small number of top female politicians. Political life is in fact a particularly bad area for British women, with only twenty-five female members of parliament out of over 600,

21

which marks an increase of just *one* on the number of women in the House of Commons in 1945. A cross-cultural comparison puts the British situation into perspective:

WOMEN IN POLITICS
a round-the-world league table

	Women as % of all MPs
Britain	3.6
Australia	4.8
USA	4.8
France	5.7
India	6.3
Israel	6.7
Italy	7.9
W. Germany	9.8
Switzerland	11.0
China	21.2
Sweden	28.0
Russia	32.5

Source: 300 Group News (1984)

These figures are the more fascinating (and damning) in view of the fact that as Leslie Abdela of the 300 Group points out, between 40 and 60 per cent of all paid-up members of political parties are women. Clearly, in Britain, a funny thing happens to them on the way to Westminster.

But power and political leadership are not confined to the public sphere. The post-war period has seen the birth of new power phenomena, the growing importance of corporate dominance of the private economic sector, and bureaucratic dominance of the body politic.

Additionally, bright and ambitious women have been able to make distinguished careers for themselves in the law, medicine and accountancy, not only because these have begun to open

22

their doors at last, but as society in general has become more 'professionalised'. The old power centres have shifted, and the women of power have not only shifted with them; they have helped this shift, indeed they have in part been responsible for it, by silently putting the weight of their ability where it will count, instead of just be counted.

Political life, then, is not a prime site for able women. The majority do not choose this traditional corridor, but find the routes to other areas of power. In the study of top women in both Britain and America carried out for this book, it was clear that some reject power politics for personal reasons. Judge Jean Graham Hall interested herself in politics sufficiently to discover, as she states, 'I couldn't be my own self. I couldn't project myself enough to satisfy my own needs.' Barbara Hosking, now Controller of Information Services at the Independent Broadcasting Association, with invaluable experience of 10 Downing Street and a Parliamentary seat in her grasp, decided not to take this up, but to concentrate on other opportunities. Jennifer Coutts Clay, now British Airways Controller Corporate Identity, with a background in running airline operations both in Britain and the USA, often finds herself solicited both by management and trade unions. 'I know I can get people's vote, get a following,' she says, 'But no. I'm not interested. It just doesn't appeal.'

Jennifer, in fact, like numbers of other top women similarly approached, could not work up any enthusiasm either for British political institutions or the men who run them. 'They're all opportunists, playing with the country's money,' she says. Others expressed much stronger disdain: 'Idiots and tricksters all!' said one with a thunderous laugh. 'Too shady for a lady,' commented Audrey Slaughter, editor of *Working Woman*, 'too many manipulations and fabrications for women.' It is clear, too, that the evolution of the House of Commons, via a series of antiquated masculine institutions from the medieval debating hall through the Inns of Court down to an inferior prep school crossed with a 'gentleman's' club, has at no point rendered it hospitable to women. 'The hours are ridiculous, totally stupid for a sane person,' said Lady Porter, leader of Westminster City Council. 'The talking side is total frustration. Women want to get things *done*. And why is it so complicated? Why don't they run it like a business? You ask yourself, am I stupid? But it's them!' Shirley Williams crisply summed it up:

> It's an old man's club and the sooner the place changes the better. It's terribly out-dated; there's too much spare time boozing and too many old men. I like politics, I like by-elections, I like campaigning and I like party work. I just don't like the Commons.

Certainly the House of Commons is no place for the faint-hearted. Its freedom from the restraints of the licensing laws makes it a sanctuary for soakers, and anyone fresh in off the street must be disturbed to find just how many of the guardians of our state are oiled, boiled, pickled and fried at all hours of the day and night. Nor are they drunk and amiable. To a woman's eye, the gross ogling and leering of ludicrously unattractive men, the frenzied posing and woeful assumption of doggish conviviality, compose a spectacle worthy of Hogarth at his grimmest.

The present writer, awaiting an MP in the Strangers' Bar of the House of Commons towards the end of 1984, met one of the strangest men in her life when a character who said he was the MP for Hartlepool descended upon her. Discovering that she was a writer, this respectable-looking old gent, all white hair and pink cheeks, used it as an excuse to discourse upon journalism in general, and Page 3 in particular. 'Tits now!' he began, 'You can't open a newspaper without seeing tits! Do you think men like looking at woman's tits? Do women like looking at men's penises?' 'No,' I replied, 'nor talking about them, either.' 'Fuck,' he burbled on undeterred, 'I can remember when you couldn't say "fuck" in front of a woman. Masturbation now" – I made an excuse and left. Such behaviour puts a new inflection on the phrase Right Honourable Member. Can any woman be expected to feel at home in a 'gentleman's club' like this?

Not surprisingly then, the reactions of top women to the question, 'Have you ever thought of going into politics?', ranged from the uproarious to the insulted; 'I take it you're joking,' was one icy response. Jean Denton, managing director of Herondrive, laughingly dismissed an MP's as 'the ultimate non-job', while Detta O'Cathain, director and general manager of the Milk Marketing Board, stated firmly that she would only

24

even consider it if she were offered a seat in the House of Commons – '*with* portfolio!' – or better still, the Lords. In America, too, many women despise the 'barking and husting, political log-rolling' as one reporter summed it up. In the public/private dichotomy, leading women can do without the huzzas and the hullaballoo, usually preferring to work low-profile. 'I don't need the publicity,' said a woman leader of Washington's business community, 'and having seen what's happened to Mary Cunningham [whose brilliant career came unstuck amid massive hostile and intrusive media coverage] I sure as hell can do without *that!*'

But for many of these women, the best reason for not seeking power through politics is that they have more where they are. Elinor Guggenheimer, described as 'one of the greatest – and the quietest – of door-openers in the US of A', has worked outside the field of elected office for most of her life. The point is expanded by Donna E. Shalala, president of Hunter College of the City University of New York and power-person extraordinaire, whose incomparable record bears witness to her experience of these issues: 'I like politics. But for me to go into politics doesn't make any sense at all. Most people who make it are in control of life – making it is the reaching for control. Political life is the opposite of all you've worked for. I have more power outside politics'. She does too.

Power is the blood and water of life itself.

Sik Hung Ng

So Where Are They?

If the majority of the female leading lights of the world are not in politics, what fields do they choose for the flowering of their talent and enterprise? The short answer is, they're everywhere. Women have quietly taken over in business, industry and the professions; they are distinguishing themselves in civil and public service; they are scientists and spacepersons; they are making their mark on the media not as pretty-face performers but as professional power-houses. US economic theorist Peter F. Drucker, writing of the need to recognise the importance of the new power centres, insists: 'An efficient society requires not political leaders but well-managed institutions.' This statement could serve as an epigraph on the careers of today's women of power.

And their rapid rise into these positions has been one of the most remarkable phenomena of the last five years. In the recently published Economic Activity Tables of the last British census, the proportion of women in the top jobs classified in the Registrar General's social class 1 had nearly *doubled*. This curve is reflected in all the advanced countries. In recent months alone women have notched up these breakthrough successes:

* Karin de Segundo-Platerink – first woman director in the history of the Shell group
* Brenda Dean – first woman General Secretary of the Society of Graphical and Allied Trades
* Simone Rozes – first woman president of the Supreme Court of Appeal, the highest post in the French judiciary
* Arlene Violet – first woman State Attorney in the history of the USA at Rhode Island
* Captain Lynn Rippelmeyer – the first woman to command a scheduled Boeing 747 transatlantic passenger flight
* Brenda Hoggett – first woman on the Law Commission of England and youngest commissioner ever
* Marna Tucker – first woman president of the Washington DC Bar Association
* Anne Mueller – appointed Permanent Secretary in the British Civil Service, the only woman at this level

Significantly, four of these eight are lawyers. In a Manhattan criminal court some months ago the judge opened the proceedings with the following comment: 'This is a day that I wondered if I'd ever live to see. The prosecutor is a woman, the defence attorney is a woman, the police officer is a woman, and the judge is a woman.' Only the defendant was male. Sadly, his view of the situation was not sought. Defence attorney Jackie Friedrich commented: 'The judge had gone to law school in the pre-1970 Stone Age, when women accounted for a mere 2.8 per cent of lawyers admitted to practice, and professors could without fear of reprisal limit women's participation in class

26

discussion to one day a year, "Ladies' Day".' Not any more. The law is now the most hotly-tipped fast-track career path for women, particularly in the US.

But women are streaking up everywhere. Dr Anna Mann, managing director of Whitehead Mann Ltd, one of the largest British executive search companies, and herself an impressive example of the new breed of top-flight women, is both encouraged and encouraging. 'We place people in the £35,000+ salary bracket,' she explains. 'Ten years ago, there were no women, they simply were not there. Only in the last ten years has it become acceptable for women with children to work, and only in the last five or six years have women been really acceptable at senior levels. It's taken five years to tap that pool of talent, but I have placed five women at that level now in the last year. Things are changing. It's accelerating. We are now often encouraged to include a woman in our recommendations. Clients say that they'd appreciate seeing some senior women, welcome them.'

Who are these talented women who are making history, money, and something special of themselves all at the same time? A close-up of three women distinguished by their own efforts and abilities in three very different fields will help to show what is putting the Mona Lisa smile on the female face of power.

Barbara S. Thomas

Barbara S. Thomas has been described as the world's leading woman merchant banker. But even this does not fully indicate her range of achievements and awards. Among them are:

* BA (University of Pennsylvania) *cum laude*;
* JD (New York University School of Law) *cum laude*; at Law School she was John Norton Pomeroy scholar, elected to the Order of the Coif, editor of the New York University Law Review, winner of the Jefferson Davis prize in Public Law, and recipient of an unprecedented eighteen American Jurisprudence prizes awarded for the highest grades in each law course.

She subsequently became a partner in a large and prestigious

New York law firm specialising in corporate and securities law. This led to her appointment at thirty-three as a Commissioner of the Securities and Exchange Commission, the youngest person ever to sit on this vitally important and high-prestige body whose task it is to maintain the integrity of US securities markets. Additionally Barbara Thomas holds or has held a dazzling array of memberships and directorships of the US Council on Foreign Relations, the Board of Overseers of the Wharton School of Finance, the Economic Club of New York, the Board of Governors of the Lauder Institute of Management and International Relations, the American Law Institute, the American Bar Association, the International Bar Association, the Institute for East-West Security Studies, the New York University Law Alumni Association, the National Museum of Women's Art, the Financial Women's Association of New York, and the Women's Economic Round Table.

Still with me? Next round. For these and other achievements too numerous (as they say) to mention, but in this case the truth, Barbara:

* was named the Outstanding Young Woman of America for Washington DC in 1981
* received a 1982 Award for Outstanding Service in Government
* in 1983 was named Woman of Achievement by the TV station WETA-FM, and identified as a leader among America's 100 Most Important Women by the editors of the Ladies' Home Journal
* in 1984 was awarded the *Esquire* magazine citation as one of the 'Best of the New Generation', the register of men and women under forty who are changing America

Barbara Thomas has now consolidated her international position by joining one of the leading merchant banks in the City of London, the ancient and distinguished Samuel Montagu and Co. Ltd. She is the first woman executive director of the bank, indeed the first woman director of any London accepting house, and president of its US subsidiary. From her offices in London, New York and Hong Kong she concentrates on what she modestly describes as 'the region', which turns out to be the whole of South-East Asia. Because of this, her expertise is now being sought after by Australian banks too. Yet she wears all this so lightly that when with her, you have to keep reminding yourself, because she won't, that this immensely likeable, lovely-looking and soft-spoken young woman is a titan of the international capital markets. If only they made men like that.

Barbara Thomas has made this brilliant international journey from what she stresses was 'a totally ordinary American family'. Yet there were some unusual, and with hindsight formative, features of her childhood. Among her earliest memories are those of her mother, who had completed half a master's degree when Barbara was born as the first child of the family, sitting at the dining-room table doing her homework as she pushed on to complete her studies. Barbara is emphatic that she benefited from having a mother who did not conform to the conventional image of kitchen-bound motherhood, but who insisted on women's rights to work 'not so much for economic survival as for psychological independence and fulfilment'. She and her mother are still close in a relationship that stretches back to include her mother's mother too – a race of strong women. Finally it was at her mother's suggestion that Barbara first considered the law. This one instance alone serves to illustrate the neglect of the distaff side in the phalliocentric research into high-achievement – it is a simple fact frequently ignored by researchers that 'Daddy's girl' by the sheer force of nature is Mummy's girl too.

Yet Barbara's background supports the general research finding that women of power choose their fathers with care. Barbara's father she recalls as 'an extraordinary man, loving and caring', patiently helping her mother with her homework, a great cook and organiser of family trips and treats. A one-hundred-per-center, he was always there for her – 'totally solid and reliable, I could call my father with any problem'. Yet he never pampered or babied her but when angry let his irritation out and never doubted she could take it.

Barbara's school experience included starring in all the school plays, but not on the games field. Nor was she accorded any genius status early on. She admits to being 'smart but not outstanding'. The turning point came when she got her first taste of the law. 'This,' she decided, 'is going to be *fun*.' As she sees it, the main prop of her achievement is that good old Anglo-Saxon four-letter word, work. 'I only did well if I worked hard,' she

29

insists. 'I worked all the time, I killed myself, and I got very good grades and it was *terrific*. I really loved it.' Yet she did not have any firm professional ambition at this stage: 'I thought I'd get married and do significant work in the community, be head of the School Board for instance, or hold some respected position. I never thought I'd work for a living in those days.'

Barbara still retains an ability to go with her life opportunities and the career rhythms which have brought her so far, and believes strongly in luck. 'I was an SEC Commissioner because at that moment I was lucky. They were looking for a woman and among the first people they asked, a number suggested my name. They could have asked different people who didn't know me. It was just luck!'

As a married woman Barbara has a normal apprehension of something happening to her husband: 'I really don't want to lose that relationship. I worry about my husband dying. I also worry that all my travelling and my concentration on my career will hurt the marriage. My worst fear is not losing my job. There's always another job. But my husband is a very special person and is clearly my best friend and supporter.' Barbara also sets high store on professional loyalty: 'I worry that someone I trust may not come through. I'm a very loyal person, and I value loyalty even above love.'

But these fears seem remote shadows on the life of a woman who has made it in every sense of the term. With the birth of her son Lloyd in 1982, her personal life is complete. Dovetailing with her business is her social life, so most evenings include a reception that is business-related, or a dinner party with clients or potential clients ('I'm glad that I like champagne!') Professionally she stands unique on a peak of deserved eminence – the world's leading woman banker.

And Barbara Thomas is still only thirty-seven.

Baroness Young

Baroness Young is Minister of State in the Foreign and Commonwealth Office, and deputy to the Foreign Secretary. Behind these dignified titles lies a career in what US Ambassador Jeane Kirkpatrick calls 'role-busting' all the more remarkable for taking place within the hallowed corridors of power of the top reaches of the British Government Service. As Janet Young, the minister became a member of Oxford City Council. Becoming the leader of the Conservatives on the council she describes as 'my first top job'. Within four years she had been granted a life peerage, and taken into central government.

From this point Baroness Young's career displays a number of important 'firsts'. She became:

* the first Conservative female Government Whip in the House of Lords
* the first woman deputy chairman of the Conservative Party
* the first woman Chancellor of the Duchy of Lancaster
* the first woman Lord Privy Seal
* the first woman deputy to the Foreign Secretary
* the first woman leader of the House of Lords

Constitutional historians debate whether Lady Young's role at the high-prestige Foreign Office, where modern ministers are still judged by the standards of Canning and Castlereagh, or her taking the leadership of the House of Lords, which has been a masculine prerogative for the best part of a millenium, is the greater of her recent role-busting activities. Her demeanour, though, is so gentle and graceful as to dispel any whiff of the iconoclast or revolutionary, and her work in the Lords has been described as 'most accomplished' by a male peer. Another elderly peer commented, 'I'm an old fogey. I didn't want them [women] in in '58 [the year that women were admitted to the House of Lords for the first time]. Don't say I said that. But she's a marvellous woman, a *marvellous* woman. You'd better not say I said that, either!'

Janet Young, the elder of two sisters, was born to a mother who was herself one of four girls, 'all very talented, very musical', she comments. Her mother was 'very supportive' in her daughters' lives, believing firmly in the education of girls, and equal educational opportunity, hardly a common attitude in the Britain of the thirties. Her faith was vindicated by both the girls becoming graduates of Oxford University. This view was shared by Lady Young's father; 'we were not pressed into

31

anything, but he wanted us to go to university'. Lady Young's relationship with her father was interrupted at the age of thirteen when she was evacuated during the war to the USA. But his continued concern expressed itself in a flow of letters across the Atlantic, in which the exhortation 'Never give up Latin and maths!' (both then essential for university entrance) found a frequent place among the more conventional pieces of paternal wisdom.

Lady Young's education as a whole followed an unconventional pattern. Perhaps her grounding in role-busting came when she attended the top-flight boys' prep school, the Dragon School in Oxford (another old 'boy' of the Dragon is Lady Antonia Fraser). She studied in New Haven, Connecticut, until she was sixteen, winning a scholarship to Mount Holyoake College where she spent one year. She then returned to England for an early entrance to St Anne's College, Oxford, from which she was a graduate in Modern Greats (politics, philosophy and economics) at the age of twenty. After marriage and motherhood, she embarked on her career on the Oxford City Council ten years later, in 1957.

'I have very good health,' Lady Young states. 'You've *got* to have that, both strength and stamina. I can be very tired, and one good night's sleep will set me up. But very good health is more than just physical. It's a mental state. You must have the temperament.' Having the temperament, in Lady Young's definition, includes both passive and active qualities. Top women must be able to withstand pressure. 'Don't ever think, what a ghastly day, this is terrible; still, it'll be better next week,' she advises. 'It never will be. At senior level, much of the work is crisis-resolution, and dealing with very serious and difficult problems. If these were capable of an easy solution, they would have been resolved before they got to you!'

Actively, in the Young formulation, women leaders must take the best advice obtainable, and learn to delegate. 'People are much more critical of women,' she observes. 'The longer I am in public life, the more I see this. Women are always noticed.' This factor, the down side of the visibility bonus remarked by ambassadors Kirkpatrick and Warburton, 'makes women work harder and become over-conscientious', as Lady Young has seen. In answer to this real difficulty she is emphatic that '*women must support women*'. 'I've always tried to do this,' she explains.

> In the chair at the Education Committee, I could see that women were interviewed and so had the chance to be considered for the top jobs. I also tried to see that the curriculum gave equal opportunities to girls, especially in maths and science. I have had three very able female Private Secretaries, which is a good jumping-off place for them, and with responsibility for the Civil Service I could put impetus behind the recommendations to help women and see them carried out.

In summing up her success so far, Lady Young attributes a good deal to having a supportive family. Her husband, like her father, is a don at Oxford University, and they have three daughters. Additionally a woman needs a bit of luck, and a lot of humour. 'You can become very tense,' she remarks. 'You must be able to laugh at yourself and your prejudices.' But finally, she says, 'I have two talents. One, I like people and can get on with them. Two, I can spot clever people and get them to work for me. If you get able people and encourage them, they will serve you well, and this is very stimulating.' In the presence of Lady Young, this is easy to believe. Her staff conduct you in with proud anticipation bubbling beneath the well-bred facade, fully conscious of the privilege they are bestowing and the pleasure in store for the visitor. She shares with Ambassador Jeane Kirkpatrick the unusual combination of intellectuality with great personal warmth. After five minutes in a room with her, most people would be ready to follow her anywhere.

Baroness Young is still nearly ten years younger than Winston Churchill was when he achieved his finest hour, and there is no retiring age in the House of Lords.

Jane Deknatel

Jane Deknatel is that unique hybrid, an Englishwoman who has become a Hollywood film producer, and her own life reads like an up-market version of *A Star Is Born*. As reporter Georgina Howell remarks, 'Talking to her is like flicking through a manual of How To Be A Successful Woman'. Beginning in management consultancy Jane Deknatel moved into the media after doing an MBA. Her appointment as director of docu-drama for CBS took her to Los Angeles, and she then became vice-president of NBC, with responsibility for movies and mini-series. Still short of forty, she became a fully-fledged movie mogul when she landed one of the best jobs in Hollywood. In 1982 Jane Deknatel became a senior vice-president of HBO, the largest pay-television cable network not only in America but in the whole world when the company went into film-making. With a salary in excess of $100,000, and a budget of around $85,000,000, Jane Deknatel had finally made good the response to the classic interview question, 'What do you want?' with which she stunned her interviewer at CBS: 'I want power, I want status, and I want money.'

When Jane was growing up, all these were in rather short supply. She was the eldest daughter of a family engaged in the other industry for which Oxford is famous, pressed steel. Her father was a trade union organiser whom Jane proudly calls 'a revolutionary, a visionary', and she grew up with men talking politics around the kitchen table. He also played professional football, and as her mother too was an athlete and swimmer, physical activities were an important part of these early years. Jane's father was deeply attached to his daughter. 'I was the apple of his eye,' she says. 'He thought I was a toy. But then, he was like a child himself.' Child or no, he had ambitions for Jane. The minute she was born he put her name down for a couple of good schools and mapped out a brilliant future for her. 'I was definitely going to be a brain surgeon,' she remembers, 'patterned on my father who always wanted to be a doctor.'

Her father's sudden death of a brain tumour when Jane was seven shattered the life of the little family. Jane's mother moved to the coast to run a small hotel, and both girls were pitched in at the deep end. The main burden fell on Jane as the elder. 'At seven I became my mother's husband. At ten I was running the hotel with her.' Mother and daughter worked very hard, in a continuing family tradition. Jane's mother had worked all her life as the fifteenth of sixteen children, and not surprisingly Jane remembers her mother's mother as 'a relentless worker'. Jane's mother wanted her daughters to stay on at school, and despite the domestic pressures Jane did well in school life, winning a

34

scholarship and becoming head girl while starring in all the school plays. But the relationship with her mother, who once told her outspoken daughter, 'With a mouth like yours, nobody will marry you,' was never easy. An attack of paralysis at Jane's birth had been followed by a nervous breakdown and Jane's aunt had to step in to look after the baby: 'Effectively, my mother gave me away.'

Jane left home at seventeen to join the Voluntary Service Overseas Corps, but even after wanderings and work experience in Malaysia, the shade of her dead father continued to influence her life. Remembering a promise he had once made to take her to America, because it was the only place in the world to be truly free, Jane decided to take herself. After completing her studies in Social Work at Southampton University, Jane set sail for New York. When she arrived, the bank to which she had wired $300, her entire fortune, had never heard of her. With only $20 to her name Jane Deknatel gritted her teeth and set about finding out what little English girls can do in the Land of the Free. And the rest is history.

Yet Jane's rise to her present position as head of her own production company, Film Partners International, has not been as easy as it looks. Her career only really began when divorce left her penniless with two small children. Casting around for a livelihood she said to the women in her exercise class, 'Somebody has to give me a job – go home and ask your husbands!' One husband worked for a major management consultancy, ADC. So began a successful and rewarding job terminated by Jane when she was refused her request to work on one assignment with the put-down, 'You're a woman, and you have no qualifications.'

Although the world would have to live with the first, Jane resolved to do something about the second, and enrolled for an MBA on a course from which the brightest graduate every year was recruited by CBS. 'I knew I would never beat the sixteen men with PhDs to this job,' Jane said, 'so I decided to talk my way into it.' Her confident start at CBS was shaken by the fact that the president who had hired her was fired a week after she began. But Jane recovered from this to work her way up through the corporate staff and was eventually asked to go out to California to head up CBS's docu-drama division.

35

From CBS Jane went to the movie department of NBC, and was in time promoted to running it. Then in one of the reversals for which this savage industry is famous, she was sacked for refusing to give a sinecure job to the big boss's mistress. She was fired on her birthday, ten days before Christmas, and did not work again for nine months. 'But I went to the gym every day, I had lunch with someone in the business every day, and came to terms with my anger against men,' she says. Finally, in one week, she received six job offers. 'What's happening?' she asked one of her callers. 'We figured we throw you out and you'd stay out,' he replied. 'But you've hung in.' MGM's David Susskind, for whom she then went to work, told her. 'You're a survivor, and too talented for the industry to waste. When can you start?'

Not for Jane the gentlemanly dealings of the City of London, or the pillared halls of the Foreign Office. You have to be able to 'hustle your little ass' in her business: 'I made a point of getting to know all the top producers as soon as I arrived in California, so that I was perceived as a "creative" person. Who you know is vital.' That is the civilised end of the industry. In the media jungle the beasts are big and sabre-toothed, so you have to know when to fight back, and when to tough it out. Nobody gives you anything, and they can always take back what you've earned. Jane was once severed from another job immediately after a substantial promotion by the only man above her, who told her, 'Our marriage isn't working.' 'So figure out how to *take* power,' she advises. 'Your boss won't give it away – would you? Tie up some territory of your own. And be prepared to fight for it.'

Fighting and struggling are two words that recur in Jane's vocabulary, usually to the accompaniment of a gleam in her eye. She has clearly found an arena worthy of her swordplay in the movie business. Not without cost – her marriage to top-drawer Bostonian John Deknatel, and long-standing relationship with lawyer Jerry Rubin foundered because both men were threatened by her success. Finding a decent man is a serious difficulty for top women, Jane says: 'We don't need what they have been trained to give.' The pace of her Hollywood life, with three phones going non-stop bringing calls from Britain, France, India or Australia (and this is only in her luxurious Los Angeles private house), sometimes makes her feel as if she is 'living in a mental asylum'. But her work and her achievement give her money, power, recognition, freedom and satisfaction.

It also, in a city where everyone is going twinkle twinkle, makes her a star. 'Jane Deknatel?' said one British film producer incredulously, 'How did you get to her?' Six individuals later tried to get to Jane through me – everyone wants a piece of her action. It must help, in image and body-conscious America, that she is quite stunningly good-looking, with the excitement of a sleeping volcano and the presence of a pagan queen. If they were casting for a woman of power, the word would go out, 'Get Deknatel. Any price.'

By setting up her own production company, Jane Deknatel has now taken the final step towards total power and control. Interested parties include French businessmen, with whom she has always had great success. At one Paris reception she was set upon by a tiny Frenchman who announced crossly, 'I do not like toll weemen.' 'You have two choices,' she told him, 'Leave this party, or stand on a chair.' He stood on a chair wherever she was for the rest of the night, and it took her the next year to shake him off. She did not want what he had been trained to give. *Pas du tout*. Jane Deknatel, power woman international, can get everything she wants for herself.

> In any sphere of action, there can be no comparison between the positions of number one, and numbers two, three and four.
>
> Winston Churchill

These three women, Barbara Thomas, Baroness Young and Jane Deknatel, have all in their different ways made themselves powerful. As such they are representatives of an entirely new race. Although so different they share with each other and with other women of power certain critical factors of background and experience which both link and identify them, and were the key to their success. How they and the rest of the new breed of women made it to the top, and how you could, will be the business of the next chapter to explain. It is a phenomenon that both women and men need to understand. For at last, after centuries of silence and suffering, as one of the new power breed puts it: '*The women are coming – with a great orgasmic roar!*'

CHAPTER 2

The New Breed

*What makes Daisy run is different from
what makes Sammy run.*
                              Barbara Hosking

Most of the research into power, leadership and high
achievement has been done on men. It is of little use or relevance
to women. The correspondence of powerful women either to the
men of power, or to the rest of the female population, is very
limited. But top women correlate well with each other. Barbara
Thomas, Baroness Young and Jane Deknatel were all the first
child of the family; all had atypical fathers, high achievement at
school, and some international perspective and experience. All
married, all have children, and all are well above average female
height. These are only a few of the critical factors. How do they
apply to top women in general? In a survey of over forty of
these women drawn from politics, business, industry, civil and
foreign services, the media and the professions in Britain and
America, I found a high degree of congruence between them,
and a clear indication of a new breed of women altogether.

This is hardly the first time historians have hailed the Rise of
the New Woman. But one contemporary social factor has
radically reshaped the lives of women in ways unknown to
history, the availability of a reliable *female* contraceptive. The
ability that this conveys not only to limit but to *determine the
moment* of childbirth has been a major instrument of women's
advancement. It produces an entirely new life profile, as follows:

Women's Life-line: The Transformation

1900

Birth	Marriage	Child-rearing	Death
0	20	45	50

1980

Birth	Begins work	1 child	Retirement	Death
0	18–21	33–6	60	75

What this means is that post-sixties women have been able to count on a forty-year work life, with the first important fifteen years under their belt before they need to think of putting anything else in that region. If they are thinking of children at all, that is. Of the women surveyed:

* 50 per cent had no children;
* 23 per cent had one child only.

Almost three-quarters, then, had broken away from the 'average 2.1'. Of the remainder, 18 per cent had two children, and just under 9 per cent had three. Only one woman had more than three children, the terrific Julia Walsh of Washington, who as a widow with four children married a widower with seven, had another to round off her family and made it twelve, some of whom are now part of the unique Julia M. Walsh and Sons Inc. investment company.

The importance of this structural factor in women's lives can hardly be overestimated. But more significant still are the psychological changes which are taking place. These women are a pioneer breed not because they are making it in non-traditional jobs and posts (although many of them are) but because they are entirely at ease with the idea of power and its practice. Donna Shalala recalls that *Ms* magazine in America once called all the top US women to get their comments on their situation, and they all refused to talk about power. 'I'm very comfortable with talking about power,' she says. 'I like power. It's fun to be at the top. Women have to be comfortable with power and, in order to help other women, comfortable with its use.' Baroness Warnock, operating in power arenas as divergent as the Warnock Committee and Girton College Cambridge, remarks, 'I was a very competitive child. Now I think I like power rather than competition.' Like Donna Shalala, Mary Warnock thinks that women should be getting to the top in every area: 'I want women to be consultants, not just school doctors, and heads of institutions, not just deputies.' Women worldwide agree with her. While British women have doubled their share of top jobs in the last ten years, the proportion of US women in top positions has risen from 18 per cent to 30.5 per cent between 1970 and 1980, according to the US Census Bureau.

These figures, as well as the subsequent research, explode the widely reported research findings that women are not high in achievement motivation, but dominated psychologically by their dependency needs. Particularly influential (and so convenient) has been the 'women's fear of success theory' propounded by Matina Horner in the early 1970s. In contradiction, these women show:

* high achievement needs and motivation towards success
* strong identification with their field or profession
* high ego strength, self-esteem and positive evaluation of their own womanhood
* confident involvement with masculine reference groups

How did they become this way? How did they escape the normal fate of women, of becoming the silent majority? In their famous study of gifted people, Terman and Oden (1959) found that 86 per cent of gifted *men* achieved prominence in professional or managerial posts. At age forty-four, 61 per cent of gifted *women* were fulltime housewives. Of the women who were employed, only 11 per cent were professionals any way in line for upward movement. James Cattell, a US experimental psychologist, calculates that of all persons who had ever become eminent, *only 3.2 per cent had been women.* So how did these women unlearn women's history of weakness, failure and non-achievement?

The Empowering Family

It is clearly demonstrable that high-achieving women come from family backgrounds where in the course of growing up they learn that they can be strong, competent and successful – in a word, powerful – rather than the reverse. This is not normally an acknowledged or even tacit aim of the parents. Nor is a girl's learning to be powerful always the result of benign influences and events; it is not a question of kind parents giving darling daughter everything she needs to help her grow up to be president of General Motors. Rather, it is a case of a series of interlocking experiences in which the parents are of central but not exclusive importance. Other relatives, particularly grand-mothers and siblings, and that indefinable entity the family ethos, all combine to turn a little girl into a woman of power.

Helpful in this context is the concept which has been developed to account for those individuals with records of public achievement, that of the 'politicised family'. This is defined as a family in which the child grows up in the belief and experience that a certain level of political activity is normal and acceptable, with the advantage of knowing from a young age not only the routes to the top, but also the highways and byways. This theory is, of course, established by reference to men: 'John Adams,' drone the commentaries, 'second President of America, was cousin of Samuel Adams, the "American Cato", and father of John Quincy Adams, sixth US President, while his grandson was Secretary of State in the Hoover administration ... ' But it also works for women. The family that produced Earl Grey, famous equally for his Reform Bill and his tea, produced the outstanding feminist, activist and reformer Josephine Butler. Women's married names eclipse these important connections – Countess Markiewicz, the first woman ever elected to parliament, was the sister of the leading suffragist and women's trades unionist Eva Gore-Booth.

Extending the idea of a family that can socialise a daughter into a positive attitude to herself and her role, and make it psychologically possible for her to crash without noticing the barriers behind which the rest of her sex wait and whimper, what are the determining factors of the empowering family? In brief, they are:

* a mother who is out of tune with domestic work and the conventional image of motherhood
* a father who is emotionally warm, but seriously committed

to his daughter's future in her own right
* a dynamic grandmother
* One younger sibling, preferably a brother

– who all live together in a little wooden house. But not in the country. Of these women, 82 per cent were born in or near a city. From the very first, it seems, their eyes were open onto the wider horizons of the 'world elsewhere'.

My Mother, My Self

Despite the popularity of recent work by Nancy Friday and others, the importance of the mother's contribution to her daughter's life has yet to be recognised in all its complexity. Research studies like that of Tangri (1972) have found a positive correlation between both a mother's education and her employment, and her daughter's choice of an atypical work life. This has led to the naive idea of the working mother as role model (responsible for her daughter's success as well as latch-key children, the rise in teenage crime, vandalism, etc.). Clearly the mother's educational background and occupation are important; 60 per cent of mothers in the survey had held paid work, and an even more unusual 37.5 per cent were graduates (a figure not true of the female population of Britain as a whole even in 1985). Daughters of working mothers report their very positive work experiences. 'Mother was fantastic,' says Anne Joy, managing director of Challoners Recruitment, 'a natural-born entre-preneur. She ran a ladies' shop, but she'd sell you a grand piano if you asked for it!' Audrey Slaughter remembers her mother going back to work for the war effort: 'She positively bloomed, she lost ten years. She took up writing and won newspaper competitions' – a forerunner of Audrey's later success in Fleet Street. Sometimes, even a memory was enough. In Australia, the magnificent Pat O'Shane drew on her mother in her struggle to qualify as the first Aboriginal ever to become a lawyer: 'What really got me through was posting photographs of my mother, who had died many years before, on the wall with little slogans saying, "She did it, I can do it." Sometimes that was the only thing that kept me going.'

42

But 40 per cent of these mothers did *not* work, and paid employment is not the key. For numbers of these women, the denial of their mother's right to a working life has been a powerful spur. As the only daughter of a family with five sons, the mother of Jennifer Coutts Clay was accustomed to working both indoors and out, all the year round – 'If the cows need to be milked, it doesn't matter if it's Christmas Day!' Not only her ambition to be a nurse, but her artistic abilities, a fine voice and a gift for writing, were thwarted in her youth. Not surprisingly, she wanted her daughters 'to work properly as part of the formal world', and get a fair reward for their efforts. It is remarkable that *both* her daughters have achieved this at the highest level. A sense of their mother's untapped potential was strong. Mary Lou Carrington, associate director of First Chicago International Capital Markets Group, says 'One of the reasons I work is that my mother so regretted staying at home. My husband says she should have run General Motors, she's one of those marshalling forces!' Mothers often conveyed, too, a very positive image of their independent work lives before they 'gave it up' to get married according to the convention of earlier days. 'She always made it clear that she had a very happy time between her university and child-bearing days, when she had money, time and interests of her own. That influenced my attitude to work a lot,' Mary Lou continued. Finally there were the harsh reminders for some of these women, through their mothers' lives, that relying on the male as breadwinner was a delusion rather than an option – following the death of her father, the mother of investment banker Helen Matthews insisted that she had to be able to stand on her own feet, and her constant message was, 'You've got a brain – *use* it!'

Far more important for women of power than the role-modelling effect of a mother's paid employment is that of her alienation from the image of traditional wife-and-mother-hood. High-achieving women, axiomatically, do not perceive themselves as fulltime home-makers, and *they learn not to do so from their mothers*. Again and again these women remembered their mothers as undomesticated, hating housework, or not performing it. The mother of Lady Porter, leader of Westminster City Council, 'had domestic help, she really loathed housework'. Audrey Slaughter's mother was 'not the slightest

43

bit interested in running a house, and a rotten cook!' The mother of Orna Ni Chionna, whizz-kid management consultant at McKinsey and Co Inc., would a thousand times rather go out to work to pay someone to clean her house than have to stay in and do it herself. Clearly these mothers agreed with Engels that 'housework is the most barbaric form of labour'.

Often, too, the mothers avoided domestic work for other reasons; Elinor Guggenheimer explained of her family's settling into American life, 'Immigrant women worked. Achievement meant *not* working.' And they usually had better things to do. Olive Barnett's mother, as the daughter of an army colonel, loved a full life and was 'very social, always entertaining' – good preparation for Olive's later career as head of training for the Savoy Group. Donna Shalala's mother would get through what had to be done, 'very well, very fast', and then hurry out to play tennis. Mary Baker, former chairman of the London Tourist Board, also had an athletic mother – she sailed, golfed, and 'wasn't the least bit interested in housework'.

Nor were the mothers uncritically loving and supportive according to the stereotype of mother love. There is a degree of ambivalence about a daughter's success; the mother of Nicky Joyce, president of the British Association and secretary-general of the World Federation of Women Executives, wanted her to have a career, 'but a *safe* career' – this did not include the stage, which Nicky's heart was set on at the time. Jean Denton reports her mother as saying wisfully, 'If I hadn't educated you, you'd be round the corner with four grandchildren for me by now.' A considerable proportion of the mothers experienced the conflict as it was expressed by Detta O'Cathain: 'My mother wanted her children to get on. She set great store by that, she wasn't tuned in to conventional definitions of womanhood.' But there was some resentment and envy of Detta's success. 'It was not an easy relationship,' comments Detta. 'I grew up in a highly competitive and intellectual atmosphere. But it *sets the daughters free*. I couldn't be a *hausfrau*.'

In some cases the maternal relationship produced intensely painful and negative experiences. For Marian Hick's mother the difficulties began with a failed attempt to terminate the pregnancy, which made her very sick. She then endured the horrors of a two-day labour with obstetric assistance of such roughness that Marian was born with broken cheekbones. As with Jane Deknatel, the relationship never recovered from this initial trauma. Another victim of a bad delivery was Sheila Needham, founder and managing director of Needham Printers. Her mother suffered from puerperal fever; 'It must have been a horrific start for her. I was a sickly, difficult child and I didn't feel loved. I couldn't please her, I was always doing the wrong thing. We clashed badly.' Sheila's words are echoed by several others, one of whom said, 'I had a domineering mother. I was the rebellious one, and we always clashed.' And nothing quite compares with a mother's power to wound. Three women mentioned a prophecy like that made by Sheila Needham's mother: 'She said no one would ever marry me.' But even as a married woman you can't always please your mother. Elinor Guggenheimer's mother got off a double-barrelled blast in her outrage when Elinor took her first paid job: 'What are you doing to your husband? If you hadn't been born at home, I wouldn't be sure you were my child.' Radical peer Baroness Wootton speaks for many when she says, 'I did not like my mother very much – see my autobiography.'

Against this may be set the fact that a far higher proportion of these mothers than the average undertook the most basic of maternal obligations: almost three-quarters of these women (73.5 per cent) breastfed their daughters, while current statistics show that less than 50 per cent of British mothers were breastfeeding their babies on discharge from hospital, a startling discrepancy even allowing for any misreporting and social change. Yet the mother–daughter relationship need not be particularly warm or close to be highly influential. The mother of Anne Mueller, Britain's top woman civil servant, had taken herself out to India to teach at the age of twenty-one. Later, the same spirit of adventure led her to join up and serve in the ATS during the war, away from her children as they were growing up. She then extended the same right of autonomy to her daughter. 'My mother was a remarkable woman', Anne comments, 'I was brought up with the assumption that I'd do my own thing, and get my own thing through the competitive route, earning scholarships.' Anne's mother also influenced her decision to read PPE at Oxford University; Mary Baker's mother went one better and organised her entry into St Andrew's altogether!

Whatever they were, these women were not conformist. Ambassador Jeane Kirkpatrick recounts with a smile the story of her mother, who, raised on a farm in Texas, left it to go to Fort Worth to study business and book-keeping ('a daring thing to do!') and became 'a quintessential flapper'. Neither by precept nor example did the mothers teach their daughters to knuckle under to the corny and crippling stereotypes of 'woman's role', but set them free from that burden to wing their own flight and sing their own song. Orna Ni Chionna remembers her mother saying that the only reason she worked (as a lecturer in physics) was because she couldn't stand her seven children for twenty-four hours a day! But this enlightened woman had a rota for the domestic tasks that applied with equal strictness to the boys as to the girls; and when Orna went off to Harvard to study for her master's in business studies, she was only following in her mother's footsteps. 'My mother – my great mentor,' said Orna. 'That's it.'

'Daddy's Girl'

The importance of a father's contribution towards his daughter's success is a more clearly identified topic, and it is consonant with previous research findings that 82 per cent of women in this survey reported themselves as close to their fathers. Often the relationship with the father was warmer and more intimate than that with the mother, in many cases reaching a degree of intensity that quite belies Joe Orton's satirical portrait of a British daughter's feelings in *What The Butler Saw*: 'I come from a normal family. I have no love for my father!' So Detta O'Cathain recalls her father as 'so terrific, I soaked him up like a sponge'. On his side, her father 'thought the sun, moon and stars shone out of me', and she is still the main focus of his life. Jean Denton says simply, 'I am my father's daughter,' adding, 'I was the cherry on the cake for him. We had a great delight in each other's company.' Shirley Porter lovingly recalls the joy of receiving a letter in her father's large handwriting, as overflowing as his generosity, and most of the women had similar accounts of feeling a deep idealising affection for these 'great', 'fine', 'gentle', 'imaginative' and 'loving' men.

Closeness was the keynote of the relationship even when its expression was more stormy. Barbara Hosking's father was an ex-soldier, 'a disciplined man, old-fashioned'. 'We were close but we had frightful rows, he used to beat me.' But he also invested a lot of love in Barbara, was keen on her career, and very positive about her future. He wanted her to be a writer and/or a teacher, and firmly believed her capable of both, as she has proved to be, and more. The father of Ambassador Kirkpatrick had ideas for his daughter that were different from her own; she always wanted to be a writer, and by the age of seven was writing second-grade compositions about this. Her father thought it ridiculous – 'He wanted me to be a conventional girl and woman.' The relationship, therefore, although close, was what the ambassador calls 'tumultuous'. 'He was an explosive person,' she comments drily. And she is now a writer, albeit at a level of intellectual distinction that she may not have envisaged at the age of seven!

What is important is the degree of faith that the father shows in his daughter. The distinguished record of Judith Hope, Washington attorney-at-law, in government service, business and the law, has borne out her father's belief; 'He thought I could do *anything* I felt like doing,' she says. 'He was very supportive and encouraging about my career.' Orna Ni Chionna remembers her father's 'extraordinary, enlightened' degree of encouragement and praise for her accomplishments. It made her mad, then, that if she came second he would always say, 'Why didn't you come first?' To an outsider, however, this looks like a very positive message. It clearly says, 'You *can* come first,' in strong contradiction to the message that young girls, especially in Britain, are used to receiving.

Like the mothers of high-achieving women, the fathers are often atypical of their time and place. Donna Shalala's father used to tell his Lebanese friends that they should educate their daughters, a strongly feminist attitude, and insisted that his daughters go to college. The father of Jennifer Coutts Clay, an Aberdeenshire doctor, would hold his three-year-old daughter spellbound with his accounts of the mysteries of the pyloric sphincter and the digestive tract. And it was no problem to Elinor Guggenheimer's father to think of her as 'the next great American poetess, floating through life'.

47

The vital element of the father's support is indicated all the more clearly by its absence. Professor Marian Hicks was her father's favourite as a girl, but his belief that it was a waste of time giving girls a university education proved a severe stumbling-block to her career. His reluctance to pay for her further education after school she overcame by winning a State Scholarship, but his pressure on her to leave school rather than stay on for another year cost her the chance to try for Oxford or Cambridge. Finally, he would only consent to a three-year period of study, so Marian's hopes of studying medicine went out of the window. Her career as an experimental scientist in cancer research is a direct result of these restrictions which her father imposed only upon his daughter; both Marian's brothers qualified as doctors.

The support of these fathers, and their active engagement in their daughters' lives, can be expressed in a number of ways. Strangely, most of them do not seem to have heard of the very masculine-orientated piece of research which argues that if you want your daughter to become a CEO, you must teach her ball-games. Margaret Pereira, controller of Forensic Science Services for the Home Office, remembers that her father played ball-games a lot with her, but that he also read, sang and talked to her. Dame Josephine Barnes, former president of the British Medical Association, played cricket and football with her brothers, and was sufficiently good at ball-games to get a hockey blue for Oxford. But the most strenuous thing she ever played with her father was golf – not exactly what the business school theorists have in mind when they go into the intricacies of team play, fighting for the ball, taking the knocks, and all the rest of that towel-snapping locker-room baloney that suggests that corporate business is being run by a bunch of blithering jocks. For the rest, fathers are remembered in gentler incarnations: Mary Baker's father 'loved cooking', Mary Lou Carrington's, although a disciplinarian at work, was a tolerant and loving person at home, and Anne Joy speaks of the childhood wonderment of being allowed to help her father sort out his collection of small electrical components, 'all lovely different colours', and playing chess for hours.

It has been argued that the father's influence is decisive in the career of a high-achieving daughter in the absence of many female role models for her to follow. So to argue ignores the importance of mothers as potential role models, and underestimates the degree of autonomy attained by women of power. As Eve Mahlab, Australian lawyer and businesswoman, puts it, 'I had two good models: my father working at home, and my mother actively enjoying the business. I just took it for granted that I had to do things for myself and be independent.' Where the father comes in is in helping his daughter to believe that she can make it. Once there, she can draw on her mother and herself.

Grand Old Mothers

Powerful women also draw on a relation whose existence has never been researched at all in connection with women's high achievement, their grandmother. The link with the father has been enthusiastically written up and dwelt on. But against the figure of 82 per cent of women reporting their closeness to their fathers is a staggering 84 per cent who reported that their grandmothers were *very important* to their careers, and 'very strong' characters in their lives. The influential grandmother is the mother's mother, who through her links with her daughter becomes an important presence in the next generation too. Many of these women are as impressive as their high-achieving granddaughters. Orna Ni Chionna's grandmother was a graduate, a rare distinction in the Ireland of the early 1900s. She was one of twelve children, and all the girls won scholarships to relieve the family finances so that all could take up their educational opportunity; all were involved, too, in the freedom fight for Ireland. Mary Baker's grandmother, 'a *very* strong character', indicates how unconventional these women reserved the right to be; she was one of a large family of sisters, a great sportswoman always out on the grouse moors, who in her advanced age insisted on sawing logs for the war effort. Often they were free-thinkers, challenging received notions of appropriate behaviour – after giving birth to seventeen children, only six of whom survived, Nicky Joyce's grandmother went off to be sterilised in 1921, even though her grandfather was so shocked by this 'wicked deed' that he would never speak to her again.

In their granddaughters' perception, these women were the

senior figures of the line of strong women in which, consciously or unconsciously, they positioned themselves. 'I see my mother and my grandmother in my face every time I look in a mirror,' says Judge Jean Graham Hall. Grandmothers were strong and capable, teaching school from a one-room school-house, running a store, active in the nursing corps in World War I. They were the repositories of fascinating knowledge – Jennifer Coutts Clay's grandmother taught her how to collect eggs, and how to put hens to sleep at nighttime by tucking their heads under their wings. They were great readers, and sometimes brilliant scholars, they loved the theatre and film, they were athletic and tough, they were landed gentry, Russian refugees, Polish emigrés and ladies of the manor. They were 'the backbone of the family'.

The formative influence of the strong line of women may be illustrated from one case study. Judith Davenport represents the fourth generation of successful businesswomen in her family, all of whom distinguished themselves in different fields. Judith's great-grandmother Charlotte, a widow with nine children, ran a large fleet of Cornish fishing smacks, turning up on the quay at 4 a.m. every day to see each boat in and auction the fish herself, during a full working life which extended into her eighties. Her daughter Amelia ran the building side of the business, raised twelve children and died at the age of ninety-one still controlling rents and properties. Amelia's daughter Elsie established a retail business in Plymouth at the height of the blitz there in World War II, and successfully developed this after the war into a chain of shops. At seventy years of age, Elsie, Judith's mother, is still working. Judith herself, a finalist in the 1984 Veuve Cliquot Businesswoman of the Year Competition, moved back into the fishing industry with her first trawler in 1969, and is now smoking fish for the nation's retail chains. At forty-five, looking back up the female line, Judith understandably feels that she is just beginning!

As with the mothers, the influence of these grandmothers was equally strong whether their granddaughters liked them or not. Some of them were obviously very trying as members of the family circle: 'a matriarch', 'a tyrant', 'an old bat', 'a queen bee of the first order' and 'a senile delinquent!' were among the observations passed by the women of power on their maternal

50

relation. Often the grandmother remained important when not physically present, or even after death. 'I never knew her, but my mother spoke of her constantly,' said Margaret Pereira. 'My mother was devoted to her. She had been a terrific mother, with a strong character, very strong impact.' So whether the grandmothers were remembered as 'a genuine horror – she always used to make my mother cry', or, as Josephine Barnes knew hers, 'like an empress – a beautiful person', the one factor that comes through again and again is the little girl's early awareness of the power of the female, and its continuance in the female line. A classic illustration of this is the family of Jill Currie, commercial director of Bass Mitchells and Butlers Ltd, and the only woman on the board of a British brewery. Her maternal grandmother, great-grandmother, her mother and her sister all lived together in the same house in what she calls a 'strong maternal line' that took these older women into their eighties and nineties. Jill's sister, accountant Barbara Cannon, is also a board director and forging ahead in business, and both women, on the family pattern, still have fifty or sixty years to go!

Power from the Family

Undoubtedly the best thing that a girl can do for her future prospects is to get herself born at the head of the family or as its sole female member. Of the women in the survey:

* 60 per cent were the eldest child
* 50 per cent were the only girl

But the would-be woman of power should not find herself at the head of a large brood. Empowering families are small, and the eldest girl typically has one sibling only – nearly half (48 per cent) of these families had two children only. For choice, a younger brother is preferable to a younger sister, but what is contra-indicated is *either* any expansion *or* reduction in the family size. Only about a third (36 per cent) of top women come from families that have three children or more, and only 16 per cent were an only child. Possibly in the larger families individual enterprise is suppressed, and girls are more likely than boys to

51

find themselves dragged down into domestic work and the female role. In the case of the only child, perhaps parents tend to be overprotective of a solitary daisy-flower. It must be added, though, that the hypothesis could not possibly be applied to the enterprising Janet Mead, managing director of Associated Research Ltd and an 'only one', whose fearless travelling throughout Europe, India and Asia was always encouraged by her mother from the moment when Janet first pushed off to foreign parts at the age of eighteen.

This, finally, is what the empowering family does; it makes it possible for its girls to do things that other girls think they can't. Janet Mead once arrived in South America without a job, a place to stay, or a command of the language. She spent a fortnight knocking on every door of every house and shop in Brazil's equivalent of Regent Street, and soon had all three. So while other women are responding apprehensively or negatively to the idea of a simple promotion, others learn to say, 'What are the qualities of a vice-president? Do I have them? YEAH!'

Growing Up

None of these girls grew up in a background of both wealth and privilege, in the interlocking network of assumptions and associates necessary to produce that unassailable sense of superiority, social or otherwise. Two families, as a result of the father's business success, were extremely well-to-do, but the benefits of this for their daughters were offset by the inescapable shadow of anti-Semitism. Of the total number only 34 per cent had 'comfortable middle-class origins'. A further 29 per cent described themselves as coming from homes where the standards were middle-class, but the income (of teacher, clerk or parson) was not. 'Money was adequate, but only just,' was one comment.

A considerable sector (18 per cent) were those from the homes of the able and aspiring working class, who in the classic motivation of social mobility 'wanted better for themselves and their children'. They got so far by themselves, then handed on to their daughters the task of gaining a university degree, for instance. More unusual is the clear indication of marked

52

financial insecurity in the childhood of a number of these women. 16 per cent talked of fathers spending most of their lives in the struggle with a rocky business which eventually failed. It is hard, under these circumstances, for women to see the responsibility for breadwinning and life management as safely left in the hands of men. And a surprising number in the survey had received the lesson of men's frailty in the cruellest way possible – one fifth of them (20 per cent) had lost their fathers by the age of twelve, a highly atypical statistic.

Growing up was not particularly easy for these girls. They tended to be advanced in infancy; such evidence as there is (it was not available for all the women in the survey) suggests that as babies they walked and talked earlier than average. What is clear is a pattern of earlier than average school entry, and an early start to reading: 82 per cent were reading before the age of five. This was usually the prelude to further academic success, which was very important both psychologically and practically. Lady Taylor, director of Taylor Woodrow PLC, won a scholarship to pay for her fees to secretarial college at the age of thirteen. Jean Denton distinctly recalls thinking, when she heard that she had passed the eleven-plus, 'We've cracked it!' Many of the women had had similar experiences.

Yet few were able to report that their schooldays were the happiest days of their lives. In Britain, girls' schools are mainly interested in producing good girls and obviously had difficulties with the talented and highly-motivated variety. So Josephine Barnes was 'too boisterous for a prefect', Shirley Porter was 'a very naughty girl, totally anti-establishment', and Jennifer Coutts Clay would get black marks for 'always roaring round the place'. In Australia, too, Eve Mahlab found that being bright made her a 'social outcast', stigmatised as a 'trouble-maker' by her teachers. As Nicky Joyce observes, 'a quick brain looks for mischief'. For many, too, there was the experience of being out of touch or sympathy with the other girls. As if in rehearsal for later eminence with its concomitant isolation, these girls tended to be leaders or loners, occasionally both. As Anne Joy expresses it: 'I felt often alone, out on a limb. I felt irritated with the other girls' passion for a variety of things. The only passion I had was Fred Astair and Gene Kelly's dancing, that was the only fantasy stuff I had. I felt great irritation with girls who were

53

fashion-conscious.' Yet Anne was also the moving spirit of the school's musical revues and once got into trouble for staging 'Tiptoe through the Tulips', instead of Shakespeare!

Do Put Your Daughter on the Stage, Mrs Worthington

It was striking how unanimously and with what pleasure the women recorded their involvement with performance activities: acting, singing, music, dancing, producing school plays or other shows. Josephine Barnes expressed the value of speech and drama lessons: 'I must have been an over-dressed little girl, but it *works*.' Marian Hicks enjoyed a heavy involvement with music while Gill Lewis, one of the three principals of Fisher Dillistone and Associates of Berkeley Square, was in all the school choirs and madrigal groups while also producing school concerts. Some were budding dramatists. Mary Baker would put on puppet plays with her father, and write the script, while Audrey Slaughter used to write and produce dramas giving herself the starring roles!

Of particular importance to many had been the ballet, and a third of the total number (33 per cent) stressed how central it had been in their early lives. Some, like Gill Lewis, were good enough to have been considered potential ballet school material, and many, like Barbara Thomas, Janet Mead and Anne Joy, wanted to be ballet dancers above all else when they grew up. The devotion to ballet cannot be explained simply as something that all little girls go through. 'Ballet is about *control*,' explains Detta O'Cathain. 'It gives confidence and a discipline,' according to Jill Currie. For Jennifer Coutts Clay the ballet meant 'something to get your teeth into and an encouragement to do better than the others so that you can dance in the front row!' Certainly to an outsider the ballet, with its demands for supreme dedication, hard work, commitment, poise and grace, seems like an image of the high achievement with which these women were later to distinguish themselves. But whatever its nature, the early experience that almost all these women had of public performance not only helped to form their taste for the spotlight and their ability to handle those pressures, but actively worked against the familiar destruction of confidence of what

Jane Deknatel scornfully calls 'English nannyspeak', *'No one's going to look at you, dear.'*

Such highlights were important in lives that in general were not uncomplicatedly happy. 'I have to tell you that I did not have a totally wonderful childhood,' said Barbara Thomas, a statement that was echoed by the majority. The reason for these feelings varied. In a surprisingly high number of cases, the distress was produced by physical setback; 39 per cent of the women had suffered serious illness in childhood, a figure high enough to support the research finding that experience of being 'out-of-phase' is one of the formative factors of high achievement. These illnesses were severe enough to keep the victims in bed, often for up to a year – with septic arthritis or rheumatic fever, nephritis, septicaemia, pleurisy or double pneumonia – and to change their lives. 'You can't be one of the gang if you haven't seen them for ten months,' was one description of the resulting alienation from peer groups. Beatrice Faust, leading Australian writer and feminist, offers this matter-of-fact summary of her alienation from a conventional girlhood: 'I was different because my mother was dead, and everyone else had mothers. I was different because I had asthma and developed a caved-in chest from being unable to breathe. I could sit and read books, which was a tremendous pleasure and relief. I had quite a rich life, but it wasn't the life of a child.' Occasionally the life change was even more marked – after a bout of whooping cough bad enough to keep her off school for three months at the age of fourteen, Debbie Moore effectively closed the chapter of her schooldays and embarked on the career of international modelling which resulted in Pineapple Dance Studios and Pineapple Broadway.

High achievement and worldly success have a dazzle effect that can make it look as if the possessor has always led a charmed life. On the contrary, a high proportion of these women suffered painful, distressing, even traumatic episodes in their lives. Gill Lewis was knocked off her bicycle at the age of nine, and the accident which severed the tendons and main nerve of her right hand kept her in and out of hospitals all over the country for a year. Such damage is emotional as well as physical. Margaret Pereira's mother, in her determination to find a good Catholic family when her children were to be evacuated in the war, made 'a most terrible mistake', billeting them with a farm labourer and his wife who took all their food rations. During this period of 'terrible unhappiness' at the age of twelve, Margaret's weight was so much reduced by this starvation diet that she stopped menstruating.

Yet it is a mark of the calibre of these women that they are able to make something positive even out of the most negative events. Elinor Guggenheimer recalls her father's death: 'I saw him fall, I saw him dead in the house. I couldn't talk about it for years, I had such a sense of lack of worth. I thought it must be my fault, I was a bad child.' But as with Jane Deknatel, later there came a positive counter-effect: 'I wanted to prove to him that I could do it,' a desire so powerfully dramatised by Barbra Streisand as 'Poppa, can you hear me?' in *Yentl*. The injury suffered by Shirley Porter was the deepest personal insult. Excelling at 'a school cast in the Roedean mould', she was made a prefect very early and showed such promise at organisation and public speaking that one of her teachers, prophetically as it now appears, said, 'You ought to become an MP, Shirley.' But when Shirley reached the top of the school, it was intimated to her that she could not be head girl, as the school had never had a Cohen on the honours board before. 'It was a spur,' she now says firmly. 'I thought, "I'll show the buggers!" ' She has.

As this suggests, embryo women of power were sparky creatures. At eleven, Lady Taylor was so keen to drive that her brother-in-law allowed her to lean over and steer his car in a field, as a prelude to teaching her the real thing as soon as she was old enough. Also at eleven, Marian Hicks acquired a horse, rode it home, put it in the paddock and announced, 'I've bought a horse from Mr Goodman, Daddy, please will you pay him £25?' Those who grew up in World War II quickly learned to be strong and self-reliant as Anne Joy did:

We grew up very quickly as children in the war, and I learned to face adversity. I remember, during the fire-bomb raids on London when I was thirteen, being put in charge of the family documents. I was quite unable to control my muscles trembling, but I just did it. Once a fire bomb landed right in front of our shelter. We could see the Air Raid Warden crawling slowly towards us on his belly, trying to shield himself with a dustbin lid, obviously terrified. My sister just picked up a sandbag, slit it open and calmly put the whole thing out.

These experiences of competence and mastery, often in contrast to some less than adequate member of the mighty male sex, helped to create a very positive self-evaluation. Important too in the majority of cases was one critical early success. Judith Hope was president of an Ohio state-wide organisation at the age of fifteen, and the first female to hold the post. At eighteen, Anne Mueller won an international competition run by the *New York Herald Tribune* to write an essay on 'The World We Want'. Her prize was a thirteen-week grand tour of the USA whose climax was a meeting with the President. Back home again, this brought journalistic and broadcasting assignments for her, tremendous and stimulating developments for one so young. Early success, reported again and again, was not necessarily in the field in which the individual was to become distinguished – Detta O'Cathain won a national art competition which did much to restore morale after a serious illness at the age of twelve. And it is remarkable that even apparently golden girls need to 'learn' success and the good feelings that go with it. A 'life breakthrough' occurred for Jane Fonda when the initiatory acting exercise she performed for Lee Strasberg at the Actors' Studio proved to be a success and won her a place in the group. As she has commented on this episode:

> My life changed radically within twenty-four hours. It was just a night-and-day difference. Before, I'd been scared and extremely self-conscious – I was one person. After that exercise I was somebody else ... It was like a light bulb going on. It's a fantastic feeling when you've finally found out where you're going. You're happier. You're more productive. You're nicer. You're channelled.

Some of these women were 'channelled' at an early age, medicos in particular being unable to remember a time when they did not want to be a doctor. But again, an early experience often proved to be formative in a highly positive way. Judith Hope's father was a Methodist minister whose church became reluctantly embroiled in civil litigation. To the young Judith sitting attentively in the courthouse throughout the proceedings

57

it was apparent that the church's interests could have been much more effectively represented. She decided that the duties of a lawyer to his client were far higher than this advocate appeared to feel, and resolved then to become one herself.

But even earlier than the stage of conscious career election, women of achievement showed a marked orientation towards power. Often this took the form of control, so that they saw themselves in charge and running things – the local council, Marks and Spencer's, a sweet shop. Often the attraction was towards where the power seemed to be; Mary Lou Carrington thought it must be a good thing to be the wife of an ambassador, and Gill Lewis wanted to be Princess Elizabeth, 'because she was going to be Queen!' Even the earliest fantasies were fantasies of female strength, not submission – Barbara Hosking, naturally enough for a coast-born Cornishwoman who had been exposed to the winds off the Atlantic at birth to strengthen her, saw herself as Grace Darling. Margaret Pereira, drawing on a Catholic culture, wanted to be a saint (N.B. *not* a martyr). From the very beginning, high-achieving women aim high. At the age of ten, Orna Ni Chionna decided to become President of the United States of America, and checked out the US citizenship requirements in her local library. 'I love fame,' said Disraeli. Clearly fame is the spur that raises the spirits of a woman every bit as high as those of a man.

Whatever the mix of setback, suffering or success, the majority of the women in this survey had concentrated in their early years upon their schoolwork, and then upon consolidating their academic position at university. Almost three-quarters of them were graduates (73 per cent) of British, American or French universities, and even more impressively, almost half (47 per cent) held a postgraduate degree as well. The clear message for ambitious women is grab as much education for yourself as you can. Favoured and fashionable are postgraduate qualifications in business studies, especially an MBA from a high-prestige school. But pole position on the starting-grid goes to lawyers. This is not only because the law is a respected and remunerative profession in its own right, but because it is the most useful route to any other area of power. Around 50 per cent of *all* state legislatures, for instance, consist of lawyers. For a woman, holding a law degree conveys an instant

58

credibility which does much to counteract the disadvantages of her sex and, as Jeane Kirkpatrick found in her pioneering study of women power-holders, enables her to surge forward without the years of party or community service that other women have to put in. This holds good not only for the US. Consider what her qualification as a barrister has done for Margaret Thatcher.

But no matter what the discipline, the key factor is getting a first-class training, according to Donna Shalala. 'This is the critical thing, you've *got* to have it,' she advises. 'It doesn't help initially, but you can't substitute for it with hard work. You must have it to fall back on.' A first-class training is indicated by the flourish of distinctions and awards tucked away discreetly on these women's *curricula vitae*; Julia Walsh, for instance, before she went into the children business, was (and is) BBA *magna cum laude* of Kent State University. At a more significant level, it is displayed in the quality of these women and their approach to life. A close acquaintance with a few of them almost seems to be confirmation of Plato's theory of the leader as one possessing a strange and rare virtue.

But a good training is not only received within the walls of the schoolhouse. Women of achievement receive a good training in life, both its good and bad elements, often to an unusually intense or extreme degree. They learn to struggle, to endure, to hold their ground, and to win. They learn to like winning. They learn to like themselves. The characteristic profile of the new-breed woman of power as a girl looks like this. She has:

* an empowering family
* a degree of early insecurity, distress, experience of being out of phase
* a growing sense of her ability to cope with this, a sense of being stronger than others, particularly men
* a concrete outside success as confirmation of promise and proof of worth
* academic achievement and validation
* a strong sense of personal autonomy, self-reliance and ability to take responsibility

With a profile like this, the young woman about to launch herself on her career looks worthy of anyone's attention. She also looks tall. Of the women surveyed, 88 per cent were above the average British adult female height of $5'3\frac{1}{2}''$, and almost a third (32 per cent) were above the adult British male height of $5'8\frac{1}{2}''$. It is well known to social scientists that height correlates structurally with social class, the privileged members of social class 1 being taller than their disadvantaged fellows in the lower social orders. But as 88 per cent of these women do not come from social class 1 their height has obviously been a factor in their advancement, to put it no higher. In addition, height correlates psychologically with dominance; despite famous exceptions like Napoleon and Hitler who have given rise to the midget theory of power, leaders at every level tend to be taller than average. The sheer fatuousness of the bulk principle was exposed as early as A.D. 235 when the Roman legions on the Rhine made an illiterate Thracian peasant, Verus Maximinus, Emperor because of his great size. It is obviously still operating to exclude massive numbers of women who do not approach as nearly as possible, or exceed, the height standards of the traditional power-holders, men.

In considering the family backgrounds and early life experiences of women of high achievement a number of interesting facts and hypotheses emerge. Perhaps most interesting is the simple fact that there are now enough of these women about to qualify as a distinct group and, as I have argued, a new breed. No longer are we looking at one exceptional woman seemingly removed from her sex by her success. The new woman not only looks good, she looks numerous. She also looks like her friend or sister. In most particulars these women are not like male power-holders; they are like themselves. Comparative figures in the 70 and 80 percentiles display a remarkable degree of consistency and homogeneity between them. Yet male standards and traditions of power, established over thousands of years, regulate their world and determine their range of action and acceptability. Inevitably, though, so many newcomers to power must question and challenge its assumptions both by their very existence and by their actions in power. Each of these women, tacitly or triumphantly, raises the fundamental question: What is power?

CHAPTER 3

What is Power?

Power is widely coveted and rarely admitted.
Generally those who have power repress
their awareness of this fact.

Rollo May

What is power? Interest in this question goes back as far as
civilisation itself. The scope and flexibility of the concept of
power make it extremely difficult to come to grips with. But
power is something it is even more difficult to be honest about.
Now that sex and death are losing their status, power looks set
fair to become the last great taboo.

The difficulty of power stems from the simple fact that where
it exists, some will necessarily have more of it than others. In an
age wedded to the myth of democratic equality, the implications
of this are too much for tender democratic consciences. The idea
that one class, one set of interests, one man, holds and exerts
power over another is, in its naked terms, unacceptable. The
challenge of women's power is even more conflict-ridden.

Power in a democratic society has to be made to look natural,
inevitable, depersonalised, invisible. So power-holders will deny
that they are powerful, power-seekers reject indignantly the
suggestion that they are after it. The really important figures are
often so entrenched in power as to be out of sight. Who runs the
civil service? The Bank of England? No politician admits that he
wants to be elected to *rule*, but to 'govern', and as Edward
Heath declared on entering 10 Downing Street, 'to govern is to
serve'. With pious platitude and self-seeking rhetoric such men
have sought to persuade that they are not taking power, when

the career of Margaret Thatcher has demonstrated the electorate's desperate hunger for someone who will.

In the manoeuvring before the election that made her leader, Margaret Thatcher displayed the classic killer instinct of the power person by going for the Heath jugular while William Whitelaw, her only serious rival, held back, feeling that he could not honourably stand against his leader in the first ballot. Yet the ruthless warrior with knives on her chariot wheels is not a role that Margaret Thatcher wants to play too often. All power-holders need to sound like St Francis of Assisi rather than Ivan the Terrible, and Margaret Thatcher has already been dubbed 'Attila the Hen'. She too, in a tradition that goes back to the birth of government, is adept at masking the face of power. Consider this exchange in an interview with journalist Anthony Shrimsley during her first year as Prime Minister:

Q: As Prime Minister do you find that you actually have the power to influence events or are you just restricted to reacting to situations?

A: Oh good heavens no. I mean, just look at what *we* have done in the first five months. *We* did in the budget what *we* said *we* were going to do ... *we* paid the police more ... changed trade union relations ... certain things in the EEC ...
None of that was reacting to events. That was *mastering* events [my italics].

Notice how skilfully Margaret Thatcher evades the direct question of how much power she has as a person, and reconstructs it as a long rhodomontade of collective government action, finally asserting control under its benign aspect, 'mastering events'.

As mistress of such events, Margaret Thatcher is past mistress of the terminology; 'I'm the custodian of the strategy' is a characteristic phrase. It is another interesting reflection on her style of power that, where Harold Wilson identified communication and vigilance as the necessary qualities for a premier (i.e. political skills), Margaret Thatcher declares for 'courage', a straight lift from Churchill, who said that courage in a leader was 'the quality that guarantees all others'. But Churchill also said that 'ambition is the motive of power', and it was in recognition of this aspect of Margaret Thatcher, accompanied by a combination of guts and gall all too often lacking in men, that led the British people to hand her power on a plate for a second term at the 1983 landslide election.

Fudging the facts of power is one of the necessary skills of politicians, male or female. In this the declarations of the governors merely answer the desires of the governed, who wish to have all such matters taken care of, along with the luxury of not being made to feel dominated in any way. So there is a ready collusion with the idea that taking up power is a *burden*, a duty, even a danger: everyone is familiar with Lord Acton's dictum that power corrupts. Thinking about power, and the individual's motivation towards power, has been very adversely affected by a facile acceptance of this one-sided pronouncement. Clearly we need a wider concept of something that relates so critically to self-actualisation and self-esteem, not to mention success, fame and money.

Arguably the idea that power corrupts is given to us to dissuade us from trying to get it. The reality is that power is so enjoyable that once people have tasted it, they strongly desire to retain or increase it, and feel very bad if they lose it. As French political theorist Michel Duverger drily observes: 'It is always advantageous to those in power to persuade others that for them to be actively involved in political action would be sordid, dishonest, unhealthy and selfish.' How do we get any nearer to a grasp on this elusive concept which masks an essential reality? One factor predominates over all others in any consideration of the subject.

Homo Called Sapiens

Power is defined by and on behalf of the masculine half of the human race. After millennia of males washing their own brains (and ours) with their delusions of superiority, it is hardly surprising that power is *thought of* as being male, and embodied in imagery wistfully reflecting men's fantasies of superman strength and sexual potency, so that a strong female is complimented with the adjective 'ballsy' or threatened with the insult 'ball-breaker'. Nor do any of the power structures of society give cause to unthink the equation that power = male. The schools that feed the universities that feed the upper echelons have as yet taken small account of women so that the great institutions, the bases of power and prestige and the chief means of exercising both, remain staffed by men who are, on any other level than the horizontal, virgin in the ways of women. Consider this indictment of psychiatrist Robert Seidenberg:

> We must recognise that our society is overwhelmingly dominated by male 'homosexuality' in religion, politics, higher education, law, big business, the armed forces and practically all other important institutions ... the reality is that men in general prefer to spend most of their time in each other's company, compete, make contracts, plan and make decisions together, and in their leisure time, play together. Very little time is spent with women; their opinions are generally held in low esteem; they are never present in the higher echelons of decision-making and are not brought into games of leisure. They are sexual partners, but this takes only a few minutes a week, just enough to establish that a male is a heterosexual, which he obviously is not, based on his apparent preferences in time-spent studies ... For most men, women are good to sleep with, not to stay awake with.

One result of this masculine monopoly of power and privilege is a blindness to the true nature of the situation that is felt as arrogance by women on the receiving end. So Walter Goldsmith, director-general of the Institute of Directors, addressed a meeting of the International Presidents of the World Association of Women Chief Executives (FCEM):

> Madam President, I have, as some of you may have noticed [they did] not complied with the request that was put to me when I was asked to address you. I have not in any way commented on the importance that I place on the role of women in commerce and industry. The reason for this is simple. I am not prepared to make any distinction.

In the same spirit Anthony Sampson, surveying *The Changing Anatomy of Britain* in 1982 after two vigorous decades of activity had produced at least some forward movement for women, came up with a ludicrously one-sided tome containing just five derisory references to women in the index. These male blinkers amount to a severe intellectual handicap. How does Bertrand Russell's reputation as a great thinker stand up in the light of a pronouncement like this: 'Love of power is almost universal but in its absolute form it is rare. A woman who enjoys power in the management of her house is likely to shrink from the sort of power enjoyed by a Prime Minister.' Well, she didn't, did she?

As power is male, the model of the most powerful becomes the quintessence of maleness, even to an absurd degree. Advisers to Edward Heath when he was Conservative leader, concerned that he lost points for being unmarried and liking classical music, had him take up sailing to masculinise his image (hello, sailor?). Similarly Margaret Thatcher's voice lessons, which took the famous tones down by many notches without diminishing the decibel output, highlighted a particular problem for women in finding the very voice of power, when the voice we are used to hearing is that of a male. Maleness is muscle is macho. Women may wonder how many steers Walter Mondale ropes a day, but he still contrived to put a spoke in the wheel of Gary Hart's success waggon during the 1984 US Presidential campaign with the simple taunt, *'Where's the beef?'*

These self-flattering male assumptions reign, for the most part unchallenged, at every level of power activity. 'The model of the successful manager in our culture is a masculine one,' burbles a business text by Douglas McGregor:

The good manager is aggressive, competitive, just. He is not feminine; he is not soft or yielding or dependent or intuitive in the womanly sense. The very expression of emotion is widely viewed as a feminine weakness that would interfere with effective business processes.

Such thinking not only works to hold back women, but equally dangerously produces a race of emotionally truncated men: men who have neither the imagination nor the intelligence to understand what they are doing, let alone question it, but who simply continue trying to reproduce the system which gives them power, no matter what the cost.

There is no doubt that the majority of men want to stay where they are. Most men feel threatened and will go on fighting to

65

prevent women from achieving a pre-eminent position.

Marjorie Proops

Women's Exclusion from Power

Power is masculine, not only in how men feel it and define it, but in what they do with it and how they continue to monopolise it. In the 1982 General Household Survey of Great Britain, figures show that 'young women are closing the gap in further education and job-hunting success, but men are still more likely to obtain top jobs and early promotion'. Among those who attend a university, men are *twice as likely* to be able to pursue a professional career. And men's advantages over women *increase* as their careers progress, since promotions go to men in preference to women. Of people with similar qualifications in the 25-29 age group there was little difference in attainment. But between 30 and 39 years the gap widens sharply as males are advanced over women and at their expense. Similar figures from other countries show that Britain is not an isolated case. A survey of women published in *Antoinette*, the journal of women unionists in the French Confederation Generale de Travail, showed that 45.8 per cent of them had *never been promoted*.

There is, then, a wildly discrepant picture of women's achievement over all. While some remain stuck at the starting-gate, others are 'spreading out into male hegemonies' in numbers too great to be ignored, according to the dynamic Patricia B. Soliman, associate publisher and vice-president of Simon and Schuster Inc. But 'women are still on the cusp,' Patricia says. '*Real* power, where the buck stops, very few women have. They get up to the edge – VP, executive VP – but still the CEO on top will be male. Especially in *business*-business, the woman will be *numero uno* minus one – as they say in men's circles. "Close, but no cigar!"' As a woman who achieved CEO status at Coward, McCann and Geoghegan before coming to Simon and Schuster, Patricia Soliman now gives, rather than receives, the metaphorical cigar. But her analysis holds good for women's advancement in the majority of areas where we are making headway.

Paradoxically, the areas where men are most highly educated

66

are those which are proving the most resistant to women, something which ought to dispel the feeble female belief that education alone will eradicate discimination. Worst of all, in Britain at least, are the professions, those super-eminent bastions of white male supremacist privilege which have for so long seemed not only unquestioned but unquestionable. The older a profession, the more its traditions have grown out of exclusively male operations: the medieval university, the practice of dialectic, the habit of sex segregation for learning and working, codified in the nineteenth century by the introduction of prep and boarding schools, all regimes posited on competitive or adversarial principles both hostile and repugnant to women. The longer the history of a profession, the more 'conservative' (read reactionary) are its traditions, and the harder they are for women to break down.

In Britain, for instance, the Church, the army and the law date from the earliest times, and only one has made the least real accommodation to women. The importance of the law goes beyond the simple question of access to its practices and rewards. In every country lawyers not only make up the most significant sector of its legislature, but supply the lion's share of the bureaucracies and are found at national and international levels in all forms of industry, trade and commerce. Women's exclusion from this vital career track clearly has the widest of repercussions. So it is a blot on Australian national life that the proportion of women practising as solicitors has risen to only 6 per cent, although women have become more than 25 per cent of law students at Sydney University, for example. Nor can Britain afford to feel smug about its recently attained 40 per cent of female law students until all those women translate their law degree into a practising certificate, and stop withdrawing or diversifying as they do now.

What is more outrageous in this context is the way that the law, in particular, operates to buoy up its old boys, and keep in practice a high volume of duds and disasters, at the same time as it keeps women down and out. The most famous case of this in recent times was that of the man at the peak of the British judiciary, Widgery LCJ. As Lord Chief Justice, Widgery was the most senior law lord and judge in England. His sudden retirement in 1980 caused surprise and was treated as premature. The truth was that Widgery had been known to be in decline. He had been inaudible, inadequate, incapable, asleep on the Bench – *for years*. But as Hugo Young disclosed in his account of this story in the *Guardian*, the law closed ranks to protect him. 'They covered up the fact that Widgery was a cipher,' a senior judicial figure said. When at last this situation, which was being treated as a private matter for the law alone, threatened to become public, Widgery LCJ was assisted to retire. At this point it emerged that he had suffered from a degenerative nervous disease for the past five years. On his departure it was revealed that the backlog of neglected cases in one court alone amounted to more than 600. Young comments:

In delay alone, Widgery's infirmity accounted for an immeasurable quantity of justice denied ... If a Lord Chief Justice has lost his marbles, he surely should not sit on the Bench a great deal longer, however painful his removal may be. [But] the law, although full of garrulous men, is a club with almost Masonic exclusiveness.

Why pick on the law? Every one of these 'men's clubs' operates some kind of security service for its members. The 1983 report of the civil service on management and personnel discreetly relates one case of 'poor attendance' in the Ministry of Agriculture, Forestries and Fisheries. This man, in his first ten years in post, took an average of fifty days' 'sick leave' per year. The response to this was simply to transfer him from department to department (eleven moves in all) as individual managers passed the dead buck. This man's career in the civil service lasted for *twenty-four years* before premature retirement took place. In this case not only the individual but his managers succeeded in raising incompetence to the level of an art. And this while women were dismissed on marriage, paced at the rate deemed appropriate for the 'weaker sex' or not admitted at all to the hallowed portals. The corridors of power – or protectionism?

In 1883, in the first ever open and competitive US Civil Service Examinations, the top of the list was a woman, Mary Francis Hoyt. She was not appointed to a post.

In Britain in 1983, women accounted for 49 per cent of those

applying to the Civil Service and 27 per cent of those appointed.
Civil Service Commission Annual Report 1983

How Does It Work?

How does the system continue to operate in such a way as to exclude women from access to power in the quantities that our numerical superiority in populations (51 per cent in Britain, 53 per cent in the US, 54 per cent in France) would lead us to expect as of right? The pat answer offers childbirth as our great disability – if you will drop out of the power struggle to indulge yourself in a task as marginal and feminine as replacing the human race, what can you expect? The reality is that the childbirth which so disadvantages us is *our own* – having had the lack of judgement, in the opinion of the power-holders, to be born into the 'opposite' sex.

Sadly, the majority of parents concur with this destructive evaluation of the capacity of their female offspring. Psychologist Elizabeth Hitchfield, in her survey of gifted children *In Search of Promise* (1973), discovered in her preliminary research when seeking to identify these children that parents nominated *twice as many boys as girls*. To be born male, it seems, is to be born gifted. What this means for girls is a two-to-one chance against being recognised right from the start.

This bias in favour of males is compounded from the moment of entry into primary school. Reports from the Equal Opportunities Commission and the Schools Council tell a dreary tale of boys effortlessly commandeering teacher time and attention:

> The fact that they lagged behind girls in intellectual development, particularly in reading skills and language development [wot, and they so gifted?] and were more prone to break rules, caused the primary schools to lay stress on girls' good behaviour to compensate for boys' needs and deficiencies.
> Judith White, *Beyond The Wendy House* (1983)

Clearly to be a Goody Two-Shoes destines a girl for a lifetime of 'compensating for boys' needs and deficiencies' – and certainly such a girl would never be out of a job. But a girl who is going anywhere, moving for herself, must be stigmatised as 'naughty', as so many of the high-achieving women in the survey reported themselves.

The low and erroneous evaluation of girls by primary school teachers continues, predictably, at the higher levels. Michele Stanworth in *Gender and Schooling* (1983) records the case of one high school girl, who was top performer in all her main subjects and who wanted a career in the diplomatic service. She was envisaged by her teachers as 'personal secretary to someone rather important'. Someone male, by any chance? By a later stage, young women have successfully internalised this poor view of their abilities and prospects. A series of research findings by Angrist, Almquist and Deaux consistently show that although university women's evaluation of themselves is low – they invariably estimate their achievements as lower than men's – nevertheless the faculty evaluation of these women is *even lower*. All the women in these studies were deemed lacking in some vital capacity (maleness?) possessed by the men, and finished with lower grades than the men overall.

This institutionalised inability to recognise the merits of women students is only part of women's problems in higher education. The first is simply one of access; in Britain males still outnumber females at entry to university, as they do in gaining the A-levels needed for admission, and in gaining the O-levels that lead to the A-levels. A greater difficulty for women lies in gaining entry to a higher education that is *recognised*. Women's colleges, even high-status sister institutions of prestige male colleges, have not prepared women for elite occupations in any systematic or structured way. A survey of the postgraduate destinations of their *alumnae* show that what they have traditionally produced are high-status educated wives for male members of the elite, not women who are members in their own right. The education that will deliver the career pay-off for women is that which delivers it for men – from a good *mixed* university, business or law school.

Education is only one of the critical factors by which masculine structures and practices restrict women's access to power. As the sex whose intellectual and career potential are routinely downgraded by parents and teachers, women are also denied access to economic resource. Where a boy will be kept at school for as long as it takes to turn him into 'my son the doctor', girls do worst in professions where the recruit has to pay privately for expensive training and equipment; even today, society will not invest in its daughters' human capital. So the vast majority of women are programmed out of the race before they get to the starting gate.

Within professions, too, for the intrepid girl who hurdles the early barriers, the systems work to restrict severely women's upward flow. Women are shown in longitudinal studies to lose out in 'status-sequence progression', the process by which a profession reviews its recruits at each step, and permits access to the next status level, where the recruit can then prepare *himself* for the next. Most elites have a deliberately unclear status sequence, in order that the in-group may retain control of progress while the out-group remain in the dark. As members of the largest out-group known to history, the majority of the human race, women are fobbed off with popular myths like 'hard work will get you there', 'the gifted will succeed', and 'you'll make it if you've got what it takes'. Meanwhile, the son also rises. The son-in-law too, on every horizon, burning off the daughters.

Bright and ambitious women *self-select* for top jobs. 'Almost every job I've had, I've *asked* for,' says Verity Lambert, production director of Thorn EMI. Women tend not to *be sought* as recruits by the power holders, and consequently not given the 'insider' information, and not selected for progression by the status judges. This is not necessarily the result of conscious discrimination by men. What they are obeying is the unwritten and usually unacknowledged principle identified by social scientists as the law of 'organisation homogeneity'. This decrees that to preserve the 'self' of the organisation, certain people must always be excluded from its executive or decision-making functions. They may be permitted to enter, in order to provide a defence against charges of discrimination. But they effectively inhabit an outland, beyond the pale, as they are deemed to be not of the kind or nature of raw material to renew or replenish the body politic. They are different in kind, and would, if promoted, change the essence of the organisation. Women would, too. We will.

Because these blocks to women's career advancement are so

institutionalised, so longstanding, so embedded in the structures and processes of society, it is easy for men to escape any charge of actively working to hold women back. But it is only recently that males have been forced to abandon a number of open and active devices which denied women equal opportunity and the right to work, such as:

* exclusion of girls from the 'best' schools;
* quotas for acceptance of women to medical and veterinary schools;
* refusal to accept women as members of professional organisations, clubs, etc.

These and other systems linger on in such practices as restricting women to the safe, 'soft' areas like the family, education, health and welfare, in government, administration or the law. As this shows, even when the doors are apparently open to women, covert restrictive practices hamper their progress. At Oxford, where all the men's colleges have nominally 'gone mixed', they are for the most part admitting women as no more than a third of their total intake. 'Just enough to break up the beer culture', comments Mary Moore, principal of St Hilda's College; not enough to change the nature of the college, or alter its balance of power.

Male power-holders have been holding women down so effectively, and maintaining their programmes of exclusion so unobtrusively, that they are not seen to be closing the doors that keep women out. The fact that it is almost invariably men who reach the top therefore looks natural, instead of the product of an unspoken collective collusion on the part of men, while the entry of one or two highly-selected women under the net 'proves' that women have the same chances as men do, could make it if they really wanted to, and so on. In the past, when male dominance went unchallenged, it was possible for men and women too to be unaware of the processes and techniques of the destruction of women's chances. Now that these matters are on the international agenda, the response 'I have never been conscious of any difference between men and women' is at best insultingly inadequate, at worst a calculated attempt to block any change in the existing situation.

In part, resistance to change springs from the simple

consideration that the maintenance of any system requires less effort, attention and cost than its alteration. Men are comfortable with the way things are, and like to think that women are too. So Richard Seifert, a leading architect responsible for London's Centre Point, talks of 'admiring women', but makes this assessment of the role of women in his firm: 'Secretarial-wise, they have a very important role to play. As architects, they are not partners or associates, and neither do I find they wish to be. Most are happy concentrating on drawing and interior design.'

With admirers like this, women can only hope to hasten the demise of the old-style gentlemen by pushing them off the mountains where they have squatted for so long. This is not easy. As Dr Johnson observed, 'Men know that women are an *overmatch* for them; and nature having given women so much power, the law has rightly given them very little.' Men have all the weight of the law, custom, and society on their side, their personal responses of fear or hostility institutionalised as structural barriers and norms. Further, all the masculine structures of power connect at an invisible subterranean level. It is no accident that captains of industry went to school with chiefs of the civil service, that barristers knew press barons at Oxford, that the interior of the Cabinet Office feels like the BBC, even *smells* like it – all these are power routes that men control and like to call their own. As the civil service attitude to promoting women was summed up in the BBC's *Yes, Minister*: 'If you go around promoting women just because they're the best person for the job, you could create a lot of resentment throughout the service.' Well yes, you can see that. The behaviour of power people worldwide illuminates the force of the dry medieval proverb, 'have, keep and hold are three good words'. The desire of a given power group to retain its power in a time of crisis will occasionally be strong enough to make it bend its own rules in order to hang on. Gloria Steinem has expressed the theory that the countries in which the 'exceptional' woman first gets to the very top are those with the strongest and most overt class or caste system (Britain or India). This is because membership of the most privileged elite can enable a woman to overcome the handicap of having been born the wrong gender. When the rise of such a woman coincides with the lack of an able man, then the power party will promote that woman rather than allow power to pass out of its hands to the opposition.

On this argument Magaret Thatcher owes less to her own 'exceptional' personal ability than to the entrenched ideology which tells the Conservative party that it is the 'natural' party of power – so much so that it will risk something as unnatural as a woman leader rather than lose its hold on power. In this lies the explanation of the phenomenon that has baffled political commentators and people at large. 'It is extraordinary that the Tories had a woman at the top before we did,' says Harold Wilson, former leader of an administration in which he promoted more women to positions of political power than any other premier before or since. But quite simply, with the failure of Heath and the reluctance of Whitelaw, Margaret Thatcher *was* 'the best man for the job'. And while her personal publicity continues to ballyhoo her as exceptional, this will ensure that the job will continue to be thought of as properly a man's for the foreseeable future. It is hardly likely that men will do anything to disturb this feeling.

> The old kind of resistance to women was ideological – that is, men simply believed that women weren't as good as they were. Now there's a new kind of anti-feminism going on. It's defensive. They think women are as good as they are, and they fear the competition.
>
> US woman sociologist

> Now I know that the higher up a woman gets, and the more she tries to do things that men haven't done, the more they slash away at you because of their own inadequacies. Sure, I'm a woman and I'm outspoken. What are you supposed to do in order to survive? At least I've blasted a trail for other women to follow. I'll tell ya what, though, there's some men that had better watch out for their bloody balls.
>
> Joy Baluch, first woman mayor of
> Port Augusta, Australia

'Why Can't a Woman Be More Like a Man?'

Among the powers that all power-holders have is the power to *define*. If therefore power itself is defined as male, then by logical extension female equates with everything that is oppositional to power. And as male-defined power is understood as strength, then women are seen as the embodiment of all kinds of weakness that threaten the power process. Women therefore loom large as a problem for men in power on the conceptual and on the practical level.

Two 'problems' in particular obsess the minds of men and are freely used as 'reasons' why women cannot reach the top:

(a) The baby business;
(b) The menstruation myth.

The baby business is our old friend, the 'biology is destiny' argument. The simple possession of a uterus renders a woman the biggest risk a manager is apparently ever called upon to take, because it makes her inherently unreliable. She is capable of having a baby *at any time*! Therefore it is not worth training, fast-tracking or promoting women, as they will just make life difficult for employers by throwing their professionalism over the windmill, reverting to type, and reproducing. The 'brood mare' theory of executive women has been enunciated by the aptly named Jeremy Bullmore, chairman of the advertising agency, J. Walter Thompson: 'I find it very difficult to know how much to invest in women. You hire them, train them, and the next thing you know they're married with kids and it's all extremely inconvenient.' As chairman in an industry which employs a large number of women, Bullmore has the power to make his views 'extremely inconvenient' to their future prospects. But he is at least attempting to think in business terms. What are we to make of this piece of rabid drivel that appeared in the *Financial Times* in June 1984?

Women and careers

From the Managing Director,
  Executive Search
  Sir.–An executive who opts to bear a child, an opportunity not open to men, becomes a mother. Physiology has specified the nature of the maternal role and the relationship to the child which, if the child were asked and given priority, should continue to be direct and

close for 5-7 years. In short, the mother should stay at home at least for that period.

If a mother does not recognise her direct responsibility and duty, she is not showing good judgment, a hallmark of the top executive. If she does, she interrupts her career.

On the other hand, perhaps the spread of feminist denial of the natural law explains why women do not often reach the upper limbs of the executive tree; they are being encouraged to revolt against their nature, an attitude inimical to fulfilment, personally and professionally, which leads to frustration.

J.M. Reid,
8a Symons Street,
Sloane Square, SW3.

Mr Reid's letter led not so much to 'frustration' as to mirth and derision among Britain's top women. The managing director of Herondrive elegantly poked fun at the 'protectionism of the male of the species' in her riposte, and concluded:

> May I reassure him that we women do not reach the upper limbs of the executive tree very often because we are not yet trained in sufficient numbers to do so. Given the current economic and management record of this country, the sooner we are, the better and, as Mrs Thatcher proves, the upper limbs will not necessarily be satisfactory: the top is where we aim.
>
> *Financial Times*, 22.6.84

Given Mr Reid's position as managing director of an executive search agency, Jean Denton adds: 'Chauvinism has always protected us from working for closed minds. It would now appear to protect us from being head-hunted by them!'

Yet apart from its comedy value, Mr Reid's letter does fulfil the function of illustrating how strongly these views are held by some men (emotional and irrational creatures that they are) in the teeth of comprehensive, readily available, up to date statistical evidence to the contrary, as follows:

* childbirth rates are falling sharply throughout the advanced world;
* the decline in childbirth is directly related to women's education level and work status: the higher, the fewer
* there is an increase in the number of women choosing not to have children at all
* of those who do, the majority have had their last or only child

by the age of twenty-six, still young enough to be in the management race and with a lifetime ahead
* fewer than 6 per cent of firms reported any problems with pregnant women employees in a Department of Employment Policy Studies Institute report of 1980
* women managers have been shown in numerous surveys to be *less* likely to leave, *more* loyal to the company, than male employees

As this shows, ambitious women are the prisoners of stale clichés and masculine non-think of epidemic proportions. Women's unsuitability for top opportunities because of their 'unreliability' and bad-risk investment status is an *idée fixe* not to be dislodged by consideration of the facts.

These archaic attitudes are the more discriminatory as bosses are quite happy to adapt to the mobility demands of male executives. In contrast with the nineteenth-century pattern, in which employees gave a lifetime of service to one company, twentieth-century employers have grown used to the idea that their ablest and most ambitious men move around. They have no problem with training a male and losing him after two years to another firm. This is partly because as all employers are roughly operating the same procedures, they may well be able to replace him with a man trained at the expense of yet another company. It is also because they are invested in the idea that a bright young man is worth having for however long he is prepared to give. A young male will even be admired for the impatience for promotion that leads him to change employers frequently in the early stages of his career as the most rapid way to gain experience and advancement. Yet women, who *will stay longer* in comparable positions, are stigmatised as 'bad risk' employees, held at levels below their qualifications and abilities, and finally stabilised below the level where they could best serve even the employers' interests. And all this for the possession of an organ which on current statistics the average woman will use *less than twice in seventy-five years*.

Maternity is an election, not an obligation.
                    slogan of MLF (France's Women's Movement)

But then, in the masculine mind, when women are not reproducing, they are menstruating. Men's fear of the deadly secrets of the female physiology goes back through the darkest recesses of Victorian ignorance to the menstrual taboos of the most primitive tribal societies. Women can be expected to become wildly unstable once a month, so this version of the 'prisoners of their biology' routine goes: they will be moody, hysterical, tearful, subject to mental aberrations, hormonal imbalance and thalamic storms. Who would put such a creature in charge of anything important? (Children obviously do not count.) The 'raging hormones' theory of women's unsuitability for top jobs received international endorsement in 1971 when Dr Edgar Berman, then a member of the Democratic National Committee's policy planning council, claimed that women's 'monthly changes' made them risks too high to take in government.

In the controversy that followed, physiologists, gynaecologists and endocrinologists (some of whom were men, even) had fun at the expense of Berman: 'What about menopausal men, or doesn't that count?' 'A woman smart enough to attain a key position would surely be smart enough to get medical advice' and, 'Peptic ulcers are cyclical too!' were among the comments of the specialists. *All* women are specialists in this particular department, an aspect of life which girls learn to handle in early teens, and certainly are not still struggling with in the executive stage. Of the women surveyed for this study, only three reported ever having had any menstrual difficulty, and none had experienced any disruption to her work efficiency: 'We were brought up in the school where period pains didn't exist, and before PMT had been invented,' was one cheerful comment. Quite a number of the women found men's attitude to the subject 'pathetic', 'incredible for this day and age', 'a real downer', and advised striking back with the same weapon: 'If they are ratty, I'll say, "Oh, I see, feeling menstrual today, I suppose?"' It is clear that women need to go on fighting hard to scotch the menstrual myth. On Geraldine Ferraro's emergence into international fame in the summer of 1984, her foreign affairs experience, voting record or electoral appeal were not more eagerly canvassed in newspapers on both sides of the Atlantic than her capacity for hot flushes. *La lutte continue*!

Women do not find their own physical lives a problem. They really do not think about it. Men do. It is men who have the problem. Countless research studies (Tiger, 1972; Harragan and Kanger, 1977) have shown that women's mere presence is regarded as extremely problematic for men. Males see them as a threat to established friendships, to pecking-order norms, to the conventions by which they live which dictate that as MD, Joe is the power figure even though to a woman he looks like a fat dope who is losing his hair. Further, the entry of women into male groups throws up the question of how the males should behave *as men*. They are forced into acts of masculine self-definition as a contrast response to distinguish themselves, and separate out from the intruding women. So if a woman is present, research shows a marked increase in

* sexual innuendo
* off-colour jokes
* 'prowess-orientation behaviour' (in plain English, showing off)

This 'masculine' behaviour, according to sociologist Rosabeth Kanter, is a regular ritual. The jokes, sexual allusions and coarse talk are generally preceded by elaborate preamble, excuses and apologies, drawing attention to the woman and her imputed embarrassment or delicacy – after which the males go ahead with it anyway. This works against a woman in two ways: she is singled out and cut off from the group by what is an alienating, not an affiliative mechanism; and she is denied any right of response since, if she tries to join in, or joke back, this will be seen as inappropriate and 'dirty' behaviour from her.

Sexuality is in fact a major part of the rationale for the exclusion of women from top positions. Male sexuality is enhanced not only by the feeling of power, but by the exclusiveness and solidarity of the masculine power world. The penetration by women of a male bastion is therefore experienced as an attack on the males' precarious feelings of sexual strength. If men are afraid of weakness in the power world, it is their own, not women's. The sexuality that women bring with them is feared for its potential to distract the individual male, to foul up

79

the running of the organisation, and to stir up sexual rivalry. The hapless female is cast as temptress and disruptor, with all the emphasis upon *her* disturbance of the work arena, rather than on *men*'s difficulties in adapting to women at work, or seeing them in any other than sex roles.

The relation of conventional male-female sex roles to the distribution and balance of power need hardly be stressed. Power is generally theorised as a social process rather than as an interpersonal activity. History has focused on the power struggles between nations, races and classes while society has turned a blind eye to the desperate imbalance of power between men and women. This has been maintained so effectively as to seem both natural and *given*, rather than man-made; more, the masculine architects of the system which privileges males everywhere from the Houses of Parliament to the humblest hearthstone, can mount from this the *post facto* argument that the system is *right*. Beaten away at last in the Western world from the claims that male dominance is either morally or legally right (though not at all in Eastern countries, or the Third World), men are making a very successful last stand on the ground that it is psychically and psychologically right. Males are equipped with more 'natural' aggression, the fuel that drives the engine of power; therefore they not only should, but need to dominate.

From this redoubt an on-going series of successful sallies convinces women of the psychological damage that they will suffer if they risk their womanhood in a 'man's world'. Another line of argument threatens women with the damage they will cause if they seek to take any of men's natural rights of power (and we all know how dangerous it is to thwart man's natural urges); women will become harpies, monsters, 'ball-breakers', castrating bitches. It's that fragile masculine sexuality again. No wonder men feel vulnerable if they think of themselves as carrying round everything that validates and empowers them in that funny little package sited in a most exposed position of their body. But how did they come to locate the source of power in this one fallible organ? How were they allowed to get away with it? What is the true nature of power, stripped of this masculine usurpation not only of its rights, but its essence?

80

Interest in this question stretches back as far as civilisation itself, and opinion from Plato, Machiavelli, Hobbes and Nietzsche agrees on certain basic principles. At its most basic, power is the ability to determine or direct the behaviour of others. By the powerful we mean those who are able to realise their will even if others resist it. Power includes not only the power to make decisions, but the power to determine what the decisions are, to set the agenda. It necessarily includes, too, the power to block the actions of others, to head off opposition and nip dissent in the bud.

Power therefore is control. Although in democracies individuals and governments are only empowered by the will and consent of the people, power is only exerted to the full when it is taxed by meeting resistance from opponents or from adverse events. So power has been defined by political commentator Brian Crozier as '*what you can get away with*'; and Dr Elliott Jacques has argued that the degree of power is to be measured by *how long* you can get away with it. For Bertrand Russell, power was 'the production of intended effects' – effects intended to enhance power and advantage the protagonist. By a logical extension, sociologist Peter Worsley persuasively argues that power-holders are '*those who benefit from the existing arrangements*'. Power can define, exclude, deprive or validate. No wonder men want to hang on to it!

But power is not a property, stamped all the way through like a stick of rock with the definition 'men only'. Power is a relative; not an absolute, but a process. Power is always interpersonal, its effects extending through the ramifications of all forms of social organisation, all structures of human life. In the public sense, power *over* people and events conveys power *to* command and to change them. Yet throughout history public life has been graced by individuals gifted with an authority not merely lent them by the external trappings of high office; and private lives have been lived with a potency inspirational to those who knew of them, however few there were. To the ancient Greeks, power meant 'being', and the power to be was a sacred right. Psychotherapist Rollo May has argued that the 'power to be' ... 'must be lived out, or neurosis, psychosis or violence will result'.

On this line then we can understand power as *being, having,* and *doing,* to the fullest extent. Power is purpose. Its denial is annihilation. This is a human, not a gender-based, need.

For women, an election for power is a vote against powerlessness, the state in which most of our sex pass their entire lives. The lack of significance or status, the helplessness to control or even to affect the course of events, the deprivation of autonomy and the denial of economic independence, amounting in sum to the exclusion from the basic human right 'to be', this is the life sentence served by the majority of women. The deep human need for personal significance was recognised by John Adams, one of the founding fathers and second President of the United States of America:

> The rewards of this life are the esteem and admiration of others – the punishments are neglect and contempt. The desire of the esteem of others is as real a want of nature as hunger – and the neglect and contempt of the world as severe a pain as the gout or the stone.

But only for men, apparently. Founding mother Abigail Adams once wrote to her husband John, 'I desire you would Remember the Ladies, and be more generous and favourable to them than your ancestors.' Her plea for 'the Ladies' to be given the same democratic rights and considerations as these gentlemen were giving themselves fell on deaf ears. At the dawn of a greater general freedom than any the world had known, the female half of the race continued to go in chains, chains of psychological and cultural subordination that we are still struggling to strike off. To reverse Acton, powerlessness tends to corrupt, and absolute impotence corrupts absolutely. Not to have power in life is to squander life's potential and submit to having a limit set upon your consciousness by your sex. Is it really so surprising, then, that when they can, women throw off the cloak of invisibility and choose the coat of many colours?

Losing sucks.
New York subway graffito

As the opposite of powerlessness, power determines the distribution of all privileges, economic and non-economic. On the material level, power brings in its train a high number of the much-coveted goods, services and activities of our society. Power people do not stand in the rain waiting for a bus; they do not iron their own blouses; they do not repeat the same soul-eroding work day by day, but travel by limousine, get valeted, breakfast at the Savoy, dine at the Ritz. As Michael Korda has written in his study of the subject:

> Some people play the power game for money, some for security or fame, some for sex ... master players seek power itself, knowing that power can be used to *obtain* money, sex, security or fame. None of these alone constitutes power: but power can be used to produce them all.

Power can also, and usually does, produce the most remarkable and welcome psychological effects, as Nietzsche insisted in 'The Will To Power': 'Joy is only a symptom of the feeling of attained power. The essence of joy is a plus-feeling of power.' Linked with this are all the related aspects of the feeling of supreme well-being, like vitality and the glow of confidence which make the power person attractive to large numbers of both sexes. On one level, this is what we call 'charisma; on another, as Henry Kissinger has boasted, and we have to believe him, power is the ultimate aphrodisiac, turning every power-holding frog into a handsome prince. Once again, there is no logical reason why the psychic benefits of power should be sex-specific. Women stand to enjoy enhanced feelings of sexuality and personal satisfaction every bit as much as men. In the blunt summary of William J. Goode, president of the American Sociological Association, 'Success is sexy ... this will apply to women as well as men.'

At the top of the power scale, where success, money, fame and applause cluster, the glamour with which the winner of all these is invested can be tremendous. Outside observers usually deem this to be the reward of high achievement. But the reward is the inner experience of which the glow is only an outward manifestation. A strong focus and goal orientation which is answered by a real achievement and recognition will combine to convey increased psychic strength. In a benign circle of accomplishment and reward, the individual progresses in self-actualisation; in the simplest terms, power makes you powerful.

Having the inner sense of power, which has been conveyed and confirmed by successful experience of power, is the characteristic *par excellence* that fits an individual for leadership. Until fairly recently, studies of leadership were constricted by concepts of the 'political personality', or the 'natural leader'. This was defined as the rare man who possessed power as an inalienable personal attribute, who was resistlessly motivated towards the public expression of a private drive, and who had an inner quality manifested as outward presence. Research into the behaviour of leaders and led over the last twenty years has, however, seriously undermined this theory by establishing a large degree of overlap between the two. In addition, a more sophisticated understanding of the ways in which individuals secure and build up their own power has exploded the naive elitism which assumed that they could only rise through what the earliest philosophers called a special 'virtue'.

The newer idea, that the leader is not born but constructed, and to a large degree self-constructed, has received support from other areas of psychology. Much recent research has shown that personality is not immutable, but flexible and situational, and likely to change in the direction of the demands of their role. Hence the person who attains a position of power is governed by, and rises to, the requirements of that post rather than by their own sex, or 'nature', or personality. Equally the position itself invests the holder with its own high attributes, as if by sympathetic magic. This view was enunciated as early as 1715 by Daniel Defoe, who argued that every ruler must be autocratic and egotistic, and declared: 'If he comes to office without these characteristics, his environment equips him with them, as surely as a diet of royal jelly transforms a worker into a queen bee.'

In support of this, leadership studies where both male and female leaders are available have shown little significant difference between the ways in which the sexes conduct themselves in office. In work on managers, administrators and high-level executives women do not score lower on aggression, professional expertise or sense of power; nor higher on subjectivity, emotionality or instability. As managers, women

84

manage. But equally and logically in Defoe's analogy, no royal jelly, no queen bee. Women's historic and continuing exclusion from situations and experiences where leadership is called forth and learned would of itself explain why women have in the past failed to display the characteristics with which power is associated.

But women today are beginning at last to learn the meaning of power and the way it works. Throughout history, power has been used against women, to tyrannise and to terrorise, to limit female horizons and to thwart ambition. Men have kept women subordinate not only by denying them access to power, but by defining women as alien in kind from the race of true power-holders, outcast in perpetuity from its exercise and its rewards. Women need now to master the use of power, to understand how to grasp and exert the power necessary to accomplish every goal. Girls must be taught to use power with determination, to build up a positive self-image, and to advance their development as confident, competent individuals. All the strengths women possess will remain under-utilised, all aspirations unrealised, until each woman can take the power to put them to effective use. For finally, the power of self-definition, with the power to get others to accept that definition, is the only power that counts, since it is the precondition of all other kinds of power, and of psychic health and survival itself.

Wherever I found the living, there I found the will to power.
                                                    Nietzsche

No one should have to dance backwards all their lives.
                                                    Jill Johnson

CHAPTER 4

Man Power

*Women must learn not to be so subservient
to the wishes of their fathers, husbands and
partners because then they don't fulfil their
own ambitions.*

Petra Kelly

Power is another country. They do things manfully there. How do women succeed in carving out a piece of this strongly defended territory for themselves, and what kind of power can they expect to enjoy? These are questions that individual women have wrestled with throughout history. Now at last women are pioneering in power in sufficient numbers to be able to give the answers that other women need so much.

The time-honoured route to power for women has been *through a man*. As wives, daughters, mistresses, secretaries or 'right hands', women have had access to power-holding males, and have used them as connections or stepping-stones towards power of their own. On occasions women have taken advantage of their proximity to the supreme position to strike out for it themselves, like the last Empress of China, Tz'u-hsi. This woman, who had been denied even the rudiments of formal education, fought her way out of the ruck of the 6000 other imperial concubines to rule China for the last fifty years of the Manchu dynasty. Her will to power was so strong that on her deathbed she gave orders for the poisoning of her successor, and the Chinese monarchy effectively ended with her. In the light of her career, her own assessment sounds not so much like arrogance as understatement:

Do you know, I have often thought that I am the cleverest woman who ever lived and that others cannot compare with me. Although I have heard much about Queen Victoria, I don't think her life is half as interesting as mine. Now look at me, I have 400 million people all dependent on my judgement.

The histories of both East and West throw up many such examples of powerful and successful women rulers, each one enough in herself to make mincemeat of the claim that only males are composed of the true metal of monarchy. In fifteenth-century Europe Isabella of Castile made herself Queen of Spain as much by her skilful dynastic union with Ferdinand of Aragon as by her great political skill and courage in arms, while Catherine the Great demonstrated that whatever needs an Empress might have of a man, the role of political adviser was not among them. The long pageant of the English monarchy, rich in the great, the good, the weak and the wicked, counts Elizabeth I as one of its brightest stars; and among Elizabeth's most brilliant achievements in making peace at home and striking terror abroad must be reckoned her decision to keep all her country matters out of reach of the husband that her advisers were constantly seeking to thrust upon her.

More commonly women were to be found not upon the throne as a surrogate man, but acting as the power behind it. This was the traditional site of women's power in high circles, operating in the orbit of the ruling males in ways that always recognised and did not threaten the authority of their men. So the great political women of the nineteenth century, for whom the conventional term 'hostesses' is far too feeble, held pivotal positions in the government of their day. It is no exaggeration to say that the ability to manipulate the male decision-makers enjoyed by Lady Melbourne, the Duchess of Devonshire or Margot Asquith, to engineer confrontations or to arrange truces, amounted to the power to make or break not only an individual's career but that of a Cabinet. This power, however, derived not from the woman in her own right but from her connection with a mighty male. It ended when his ended, as end it must, no matter how hard Catherine Gladstone, say, fought to get 'her William' to stay on as Prime Minister. Furthermore, this was always perforce the power 'that dare not speak its name':

these women had to veil their activities, and always, in public at least, defer to the men in whose name and for whose sake they acted.

The role of *eminence grise* was, in times past, one of the few power options open to women, when law, custom and personal circumstance so strongly inhibited any active or overt bid for power from the distaff side. Today, when social change has removed at least some of the stumbling blocks, numbers of women still *choose* to exert power off stage, as influence, and their success shows that this is a highly viable pathway to power in a variety of ways. As the personal secretary and political adviser to Harold Wilson, Lady Falkender (then Marcia Williams) had to endure the bitter hostility of the civil service, which was unused to the idea of a woman filling a role traditionally held by a man. She was subject, too, to the vicissitudes of her leader, which included the shattering electoral defeat of 1973. Yet she had no hesitation in telling reporter Melanie Phillips:

> I never had any desire to be an MP ... I don't like the atmosphere of the House; it's unruly, I loathe the shouting and the debates. Everyone works themselves up artificially, and in a sense that's not where the real work is done ... I enjoyed the constituency business that is part of an MP's work. I also enjoyed the backroom political stuff – the briefs, the propaganda work, what strategies to employ.

On the other side of the political spectrum, Mary Baker has described how her participation in a discussion group for Conservative women founded by Elspeth Howe, former deputy chairman of the Equal Opportunities Commission, proved to be 'the transition' for her, after six years of teaching, into public life: 'The meeting, the talking, the research moved me forward into other outside areas of activity.' The group was originally founded for the benefit of the women themselves, 'to be better briefed, to be more useful and knowledgeable'. But as the wives of senior members of the Conservative administration, these women are in constant contact with the policy-makers and ideally placed to be very influential behind the scenes.

Women's traditional exercise of power as influence has recently received a striking update in America, where two not-so-grey eminences have put a brilliant new inflection on the whole activity. Anne Wexler and Nancy Clark Reynolds have been summed up by Marylouise Oates of the *Los Angeles Times* as 'that first breaking wave of women who hold power in both the front parlors and the back rooms of politics'. They are, in US government and business circles, two of the new breed of super-lobbyists, high-priced professional power-brokers mapping out long-term strategies and multi-front campaigns for clients as diverse as General Foods and General Motors, Kelloggs and the New York Power Authority. Together they run what they demurely call 'a bi-partisan consulting firm' (Wexler is a Democrat, Reynolds a Republican). But then they can hardly have on their business letterheads the sheaves of compliments that have come their way since they joined forces in 1982 to become 'the hottest firm in town', in the words of one of their many admirers.

Each of these women separately has a *curriculum vitae* that reads like a blueprint for Superwoman. With a background in public work and political organisation that has led to her being dubbed 'the queen of the grass roots', Anne Wexler served in the Carter administration and is known as 'the most prominent woman in the behind-the-scenes Democratic brains trust'. In addition she holds down business, educational and committee activities of an astonishing variety. Nancy Clark Reynolds was one of the first women to break into radio and television broadcasting in a big way, and it was while working as a news reporter and anchorwoman that she first met the then plain Ronald Reagan. This was the start of a long and close professional relationship during which she saw the one-time candidate for governor of California become President of the USA, herself becoming 'the other Nancy' to the Reagans and 'the First Friend' to the Washington press corps. She also in these years gained invaluable corporate experience, a cluster of awards as a woman of achievement, a Presidential appointment as US representative to the United Nations Commission on the Status of Women, and was working as the first woman vice-president for the Bendix Corporation when lured away by Anne Wexler to become president of the company of which Wexler is founder and chairman.

If each woman is a power figure in her own right, together,

'working both sides of the aisle' as Wexler puts it, they are dynamite. Where others manage political campaigns or individual careers, 'we manage issues', says Wexler. 'They're very much the power brokers in Washington, and they have not hit their peak in any way,' was the comment of the chairman of the Democratic Campaign Committee, one of many taken by surprise at the way in which these women have developed careers following on from their White House experience, capitalised on their political access and shown such a confident grasp of the intricate connections between business and politics peculiar to the American system. Commentators agree that, as insiders in circles composed mainly of men, as successful lobbyists whose targets are mainly men, and as power-brokers in a world where those with power are men, Anne Wexler and Nancy Clark Reynolds have raised the exercise of women's influence to the level of an art.

But what is possibly even more impressive is the consummate skill with which the partnership has converted influence-power into power-power; the firm of Wexler, Reynolds, Harrison and Schule Inc. is now turning away clients, and estimates that it handled $1.5m in business last year. And they are still only beginning. They intend to tread carefully, aware that this kind of power is still new to women: 'I think sometimes it's harder to use it, it's not as instinctive,' was Wexler's comment and in the 'cannibalistic, fickle city' of Washington, Reynolds adds, 'If you have power, you keep it by not abusing it.' But the issues that they deal with are, they insist, 'gender-neutral', and in Anne Wexler's experience, 'when it comes to toughness, there is no gender for that, my dear!'

Toughness is an attribute that both would like to encourage in other women. As Nancy Clark Reynolds explains:

> What Anne and I basically are – we're risk-takers, and I think we're willing to jump into things sometimes. And maybe we can encourage other women to…well, to risk a few things and be willing to lose, to get a setback or two and learn from it and not take it as the whole end of the world.

To this her partner adds, 'The other thing – and I think it's harder for women to learn than it is for men – just don't take no for an answer. If someone says no to you the first time, just regroup and go back and ask again!' Both women are united in a strong belief about the importance of helping other women, and personally direct or advise on the careers of younger women where they can. But perhaps their greatest contribution towards opening up the road to power for other women is simply in what they are achieving themselves. At a stage where most high-visibility, high-earning firms are still run by men, and where damaging stereotypes still linger about women's unsuitability for high office and inability to work with or for another high-powered woman, the partnership of Wexler and Reynolds is not simply a new model but a beacon light.

Leading Men

But while some women are rewriting the rules, others are still working by the old ones, and as virtually all the power in our society is still held by men, access to power for women continues to be in the male line. As a result those women who are either born or marry into the world of a top male power-holder often look as if they have had a short-cut, a special personalised pathway to power arranged for them with no effort on their part. In reality there is no alternative to keen application from an early age, as Cosmo-woman Helen Gurley Brown warns:

> Restless young people (you?) tend to think other people do it some other way than through child slavery – that the others are not only luckier and cleverer but that 'it' somehow just falls on them and presto they are in the 'big time'. Almost *never* does that happen. Nearly every glamorous, wealthy, successful career woman you might envy *now* started as some kind of schlep.

In other words, nobody is handed power on a plate, no matter whose daughter or wife they are, as the careers of a number of these women illustrate. Clearly it helps an ambitious girl to be born into a family that knows the ropes – Margaret Thatcher, Shirley Williams, Barbara Castle and Lynda Chalker were all daughters of 'politicised families' well up in issues and techniques, *au fait* with the personnel and the points of leverage. This concept translates easily to other areas of human activity –

91

if your daddy is in the fight business, you should be able to get a ringside seat.

But none of this translates quite so simply into direct power for the woman concerned. For know-how in a key area may be a great dowry of personal or cultural capital, but it still has to be invested and made to pay dividends; it will not of itself turn a girl into a top politician. Rather than feeling that the mayor of Grantham gave his little Margaret a head start, we should be asking why so few of the daughters of other politicians have managed to make use of this entry route. In other walks of life, too, being born into a house of power will not usually offset the disadvantage of being born female. How many businessmen ever dream of grooming their girls to succeed them? When shall we see 'Smith and Daughters' as frequently as 'Jones and Sons'? For individual women, too, the relation to the powerful man can be as much of a handicap as a help. Jane Fonda certainly knew where to start out in films, but found the star status of her father almost overwhelming in her early years. Nor was the self-absorbed Henry, with his spectacular trail of private life wreckage, either any support for Jane as an actress or any useful model for her as a manager and businesswoman.

Power is not static. However much a young woman may inherit, she has to keep the enterprise powerful by her own efforts; more, since it is in the nature of the power dynamic either to keep growing or to wither and fail, she has to keep working to come up with her own contributions and adaptations. So Christina Foyle inherited the world-famous bookshop in Charing Cross Road and inherited also book-business knowledge from both sides of the family (her mother had her own bookshop in New Oxford Street before meeting Christina's father). But she sparked off by herself some of the firm's most significant cultural and financial initiatives, like the legendary Foyles' Literary Luncheons, and it is under her guidance that a shop founded in 1904 has metamorphosed into a high-earning international concern in the second half of the twentieth century.

At least Foyle père ran a clean and classy outfit. For Christie Hefner, hopping rather higher in her father Hugh's Playboy empire than any girl bunny has ever done before led to unenviable press coverage and snickering derogation as 'hare apparent' and 'workmate of the year'. Christie's elevation to the position of president of Playboy Enterprises Inc. reads like the ultimate silver-spoon fantasy – daughter of multi-millionaire shoe-horned into big-lolly sinecure. Newspapers delighted in reporting that Christie had ousted the previous incumbent by the simple expedient of asking her father for the job. In fact, so far from being the spoiled darling of a rich man, Christie was strictly brought up, hardly knowing her father, whom her mother divorced when she was two, and without any special allowance, since both her parents believed in the work, not the safety-net, ethic. Graduating from Boston University, Christie worked elsewhere before joining the Playboy group as a trainee, where her reported IQ of 145 must have done more for her than the possession of a handy surname. And when her father made her president because of her 'exceptional business acumen and skill', he was hardly doing her a favour. Profits were plunging, the magazine's circulation was dwindling, and the London casino operation was collapsing in a shambles of bad debts and worse publicity. Christie has had to pull round a worldwide empire of casinos, different editions of the magazine, cable television and 15,000 employees. She has done this by slashing operating expenses, purging 100 or so executives, refocusing the company on its publishing activities and launching a whole new business of video cassettes and programmes for cable TV. Those who came to sneer have stayed to applaud as 'Little Miss Bunny Girl' has proved herself to be more of a hefter than a Hefner.

As this shows, taking up the mantle of 'poppa-power' is by no means an easy operation. It can indeed be in the nature of a sacred charge that rules out the element of personal freedom, even a dangerous burden. As the daughter of the Prime Minister of Pakistan, Benazir Bhutto enjoyed exceptional status and opportunity for a woman of her country or any other, including an education at Oxford University, where she became president of the Oxford Union. But it was hardly a privilege for Benazir to accede to the leadership of the Pakistan People's Party after the execution of Zulfikar Ali Bhutto by his opponent General Zia, nor to endure the persecution, house arrest and imprisonment by which Zia attempted to harass her opposition out of existence. As a woman, too, Benazir is condemned by the general to fight on two fronts, the political and the personal; General Zia's 1984 programme for Islamic renewal includes laws which totally undermine the rights and status of women, an action which in the words of Hinna Jilani, leader of the Pakistani Women Lawyers' Association, turns women into 'second-class citizens' and 'enforces cruelty to them'. Benazir Bhutto has frequently been invited, with varying degrees of force, to lay down her succession to her father. It is a tribute to her power as a woman that she does not do so.

Carrying On

The story of Benazir Bhutto is both poignant and highly peculiar to her national and family situation. But many women come to their envied power and success through their men in circumstances of such sadness that they cannot feel the achievement worth the price that they had to pay for it. Widow-power is a large and growing business phenomenon, especially in America, where at present there are over one million widows aged under fifty-four, and over three million widows aged under sixty-five. Many of these widows choose to carry on the business for which in some cases their husband sacrificed his life, partly as an act of respect to his memory and as a tribute to his life's work, but mainly, it appears, to give expression to their own drives and abilities, which particularly need an outlet in the wake of bereavement. 'Fortunately I've got the business, and that's filled a void', says Gertrude Crain, now chairman of her late husband's publication empire, Crain Communications of Chicago.

Gertrude's first experience of her husband's business came when after her marriage she used her secretarial skills in the task of signing the employees' salary cheques. Soon afterwards she became 'secretary/treasurer', a post she held for thirty-two years. From this vantage point she mastered the critical financial skills necessary to a growing business, handling the company's profits, pensions and investment strategy. 'It wasn't so awesome,' she says. 'My husband always believed I should know all there was to running the business, to keep it in the family.' Gertrude's acumen was obviously of great advantage to a busy man: 'He used to tell me, "I'm too busy being a publisher, you handle the investments," ' she recalls. G.D. Crain Jr is still, ten years after his death, a strong presence in the life of his widow. 'Often on my way out of the office I'll look at his picture and review the day and wonder what he would have thought,' she says.

It is hard to imagine that the man she calls 'D' would be anything other than delighted. In the ten years since she became chairman, Gertrude Crain has built her inheritance of five trade papers and a turnover of $10 million a year into an empire of twenty-two titles read by half a million people and grossing $80 million annually. She has done so by a series of brilliant and bold business strokes, like gambling $3 million on a new launch in an area where others had fallen away with cold feet, and coming out triumphant – a far cry from the conventional widow's image of the little old lady in bonnet and shawl quietly minding the shop.

Again and again women rise to the challenge of this situation, interpreting their inherited power as opportunity, and seizing it by the forelock in an active assertion of their own ability, their own grit and gumption, their own will. Perhaps the mother of them all was Mary Reibey, Australia's first woman tycoon. Married to a ship's officer who had become a ship-owner, and left unprotected with seven children when he died in 1811, Mary turned to, and built up, her husband's modest beginnings into a vast property and business empire. Many women not accustomed to business life find its risk elements frightening. Mary had built up her business nerve in a hard school, having been sentenced to death in England at the age of thirteen for stealing a horse, transported to Australia as an orphan child, and serving forced labour as a convict before she obtained her freedom. Even the worst of the worries over her new concerns as 'widow Reibey' must have seemed a paradise to this.

For most women, the route to the top will not open up in this particularly painful and conflicting way, where the shoes of the dead power-holder into which you step are those you have been accustomed to seeing under the other side of the bed every night. Yet the workings of widow-power have an important message for other women not in their situation. All these individuals suffered one of the severest of life's blows, and doggedly turned it round into something positive. In some cases, they convert their anger into energy. Fran Muncey used to tell her husband Bill, who was known as 'the winningest driver in the sport of hydroplane racing', 'If anything ever happens to you, I'm going to be really mad.' When Bill was killed during a race, Fran used her 'feelings of anger' to fuel her determination not to let his business die with him.

Like Gertrude Crain, Fran already had her own power base in the firm from her previous experience of handling the finances and working alongside her husband. With the Seattle-based Bill Muncey Industries all but wiped out, she rebuilt it into a new and stronger outfit, with solid financing, different strategies and innovative developments. As her principal driver observed, 'What comes naturally to her, most people go to management seminars to learn.' And what the career of Fran Muncey and others illustrates is that even the most terrible loss can be reconstructed as a gain, that a woman never knows the extent of her power until she comes to call on it, and that there is life after man. Finally, consider what a loss it would have been to the world had Nicole-Barbe sat around wringing her hands after the premature death of her vintner husband, M. Cliquot. It was the astute widow who not only took over the business, but invented *la méthode champenoise* and gave the world the most celebrated widow's mite, Veuve Cliquot!

My Husband and I

Of all the pathways to power through the male of the species, marrying the man of might often seems both the easiest and the most attractive. Psychologists have observed that when the average man fantasises about obtaining power, he sees himself like Walter Mitty translated into the active and heroic role, both being and doing in the power mode. The female subject, however, fantasises herself as plucked from her powerless state by a powerful man, who discovers her and snatches her up in circumstances which *accentuate* her weakness and helplessness – Cinderella, Sleeping Beauty, Snow White. The highest that women can dream of is *attaching* themselves to power, while men can imagine power itself. A girl wants to marry, not to become, the chairman of the board.

Clearly women can sublimate their own drives and desires through attachment to a powerful man, and in the past have usually found it either convenient or expedient to do so. English history abounds in examples of wives who threw their own considerable weight, personal, social and financial, unhesitatingly into their husband's career. Hannah Rothschild carried her husband, Lord Rosebery, to the forefront of political life, and eventually into 10 Downing Street, as much by her skilful management, vigorous promotion and shrewd counsel as by her personal fortune of £2,000,000. The Roseberys' was the model of a successful union of this type. It was indeed considered a great blunder by a would-be man of power not to take an able and ambitious wife who would make his achievement her life's work.

The comforting belief that women are endowed with attributes of power only in order to place them at the service of a male has undergone some revision in recent years; women who see a chance to make their own way up the mountain are less likely to do so roped behind a man. Yet the obsession of the image-makers and opinion-managers with presenting a public or powerful figure as a 'family man' continues to exert its old tyranny over women's lives, with the confident expectation that the woman will uncritically invest in her husband's career, and shore up that end of his operation no matter what he does to undermine it. It is ironic that nowhere is this 'good partnership' myth more cherished and heavily promoted than in America, the land of divorce, a country re-echoing with the sound of crashing marriages from shore to shore. The wife who cannot or will not obligingly carry out the conventional 'junior partner' performance in public life, like Betty Ford or Ethel Kennedy, is subjected to punitive media coverage as a 'liability' to her husband – her life is seen as his, however she tries to play it.

This old stereotype of the strong and single-minded wife devoting her all to her husband's cause, to the selfless exclusion of her own desires, has served the male power-holders and brokers very well over the years. Since naturally enough they have not seen fit to dispense with it, it is still very much with us and remains a power option for a woman who would be unlikely to ascend the peaks of power on her own. In one contemporary example, even with a penchant for old film stars, would the US ever have made *Nancy* Reagan President? And of all recent First Ladies, she has played the part with the greatest conviction upon the world stage, apparently unthreatened by any sneaking suspicion that the 'loyal wife' number, in its creepy, vicarious and essentially neurotic nature, is a role somewhere between Lady Macbeth and Little Nell.

In rare cases it is possible for women partners of greatness to use their wife-power in such a constructive way as to benefit their husbands, their country *and* themselves. Few women could have had more against them than Eleanor Roosevelt. After an unhappy childhood the young Eleanor, shy, awkward and so terribly plain as to make 'ugly duckling' sound like a compliment, was *not* rescued into 'happy ever after' by her marriage to Franklin D. Her mother-in-law ruined her early married life with the kind of domestic despotism that would put a pasha to shame, and her husband became paralysed for life following an attack of polio – a stroke of fate no less crippling to Eleanor's peace of mind than the discovery that he had formed and continued a love affair with another woman.

Yet Eleanor Roosevelt's deep commitment to ideals of personal dignity and freedom enabled her to triumph over all this. She it was, when her mother-in-law decided that Franklin's paralysis meant that he would have to retire from politics, who determined that on the contrary, he must live as active a life as possible. On his behalf she lobbied and campaigned tirelessly, even undertaking the nationwide 'Presidential' tours that he could not. In doing so she discovered her own power and developed her experience of it – a long journey for a woman who had been so systematically undermined in her younger days.

But nothing is ever wasted in the growth into power. These early experiences clearly formed her sympathies for the weak and down-trodden in society which were so marked and inspirational a feature of her life's work. She used the platform of power which fate had offered her to change her world for the better. Eleanor Roosevelt, by constant hard work, courage and application, graduated from 'wife power' as First Lady to a power constituency of her own. Her stature, although already higher than that of any other US President's wife, rose even more after the death of FDR in 1945. It was in recognition of

98

her own unstinting commitment and absolute independence of mind that she was appointed as US delegate to the UN, where her work in drafting and pushing through the Universal Declaration of Human Rights brought her a standing ovation and made her, in the words of President Truman, 'First Lady of the World'.

Yet even for a woman of Eleanor Roosevelt's outstanding capacity there was still a reluctance, on the part of the men around her, to recognise her free right of action. In her revealingly entitled book, *On My Own*, she tells of the deputation of self-styled minders who descended upon her after her husband's death. To a woman who had had thirty years of top-level political experience, who had run her own life and that of a President of the USA, the spokesman announced:

'We have appointed ourselves a kind of committee to help you ... to consider how your life is to be planned.'

'Did I hear you correctly?' asked Miss Thompson [Eleanor's assistant]. 'You want to plan her life?'

'Exactly,' Mr Golden replied ...

Nothing speaks so clearly of Eleanor Roosevelt's warmth and grace as the fact that she considered these men 'kind friends' rather than a pack of meddling busybodies. But the insulting idea that the wife of a top man is no more than some kind of domestic adjunct to him, and has no rights or claims on her own account, dies hard. Of all First Ladies since Eleanor Roosevelt, none has stood so close to the heart of American government as Rosalynn Carter. No other has worked so hard, on so many fronts, to earn her place at the right hand of power. As a fatherless girl from the rural South, with no higher qualifications than junior college, Rosalynn became Jimmy Carter's treasurer, deputy, campaign manager, special envoy and alter ego. She had been attacked in the waves of racial hatred engendered by Carter's stand on integration; she had been reviled and spat upon; as she relates in her honest and moving account, *First Lady from Plains*, she knew what it was like to sit there 'with my chin up' while 'I was crying inside'. But in spite of it all, she says: 'I liked being a political wife ... I never felt burdened. I had an important task ... I was more a political partner than a political wife, and I never felt put upon.'

And there's the rub. Rosalynn Carter's record amply vindicates her claim to be considered a partner to her husband in the truest sense. But the contribution of this able, experienced woman, a person of deep integrity and commitment, was bitterly resented and resisted in Washington. Nothing more plainly illustrates the anti-feminist and essentially homosexual nature of systems of power than the reaction of the American establishment to Rosalynn Carter. When she went to South America on a goodwill and fact-finding mission for her country, a European diplomat was reported in the US press as saying, 'I don't think any Latin-American statesman will take her seriously, even if she is the wife of the President of the United States.'

Nor was the support any stronger on her own side of the pond; officials at the State Department were in a tizz in case she 'inadvertently' shot her mouth off and committed the US to some untenable position. When US expertise was invited to assist her, one Florida congressman's contribution to her briefing consisted of, 'The Latins are macho and they hate gringos and women. What else do you want to know?' Finally, her attendance at Cabinet meetings, even though numbers of other aides and secretaries were also present, and even though she never spoke or contributed in any way, was consistently feared, attacked and misrepresented, so that eventually not only was her position undermined, but that of the President as well.

> Is there not a grave risk of encouraging her in ideas of her personal power?
>
> Foreign Secretary remonstrating with Prime Minister Disraeli for his habit of taking Queen Victoria's opinion on matters of state

The experience of Rosalynn Carter throws into relief the heavy, painful and often contradictory demands made upon women who gain access to power through their men. In her case, while her husband was able to give her power, a male establishment and a male-dominated media, running scared, conspired to take it away. Yet paradoxically, where a wife will serve the interests of her husband's power group, there will be no hesitation in promoting her. Certain women have found themselves in

100

prominent positions by undertaking to run for office as, for, and instead of their husbands. This pattern was initiated from the earliest days of women's breakthrough into political power, when the first woman ever to sit in the House of Commons, Nancy Astor, did so only by taking over her husband's seat when the inheritance of a peerage meant that he had to move up to the House of Lords. A more bizarre example was the election of Mrs Lurleen Wallace as Governor of Alabama in 1967, when her husband, who had dominated power politics in the state for many years, was not eligible to run for another term. 'MRS WALLACE WILL OBEY THE BOSS' and 'GEORGE IN COMMAND AGAIN' were reactions of the British press to Governor Lurleen.

These comments illustrate the essentially inferior and demeaning nature of this kind of power for women. The female is only brought in because for some reason her male is not available, so she starts out as second-best. Then, in office, she is expected to carry on his work, move along the lines he has previously determined, acting all along as his equivalent or surrogate; and when she no longer meets the needs of her masters, she is ditched without hesitation and forgotten without regret. *What men have power to give, they can also withdraw.* Nancy Astor fought hard to assert her independence – 'If you want a party hack,' she told her husband's people, 'don't elect me!' She succeeded in pursuing her own often highly original line on most matters throughout her long parliamentary life. But when husband Waldorf decided that the time had come for her to retire, retired she was. The bitterness she felt at being forcibly put out to grass poisoned the rest of her life.

> Power cannot, strictly speaking, be *given* to another, for then the recipient still owes it to the giver. It must in some sense be assumed, taken, asserted. For unless it can be held *against* opposition, it is not power and will never be experienced as real on the part of the recipient.
>
> Rollo May

La Presidenta

Undoubtedly the most extraordinary and compelling example of a woman's use of 'wife power' is that of Eva Peron. Yet her story also clearly demonstrates that in the last resort such power is ultimately *man* power. Even the most brilliant and self-dedicated of female partners will eventually chafe against the restrictions of her husband, and ironically it will be at the height of her achievement that she will feel the curb. Eva Peron's rise to power in the 1940s, as the wife of Argentina's political strong man, remains a dazzling phenomenon. In the words of American reporter Lois Gould:

> Eva had, and was permitted to show, more naked ambition and brains than Marilyn Monroe, more personality and political acumen than Jacqueline Kennedy, more fire and ice than Eleanor Roosevelt. This was so even though she lived in a myth-obsessed, super-macho culture where a Madonna and whore might, in the abstract, wield extraordinary power, but where an ordinary real woman had none.

Eva Peron claimed her authority as the right of the President's wife and First Lady of Argentina. But this was a power and status never before assumed by the wives of Argentinian presidents. Eva's bold and ambitious step in striking out for her own personal platform was the first public signal of her unique style and aims. Riding roughshod over the howls of her opponents at this presumption by a jumped-up radio starlet and amateur tartlet, Eva then proceeded to build up her power bases with a mature political skill astonishing in a twenty-seven-year-old. Forty years before Reagan she saw the personal and political capital to be made out of the gender gap; her enfranchisement of Argentinian women and her formation of the Peronist Women's Party not only delivered to Peron 64 per cent of the new women's vote; it gave her, in its presidency, her first real political post and also the recognition of her power in Argentina on a basis separate from Peron's. Her creation of the Eva Peron Foundation for social assistance and the scale on which she operated it made her a magical figure in the lives of the poor. Despite these two heavy responsibilities, Eva also made time to carry on her original occupation in the Ministry of Labour, receiving workers, union officials and labour delegates in their hundreds during an average week. Together these power bases in feminism, social welfare and labour dealt her an enormous constituency.

Eva's supremacy in the short years of her 'reign', and its quasi-royal nature, are evident in the hyperbolic handles in which she rejoiced:

* First Worker of Argentina
* Queen of Labour
* The Workers' Plenipotentiary
* Queen of the *Descamisados* (Shirtless Ones)
* Lady of Hope

Like the superb *politica* that she was, Eva also succeeded in capitalising on her adverse publicity, personal attacks of such appalling venom as to have had any other woman running for the hills. 'You see what I suffer for you, my people,' she would incant in her special vein of supercharged emotion to the besotted crowds, 'but nothing will deflect me from your service.'

When Eva died, at the tragically young age of thirty-three, she was the most powerful woman in the world. Yet even all this, at a level of personal power and political activity quite unprecedented in Argentinian history, was not in the end enough. For Eva's ultimate power base was not her own; it lay in Peron, and her authority derived from him. This was indeed the theme of the whole of her public life: 'I am a fanatic for Peron ... to be a Peronist is for a woman to have blind confidence in Peron ... all I do is for Peron, to be a bridge of love between him and his people.' Eventually Eva became the prisoner of her own rhetoric, held at the level of La Presidenta, confirmed as no more than a female extension of the President and confined to operating within his shadow. For when she made a bid for a recognised power position, the office of Vice-President, which would have institutionalised her power only a heartbeat away from the Presidency itself (as on the US model), she was sharply cut down to wife-size again. As the huge crowds roared and screamed their demands for 'Evita' to accept the nomination, the inflamed Peron, his resistance stiffened by the manic opposition of the military to a woman in power, delivered his interdict: '*Stop this act!*'

Perhaps in blocking Eva's path the Generalissimo, famous both before and after his marriage to Eva for his loving kindness to the female sex, was only showing a husband's concern for a sick woman. Six months before this event, Eva had had a hysterectomy in response to the cancer which was to kill her within two years. But in retrospect it seems the chief of the many ironies of Eva's paradoxical career that the honour which he withheld from the brilliant Evita, Peron was prepared to grant twenty years later to his second wife Maria ('Isabelita'). The calamitous incompetence of this *ersatz* Evita brought the country to the verge of ruin, precipitated a military coup and put Isabelita in prison for the abuse of power and public property.

The careers of the two Mrs Perons have almost nothing in common except the power drive of a man who, like Governor George Wallace, found the wife-card such an ace that he attempted to play it twice. In these circumstances the individual woman, however much she appears to exert power, is in reality only acting as an extension of the man, as an implement of his power. At the deepest level, she is not even his puppet – she is his creature. Peron himself drew attention to the truth of Eva's situation with brutal directness: 'Eva Peron is an instrument of my creation. I prepared her so that she would do what she did. I needed her in the sector of social work within my leadership ... a leader must imitate nature, or God.'

Of course Eva threw herself into the hands of her hideous Svengali with what amounted in the end to a passion for self-annihilation. It is no accident that when Peron picked her up, she was starring in a radio series of 'Heroines of History', playing famous women like Elizabeth I and the last Tzarina. Peron offered her the female lead of all Argentina, a part she could play on the world stage, and in so doing could transmute and transcend the searing poverty and deprivation of her wretched childhood. By her workaholic commitment to the cause of the 'shirtless ones' she made herself a saint; by her paranoid refusal to accept medical advice ('They all want me out of politics – they won't succeed!') she made herself a martyr. With her genius for cueing into all the myths of womanhood that continue to tyrannise the female victims of South American culture, Eva Peron ultimately assumed a heroic status greater than any woman of her country before or since. But she could not convert this into power *of her own*. As her power derived from Peron, it remained, in the last resort, his.

It is undeniable that a fortunate accident of birth, or a shrewd marriage, can bring a woman into the charmed circles of power normally reserved with jealous exclusivity to men. From this vantage point she can also learn the tricks of the trade, the insiders' skills of the powerful. But this close relation and the intimate access that it affords will not in itself empower her. She has to experience the growth into power, both personal and professional. Many women have come from unpromising origins, at the side of a power-holder or in his shade, to develop great personal authority and demonstrate ruling ability to the level of genius.

But power derived from men, as fathers or husbands, alive or dead, remains in the last analysis men's power. The inheriting woman has to want it, take it and work hard and long to prove her hold on it – yet she can always be denied the final accolade of having made it on her own, by virtue of her own talents. Unless she can succeed in carving out her own independent power base, she is denied the only real prerogative of power, the ability to implement by your own deeds your own will and desire. She remains an aberration, the 'lucky one' who can be explained away. As one who seems to have had a rare and privileged access route, she cannot provide any kind of model for other women, but can even confirm them in a sense of powerlessness ('If you have to be the wife/daughter of the chairman of the board … '). The males who give power, take credibility. The woman recipient is undermined from the start. However good she is, the system remains a masculine system and power remains male. For one primary definition of power is *the power to hand it on*, and this is what these honorary or surrogate men never have.

CHAPTER 5

Whores' Power

Every normal healthy male thinks about
fucking a woman the second she walks into a
room. Women know that, surely?
Male managing director, advertising agency

In the long litany of women's powerlessness, one source of power has always remained both available and peculiar to the female of the species: her sex. It is remarkable that throughout history the very breasts, uterus and vagina which disqualify women from holding power yet constitute a source of it. A woman's sexuality can be her passport out of her inferior and subordinate status, taking her from nowhere to the top. It can also, in its unbridled expression, be a statement of pure female power in itself. This is one area where women can reign supreme, one function that men cannot usurp, one attribute that may not be taken away. In a world where men dominate, looming from the high places and lurking in the low, her sex is all that a woman can truly call her own. It is, so to speak, the bare essential. But it has often been more than enough.

At its simplest level, trading sex for power was of tremendous importance to women historically, when other avenues were closed to them or had never been open. If a woman could not go to college, stand for election, set up a business or even work outside the house, her options were strictly limited to the respectable concubinage of matrimony, or the dangerous but more potentially rewarding path of the freelance. In former times, if a woman cherished any ambitions higher than a lifetime of domestic service to her husband, with the dubious pleasure of being what Sonia Tolstoy bitterly called 'a vessel' for his children, then she had to put her sexuality to work for her. This selling of sex for self-advancement was a strictly professional, not a romantic, deal. Only Eva Braun and Tony Curtis know what it was like kissing Hitler, but hundreds and thousands of women have laid end to end a succession of the kind of men who make Hitler look like Mr Wonderful, just to get on, get up or get out.

Men of course love to think that even the hired cocotte takes them for pleasure as well as money. On the contrary, the history of successful courtesans shows that their passion is for power rather than for the individual who holds it. The skilfully calculated use of sex enabled a woman to leap over all the barriers dividing the ruler from the ruled. It also provided the only way of converting the fact of being a woman, and therefore one of the race foreordained to exclusion from power, into an advantage. For Theodora, the first of the high-class courtesans to rise to the top in around A.D. 500, the jump was from orphaned daughter of the circus bear-keeper to Empress of Rome. As a prostitute she took only highly-placed men, using them for her education, not for her satisfaction, abandoning the life when it had given her what she sought. When the Emperor Justinian met her, she had made herself into a woman he seized on to become his Empress. Prostitution for Theodora had been a means, not an end.

As 'decent' women gave sex to get marriage, so their indecent sisters gave sex to get control. One mistress whom even her enemies acquitted of the charge of enjoying her duties was Madame de Maintenon, the most powerful of the many moons of the Sun King, Louis XIV. She was a woman of such strenuous devotion to her Roman Catholicism that Louis's brother quipped that the King must have been set her for a penance. Yet after a full diet of luxurious, tempestuous and wanton women, it was de Maintenon whom Louis married following the death of his queen. For her, too, the liaison was a pathway, not a pastime. With the assiduous aid of her confessors, Françoise de Maintenon was only able to square her Catholic soul to this egregious adultery by focusing on the power it gave her to pursue her aims for social reform, to bring up the royal children in the faith, and to catch the conscience of the King.

In all these aims Madame de Maintenon was successful. Nevertheless the history of her 'ministry' reveals the same problem for the women who seek to go this route as for all others who essentially enjoy their power at second hand, derived from their man. The real power is, and remains, his. De Maintenon showed her own shrewd sense of this fact by steering clear of any issues of statecraft or politics, concentrating instead upon her pet project, the girls' school she had founded. This did not protect her from becoming the whipping girl for all the King's mistakes in foreign or domestic policy. Whenever anything went wrong, it was blamed on her malignant influence. As with so many other situations which women experience in public life, the courtesan companion to power is 'damned if she does, damned if she doesn't'.

In modern times there are fewer kings and princelings, and as government has become more bureaucratic, it has also become less open to the bold adventuress. Simultaneously, the opening of the more formal pathways to political power to women, via elective office, for example, means that they no longer have to work their passage to the top in the time-honoured way. The last British woman to hold a place not only behind the throne but under the canopy was Frances Stevenson, the 'kept woman' of 10 Downing Street. Joining the household of Lloyd George as a summer governess to his children, she became his mistress and then his secretary, to give colour to her continuing presence at the side of the goatish gloryboy. As 'L.G.'s' *maitresse en titre* and London partner, while his disgusted wife kept her welcome back home in the valleys, Frances stood at the heart of the British government in the critical period during and after World War I. The personal and political secrets of a Prime Minister in one of England's darkest hours were in her keeping.

Yet as in so many of these cases the role of royal courtesan combined prestige and power with heavy penalties. Whatever magic the so-called 'Welsh wizard' brought to their private hours, the public life of Frances Stevenson was fraught with the kind of duplicity and hypocrisy only possible in those days of a subservient press and a credulous public. During a long relationship of over forty years, she lived the pretence of a purely professional connection that denied the central truth of her existence. Lloyd George's demands that the affaire be kept *sub rosa* denied Frances also the chance of a normal home and family life. Meanwhile, as the first-ever woman to serve as private secretary to a Minister of the Crown, and first woman personal secretary to a Prime Minister, Frances endured alone the rabid hostility to women of the British civil service that was still finding vigorous expression in the resistance to Marcia Williams, secretary to Harold Wilson, over forty years later. Nevertheless the attractions outweighed all these drawbacks. Frances chose this life, refusing a conventional offer of marriage from a conventional (and much younger) man. What it gave her was an exciting and worthwhile job, a place at the power centre and a 'magnetic' lover, in her own words. How would washing dishes and raising children in the suburbs have compared with this as a way of life?

It is quite clear that the women who strike out for power in this way do so as a reaction to powerlessness and a move against mediocrity. Their first real success and the first proof of their star quality lies in capturing the attention of a leader who in the nature of things will not be short of female admirers. So Eva Duarte had already succeeded in making herself into a leading lady of Argentine radio when Peron noticed her, and she reached out immediately for the greater opportunity he offered, driving his incumbent mistress out of the Presidential palace by main force.

Actresses will naturally have an advantage here over other women, and can use their flamboyance, their professional cunning, and their training in the arts of enslavement to entrap the male leader in their coils. That at least is the explanation given to account for the rise to power in China of the extraordinary Jiang Qing, 'evil demon' of the Communist leader Mao Tse-Tung. Jiang Qing is the only woman to have secured major power in the modern world through the world's most ancient means. The ruthless use of whores' power is a striking feature of Chinese tradition from the most ancient times – over twelve hundred years separate two famous ex-concubine Empresses, the last in the line, Tz'u-hsi, and Wu Chao, who began as a thirteen-year-old imperial prostitute a career of power in China which lasted for almost all of the seventh century. But the custom of concubinage, though plainly a fertile breeding-ground for ambitious young Chinese women, went the way of the Emperors whom the 'little lilies' had served. Only Jiang Qing has managed to make herself heir to this tradition with any notable success.

Jiang Qing was a film and stage actress whose leading roles had, ironically enough, included the part of the radicalised wife Nora in Ibsen's *A Doll's House*. As the daughter of a concubine growing up equivocally in the households of rich, uncaring men, Jiang Qing had good motives for wanting revenge on the male power-holders of Chinese society. Joining the Communist Party, she studied Marx and Lenin and underwent military training. None of this was enough to dispel the deep suspicion of her among the other party leaders, which quickly turned to outrage as this new arrival from the bohemian stage circles of Shanghai set her cap at Chairman Mao, landed him, and moved herself into his wartime cave. The central committee of the Communist Party was forced to accept their chairman's action and grudgingly issued a marriage licence. But it came only on the strict understanding that Jiang Qing was barred for life from politics.

The energy and drive that the party stalwarts were so right to fear were held in check for the first ten years or so of her marriage. But then Jiang Qing began to take an apparently innocent interest in art and literature. In 1966 she became cultural adviser to the People's Liberation Army and from this bland-sounding base constructed the ferocious weapon of 'reconstruction' and destruction that became known as the Cultural Revolution. Her involvement as one of the key leaders gave her an enormous, nationwide platform of personal power. To this she increasingly added the role of interpreter and spokeswoman for the ageing Mao, and guardian of his revolutionary tradition and thought. As an indication of her unprecedented power, she was elected to the Central Politburo of the Chinese Communist Party. She seemed unassailable.

But the death of Mao in 1976, hardly an unforeseen event, showed how tenuous her power was, and how little she had been able to prepare for solo flight without her protector and keeper. Within ten days she was in prison, charged as the leader of the 'Gang of Four' with a variety of offences, ranging from subversion of the government to violence against individuals.

Running beneath the official charge sheet, however, are the deeper accusations: of being an evil, worthless, destructive person; of usurping power not rightly hers; of being unfit to be a member of either community or party, unfit to govern, even to live (Jiang Qing was sentenced to death in 1981, suspended for two years). Of being a whore, in short, who is all these things.

As the history of Jiang Qing indicates, the trade-off of sex for power has certain severe limitations for women power-seekers. As with the power that a woman marries into or inherits, it only rarely becomes the woman's power in her own right but like a fantasy of cloud-capped palaces can shiver and dissolve in an instant, leaving not a trace behind. But even at the height of her power a woman from such beginnings is *never* seen as its rightful possessor. She is never trusted, never taken seriously, never felt to be legitimate. Perhaps it is as well for women that this pathway to power, so time-honoured and well-worn, is at last falling into disuse. It is a route that has suffered the law of diminishing returns by steady decline throughout this century. In the past the great courtesans could expect not only the King but all his government to pay court to them, in recognition of their important place in the scheme of things. But where they played for crowns and coronets, today's good-time girls play for minor US congressmen or disaffected members of the lower British aristocracy. Naturally this has reduced the attraction of power politics as a spectator sport. But it has immeasurably increased the chances for women to find other ways of expressing both their drive towards power, and their own sexuality.

The Life Force

The connection of power with sexuality has found many other expressions than this system of the oldest barter the world has known. On the simplest level, power provides an individual with all that is necessary to indulge sexual desires and fantasies, and there is no evidence that women are exempt from this kind of power behaviour. The different but equally dedicated sagas of Messalina and Catherine the Great show that males do not have

111

a monopoly of the ability to use their position to sexual advantage, nor of the energy to enjoy it. The possession of power enhances feelings of well-being and consequently of sexuality. Conversely, the free expression of her sexuality for a woman can convey an enormous sense of power over all these little fish positively gasping for the hook. Despite the efforts of males everywhere to persuade women that their sex equals weakness and disability, many women have made the interesting discovery that sex *is* power, and have exploited it to the full.

Chief among these are the legendary *grandes horizontales* who took nineteenth-century Europe by the ears with a fanfare of strumpets. Never before had women peddled their primary asset with such success, achieving fame, adulation and social eminence to an unprecedented degree. Their reputation for sexual prowess gave them the entrée into the highest circles; La Belle Otero was at different times consort to Edward, Prince of Wales, Prince William of Prussia and Grand Duke Nicholas, later Tzar of Russia. Cora Pearl, who had begun life as Eliza Emma Crouch in a back street of Plymouth, counted five princes, three dukes, two counts and a marquis among her clientele, plus untitled millionaire bankers and beys of the Emperor Napoleon III, in a raffish *Who's Who* of the contemporary aristocracy.

These women also employed 'that one talent which 'tis death to hide' to amass the kind of money that makes even the salary of the highest corporate woman today look like underpayment. The famous 'Skittles' obtained from the eighth Duke of Devonshire an annuity of £2000, worth at least ten times that in today's money, and lived to collect it for the next *sixty years*. Cora, the pearl of them all, relieved an Irish heir of £80,000 inside two months, and at the age of thirty-seven so enslaved a young Frenchman that he parted with his entire fortune of £500,000 to her. But the palm for Businesswoman of the Year must go to the demure and gentle Laura Bell, who with her Madonna face and Magdalen demeanour managed to shake down the Nepalese envoy, General HRH Prince Jung Bahadur, for £250,000 – *in one night!*

Such wealth, on a literally fabulous scale, brought power in itself. While London dockers were moved to a desperation strike for a minimum wage of 6d an hour, these darlings of delight would spend hundreds and even thousands of pounds on the flowers for one evening's dinner party. But conspicuous consumption did not account for all the take. Many invested shrewdly in jewels, property or horseflesh; Laura Bell accomplished the impossible with her £250,000, using it as a dowry to cancel her position as 'the Queen of London Whoredom' by marrying into the British aristocracy where she was accepted by such worthies as the Bishop of Norwich and the 'Grand Old Man' of England, Gladstone himself.

As this shows, the women of what contemporary hypocrisy ludicrously entitled the 'Frail Sisterhood' knew their own power, and knew too the points of leverage. They were not, however, at all interested in using it for political purposes: when Leonide Leblanc was simultaneously favouring a French prince, the Duc d'Aumerle, and his bitter opponent, the socialist politician Clemenceau, she enjoyed her situation for its irony rather than for its influence. Yet they could and did rejoice in the untrammelled expression of their dominance, both personal and social. Cora Pearl's only response to the man who shot himself, not because she fleeced him of his fortune but because she then cast him off, was, 'The pig! He might have done it in the ante-room and not ruined my carpet.'

Cora was also adept at using the personal clout of her respective men to make a public statement of her own power. One such occasion took place at Baden-Baden, then the centre of the fashionable world. In the words of a delighted observer:

> Cora was sailing gracefully into the Kursaal, all dressed in white satin and white lace, on the arm of Salamanca [a millionaire Spanish-Jewish banker] when they were very politely and firmly stopped by an official with a big gold chain round his neck, and Cora was told her presence would cause a scandal and she must retire ... Lo and behold! within half an hour, Cora and her red hair and white jewels and her interminable white dress again appeared at the door triumphant, for this time, being on the arm of the Duke of Hamilton, whose mother was a Princess of Baden, her progress was unimpeded; in fact all the Casino officials bowed to the ground as she advanced.

Cora ate little men like flunkeys and major-domos for breakfast. As she herself boasted: 'Your princes and kings! –

I've trampled on them! And then they crawled off for consolation to the Tweeleries [les Tuileries, the palace where the Emperor held court]. The Tweeleries! Why, the Tweeleries is my *lumber-room!*' Not a bad boast for a woman who was described as 'very ugly, amiable but very stupid and fond of playing coarse silly monkey tricks'. Whatever else she was, Cora could not have been stupid, and like all these women she seems to have grafted herself onto the life of high-class whoredom not for the sport, nor even wholly for the spondulix, but for the opportunity it gave her to actualise herself to the height of her bent. Whatever she wanted to think, be, or do, she could, without any man's let or hindrance. Her sexuality gave her power not only over men and a man-made society, but over and in *herself*. Again and again examples crop up of women using their sex as an instrument of self-discovery and self-assertion. The French actress and *grande cocotte* Rachel, although reviled as 'small, hideous, narrow-chested and Jewish', was reported as having 'willed her features to be beautiful' as she embarked on the career that arose out of her realisation, *'J'ai besoin de m'encanailler'* ('I need to make a bitch of myself').

With the honest recognition of needs and drives, and their often extravagant fulfilment, came a poise and assurance rare among the women of Victorian England, where the captive rosebud maiden was the order of the day. The knowledge of their success, personal and financial, gave them a proud sense of self-worth and often put an enviable edge on their wit. La Belle Otero, insulted on one occasion by a rejected suitor demanding, 'How can women be so beautiful and so stupid?' replied, 'God made us beautiful so that men would love us – He made us stupid so that we could love them.' Sentimental moralists have painted warning pictures of the great whores as ruining their lives, and dying of consumption in a garret like *La Dame aux Camélias*. The reality is of Otero, Pearl and many others living in style until their eighties and nineties, and in the exuberant joy of life that made 'Skittles' sing out to an aristocratic Master of the Hunt when he complimented her on the colour in her cheeks after a strenuous day in the saddle, 'That's nothing. *You should see my arse!*'

What these women embraced was not so much *la vie horizontale* – both 'Baby' Jordan and La Paiva claimed that they had sex less often than the average downtrodden wife, because they could choose *not to* – but a life which enabled them to make all their own choices, not simply those of sexual selection and rejection. The freedom which they enjoyed to choose their houses, their companions, their country of residence and their way of life amounts to the kind of independence and autonomy through which an individual discovers and masters soul and self. Set this in contrast with the almost intolerable restrictions of the standard Victorian marriage, entry into which cost a woman the few meagre civil rights which she possessed, and the 'whores' option' looks less like a disgusting and deviant means of self-destruction than an entirely rational and functional response to a set of highly adverse circumstances. For these women, whores' power was the only kind of power they would ever succeed in getting their hands on. The wonder is that more of the beaten-down brigade of Victorian females, corseted physically and strait-jacketed mentally into caricatures of normal womanhood, did not also rush to tread the primrose path.

> Men, some to business, some to pleasure take,
> But every woman is at heart a rake.
>
> Alexander Pope

The greatest whores were those who manipulated not only their 'Toms' and the rules of their society, but the very symbols and ideology that subordinated the rest of their sex. For while conventional wisdom constructed the myth of the innocent girl-child, the pure maiden, the chaste wife and the devoted mother, all familiar gooey stereotypes from the sickbag of Victorian stock, this automatically placed a rarity value on the women who broke the mould. Surrounded as he was by women who 'wouldn't', and couldn't even be expected to, the nineteenth-century male was an absolute pushover for a woman who both would and *did*. Such women undoubtedly possessed in real life strong drives, appetites and energies, all of which, for very good reasons of their own, men have seen fit traditionally to repress in the 'gentler', 'weaker' or 'softer' sex.

Women of high sexuality therefore hold a very special charm and challenge for men, who find it hard to believe that all this vitality and sexual promise has not been created for them, and

115

yet are terrorised by the thought of its rampant, unbridled expression. On one level the sexual woman is a man's to do with as he likes, infantilised and domesticated by nicknames like *fille de joie*, bunny girl, *poule de luxe* or playmate. But with only a slight shift of perspective she becomes evil and dangerous, insatiable in the clutch of her unconquerable eroticism, governed by emotions and irrational female instincts, dominated by her sex with which she seeks to dominate men. All this is nothing but the product of the male's deep fear of impotence and his rage against supposedly inferior women who yet, at this most basic level, never sexually fail.

The Dominatrix

Men's reaction to their self-imposed nightmare of sexual weakness in contrast with women's perpetual sexual strength is incarnated in the powerful fantasy of the dominatrix.

'Madame La Domina' represents the idea of women's sexual power in its most extreme and threatening form. She is the cruel female authority figure intent on punishing males and making them suffer and cry out; she is the bitch with the birch, the witch with the whip. Yet at the same time she is, in the classic pornographic realisation of this classic masculine fantasy, young, sexually attractive, abundantly revealed by a little black dress of studded leather, and most heavily clad around the nether extremities that are cased in black boots, heeled and spurred. With these, and the rest of her ingenious array of instruments of correction she domineers over men, punishes them for their opposition, rides roughshod over them physically and psychologically and makes them do her will.

This figure, rich in erotic promise and terror, has a long pedigree. It springs in part from European habits of punishment unthinkingly continued since medieval times, when every dame school gave power to a woman like that celebrated by William Shenstone in *The School-Mistress* (1752):

A matron, whom we school-mistress name,
Who boasts unruly brats with birch to tame.

It picks up, too, on all the myths of the 'other' mother, the wicked step-mother, the cruel killing woman as opposed to the ever-loving life-giver, that run back to the dawn of time. But it is also a current modern preoccupation of pornographers and professionals in the sexual trades. Any sex shop has a wide range of 'dominatrix literature' and videos, any contact magazine has a rash of desperate males requiring the specialist attention of 'governess', 'nanny', 'strict teacher' or 'disciplinarian'. The 'whip lady' is an attractive role for prostitutes, for they are much less likely to end up being beaten or battered themselves by the 'punters', because they hold the power and control. As one London 'specialist' commented, 'I'd rather see them grovel than have to grovel myself!'

The implications of this puerile and impoverished male fantasy go far beyond the confines of modern pornographic dystopia. The whole issue is highly revealing about men's thinking (if the process can be graced by such a term) on the subject of women and power. So strong is the association between ideas of power, sexuality, women's dominance and their unchecked will, that frequently an unspoken assumption arises that if a woman as both power and sexuality, she must be a whore. The strain that such a woman imposes upon the men around her and the male public at large is almost intolerable; they can accommodate a woman either as a sex object or as a leader, but not as both without feeling deeply threatened and reaching for the crude explanation and derogation of 'whore'. Lois Gould, in her perceptive analysis in *MS* magazine in September 1979, has drawn attention to a classic manifestation of this:

> Whatever else they were and did, Joan of Arc and the other certified saints (including the Virgin herself) and in recent times Eleanor Roosevelt, Golda Meir, Indira Gandhi, Margaret Thatcher and Governor Ella T. Grasso – none of these women was ever described or, presumably, fantasised about as a hot number. Whereas Eva Peron, whatever else *she* was and did, was emphatically that too, and with a vengeance.

So Aristotle Onassis could boast that on Eva Peron's European tour, when in fact she was enjoying widespread personal and political success, he hired her to have sex with him and paid her with a cheque for her charitable foundation, a characteristic Onassis vulgarism that Eva's latest biographers point to as indicating the extent to which she continued to be seen as a sex object despite her political ability and record. Even today these subterranean connections seem to be inescapable. The character of the hard-driving woman TV producer played by Faye Dunaway in *Network* is a mindless reworking of the myth that high-achieving women inextricably confuse their sex and business lives – this character is so obsessive that she thinks about the ratings even when she is screwing. Power and success make women monsters, and they give decent chaps like Peter Finch heart attacks. Despite the modish trappings of this overrated tale, at heart it remains a Victorian melodrama with an awful warning about the dangers of messing with a Bad Girl.

However dubious its application, the slur of 'whore' is always available to men, ready to hand as a weapon against women who are in power, or have any prospect of rising to it. Ann Clwyd, the first woman ever to be returned to parliament from a seat in the Welsh valleys, had only been in parliament long enough to draw approval for her promising start when she found herself viciously attacked in *Private Eye*. The gist of the smear was that Clwyd had achieved success only because she had slept her way to it: 'the reference contained a large number of allegations of sexual immorality,' states Ann Clwyd's solicitor, Bernard Simons. Clwyd immediately took legal action to obtain redress against this gross libel, and was further vindicated by widespread expressions of support from both sides of the House of Commons. But such incidents are fairly common in the 'man's world' of power politics. Petra Kelly, leader of the Green Party in Germany, has on several occasions successfully sued West German publications over sexual lampoons, and illustrations in which her head was superimposed on a nude photograph of another woman.

The experiences of these two women highlight the danger area of sexuality for women in power. They are always vulnerable to the vileness of men who turn their sex against them and use it as an insult. This most ancient term of abuse for a woman, 'whore', is employed in this context as a means not only of hurting an individual woman, but also of frightening off the whole sex. 'If you go forward to power,' the message is, 'this is what will happen to you.' It is both an expression of men's hostility and a weapon of deterrence in the power struggle, a vicious and small-minded tactic of power-game sex harassment. Sadly but predictably, all too often it works. Lois Gould stresses: 'The fact is that while we revere – and revel in – the sexual exploits of male leaders, it's almost impossible to recall a politically prominent woman who was also perceived as sexually active without being destroyed by it.'

Sir, the woman's a whore, and that's the end of it.

Dr Johnson

What Really Happened at Bendix

One woman who has suffered in very recent times from the dual standard of morality, and from the overriding preoccupation with women's sexuality, is American businesswoman Mary Cunningham. After a brilliant career at Harvard Business School Cunningham was in the unique position of choosing between thirty-two top job offers, and tipped to become Harvard's first female graduate to be the chairman of a non-cosmetics company. She turned down a post in investment banking starting at $55,000 a year to go to Bendix to work for its whizz-kid chairman, Bill Agee. As his executive assistant Mary Cunningham rose to become at twenty-nine the youngest female corporate vice-president of a Fortune 500 company in America. But suddenly Bendix became more famous for dirty linen than for washing machines as Mary Cunningham was dragged through the mud for what she calls 'the oldest sin in the business', 'sleeping her way to the top'.

Mary Cunningham was fired from Bendix by a board desperate to put an end to a rising epidemic of gossip and media speculation about the relationship between her and Agee. She herself strenuously denied the allegations, but as she sardonically noted in her account of it all, *Powerplay*, 'what could be more titillating than the notion that this *Wunderkind* was having an affair with his blond executive assistant?' Once the rumours had taken hold, it became immaterial whether or not the much-canvassed affair was a reality or a fiction. As Mary Cunningham's ex-husband grimly observed, they were going to slaughter her either way.

With Mary Cunningham's public designation as the floozy, tart or corporate crumpet came the classic masculine reaction to pay her off and save the man's hide. 'So you piddled on the floor. But you don't have to have your face wiped in it. She's got to go,' Agee was advised, 'Get rid of her. Give her a nice fat settlement. She'll survive ... You've got a company to run. Think of your obligations ... your neck ... ' Other men too were thinking of the sacred masculine corporate neck. After issuing a pious statement that the board had complete confidence in Ms Cunningham, and considered it 'unjust to respond to speculation in the media' with any action against her, the brass at Bendix did just that. At a meeting of what Cunningham describes as a 'kangaroo court' at which 'character witnesses' were called against her without her being present or having a chance to respond, she was given her options: resign or get the boot. In the circumstances it is hard not to agree with Gloria Steinem, who called Mary Cunningham to lend her support: 'I hope to God that you two are having an affair, because you're sure paying the price for it!'

Whether or not Mary Cunningham was having an affair with Bill Agee she was certainly paying the price for being a woman. This painful saga exposes the deep vein of hostility to women in business which can take on a rabid intensity when the hunt is up and a victim comes into sight. Warnings of this had reached Cunningham from the start, when she arrived at Bendix to discover the key executives either resented or feared her. 'We had one other feisty woman round here and we took care of her,' she was told. 'They're making 'em better-looking all the time!' was her welcome to another meeting. Bill Agee, himself entrusted with great power at the age of twenty-nine, attempted to defend his advancement of a young, attractive woman: 'Is that any reason not to promote her? Should I make her wait another five years even though she's better able to do the job than the rest of the people on my executive staff – men who are twice her age?' As Cunningham adds, 'Why penalise the woman?' The obvious answer is, because she's a woman. During Cunningham's trial by ordeal, letters poured in from all over America, from hundreds of women who had had similar experiences. She realised then how common was this slur tactic as a weapon against women in corporate warfare, the undermining of their professional credibility along with their personal reputation.

This nudge-nudge anti-feminism and rooted refusal to consider women on other than a sexual level was both restated and returned with interest by the press. Mary Cunningham recognised from the outset that the combination of circumstances made this story vulnerable to press exploitation: 'It had power, sex, divorce, money, everything that sells papers.' During the course of the massive coast-to-coast coverage she found herself transformed from 'wholesome Mary Cunningham', 'Vermont Maid look-alike' to 'shapely VP' and 'femme fatale'. Of the rag-bag of stale clichés and restrictive stereotypes available to the 'gentlemen' of the fourth estate, clearly siren-temptress was more appropriate to Cunningham's new and exciting sexual status than squeaky-clean country cousin. And so it came to pass.

But chief among the object lessons of the Cunningham affair, in any relevant sense of that word, is the danger for women of being primarily perceived and subsequently trapped *within the female role*. Mary Cunningham tells how she was from the first looked to for 'the female touch', drawn into the 'business wife' routine so familiar to the lone woman at the top: 'When Agee wanted someone with him to ease a conversation or welcome a new face he'd summon me up to the dais.' She made herself available for all aspects of Agee's work, abandoning her own business and political life for his. When Agee's wife left, she found herself hiring him a cleaning woman. And when the crisis came, in the true spirit of female sacrifice, she 'took the bullet for Agee'. If the board of Bendix failed to separate Mary the business executive and vice-president for strategic planning from Mary the woman, then it seems clear that both Agee and Mary herself had had difficulty with this issue too.

The Personal is Political

This old saw of the women's movement takes on a new dimension in relation to women's achieving or holding top jobs, especially in what is thought of as 'big' business, where the stakes are highest and the ante is up. Mary Cunningham and Bill

Agee are not alone with this clichéd but yet unresolved problem of a 'woman's role', even if they have become the most spectacular victims of its mismanagement to date.

The confusion between women's specifically female roles and their business life is one of the most serious of the disadvantages that high-achieving women have to face. Traditional social and cultural expectations run deep in both sexes, and surface in the assumption that even in the top flights of employment a woman will continue to perform the kind of work that is dictated by her female function. This is not simply the pinprick irritation of being asked to take notes or make the coffee, although even the most highly placed woman in the civil service, Anne Mueller, reports being taken for a secretary. It is rather the quite unexamined and taken-for-granted feeling among men that a woman will always behave like a woman no matter what the nature or demands of her job.

What this means is that male employers unthinkingly consider themselves entitled to expect that in addition to her professional work a woman will also always be ready to contribute her personal female skills of caring, managing and soothing. So top women wryly relate being instructed, 'You'd better go and pour some oil on Joe, he's very angry about the new plan, be nice to him.' Kiss him better, perhaps? This frequent practice of using women in a female rather than a business role also includes the self-serving masculine assumption that women will unquestioningly perform the shit-work of the organisation too. When one woman decided to visit a female employee in hospital, she discovered that she was expected by her fellow directors to carry the letter giving notice of redundancy. It would somehow be 'easier' for her to soften the blow. It is also obviously easier for men to get someone else to clear up their messes by invoking the mystique of female magic!

The reliance of male employers on women's ability to 'be nice' is reflected in the clustering of women in work areas like public relations and personnel. But women not engaged in these areas still find that they are expected to 'smile', 'be kind', not give male colleagues 'a hard time' but on the contrary devote their energies to making the men they deal with feel good and look good. Rising in power and prestige does not relieve a woman of this sacred responsibility for the masculine ego. 'I'm the most senior woman in his organisation, so he expects me to be especially grateful to him – half geisha, half mother, would just about sum up what I have to do,' was one female director's comment.

The unspoken demand that women will carry over their female bolstering and stroking functions into the work-place makes itself felt in a number of ways. Often it means that the highest that a woman can rise will be to some institutionalised support-dependency role, however flatteringly it is tricked out as 'executive assistant' or 'the chairman's right hand'. It can also actively block women's promotion by the tunnel-vision males whose egos they have worked so hard massaging. In one instance, a male director of personnel leaving for a new job called his female assistant in and told her that he was giving her a glowing review in which he recommended her as interim director until his successor could be found. The ensuing dialogue went like this:

She: Why haven't you nominated me as permanent director if I'm that good?
He (*astounded*): It never occurred to me you'd want the job.
She: Why do you think I've stayed here for five years?
He (*hurt*): I thought you liked working with me.

Well, he would, wouldn't he?

The fundamental problems for women are being seen all the time as a woman, in fact, on the deepest level, simply being *seen*. Research by Rosabeth Kanter has shown that male colleagues consistently obliterate details of women's credentials and expertise, but recall every aspect of her physical appearance. Brutally, while you're talking balance sheets, they're thinking about your breasts. Given that male minds can only run on one track at a time, it is not surprising that women's 'visibility', according to management theorists, creates communication distortions and dysfunctions which either erase what the female executive has said, or ensure its misunderstanding. Simultaneously women's high visibility brings with it built-in performance pressures which mean that as a woman you will always be more strictly evaluated than a comparable male, and this on the basis of a performance that the men present could neither hear properly nor remember clearly, obsessed as they are with your sex!

There is no point in minimising the struggle for women to win a

123

new working relationship out of the old sexpectations. The struggle is not to get men to take us 'seriously' or as business *persons*, since that implies a fundamental *unseriousness* of women and an illusory neutral or sexless occupational world. The fight is to break down the idea that the caring work of society is only or properly women's. If women are to humanise the wider world through their professional lives, we will do so not by performing all that emotional and psychological work but by getting men to take their responsibility for it, and teaching them how.

Further, while sexual awareness is still in its present Neanderthal state, women must be aware of the negative constructions that can and will be placed upon their sex and their actions. As long as men are still shuffling through the worn-out pack of dog-eared sexual attitudes and definitions that they were issued at birth, the 'whore' card will continue to surface and continue to be played. If this situation threatens, try to be as open and disarming as Sian Vickers, the only woman on the board of the advertising agency Young and Rubicam. Vickers, who joined the board to the muttered accompaniment of 'We'll be having blacks next!', lives with the agency's creative director and deputy chairman. She engagingly comments: 'I am occasionally asked if I slept my way to the top – a suggestion I find rather flattering, but I don't think I did because I know lots of women who slept with the same people without getting promoted.'

That, finally, is the drawback in resorting to the sexual option. It doesn't make you chairman of the board, it just makes you a (not even *the*) woman who slept with the chairman. Don't take it, or trust it. Whores' power was only ever an avenue worth considering for women when all others were barred, and the alternative, of respectable wifehood, so deeply unattractive. Now, especially in the higher reaches of the more competitive or cut-throat professions, it is a game too dangerous to be worth any man's candle, potentially costing you not only your status and credibility, but even your job. And no matter what the short-term rewards, power derived from a man is not yours, and it is not the real thing – boudoir power never equates with boardroom power. So instead of saying, in the celebrated *bon mot* of the Hollywood actress, 'Who do you have to sleep with to get *out* of this movie?', resolve to get off your Madame de Pompadour and make it by unassisted woman power – your own.

CHAPTER 6

Pathways to Power

There are more ways than one to the wood.
Russian proverb

The lessons of history are of limited use to the modern woman power-seeker. Past models are either inapplicable or illegitimate in today's world, and the woman embarking on her journey not only has to plan her own route, but in many cases draw the map too. How to find the way, and how to get there, increasingly concern the numbers of women who are no longer content to stand on the sidelines while the male long-distance runners embark on the race for the top. Some of the do's and don'ts are becoming clear from the example of those women who have made the journey.

First, do all you can to come in with as high a profile as possible. Many women do not choose their entry gate into the world of work, but have it chosen for them by circumstance, particularly short-term thinking, their own or that of those around them. On the day that my grandfather received a letter from my mother's school stating their intention to enter her for a university scholarship he terminated her education, saying that what she obviously had to learn was how to wash the pots and pans. Many women, even today, relate similar experiences, and even though they later make a success in business, as she did, their struggle is so much harder for having to start farther back. The errand-boy-to-boss success story is a dearly cherished myth, particularly in America where it does not exclude even the highest office in the land (log cabin to White House). But tea-lady to chief executive?

One key factor is to obtain education, not just in quantity, but in quality. Although female graduates do better in the employment market than non-graduates on the whole, not all female graduates do equally well. Certain subject areas are strongly favoured over others for pure success, as opposed to emotional fulfilment, and the girls who take the standard female school options like English and modern languages usually find that something more is needed to put a glint into an employer's eye, not to mention a thrust to their own performance. For this reason, any subject with a hard vocational edge offers a good foot on the ladder. To get into business or law school, to be seen 'eating dinners' in the Inns of Court, has another advantage too; it gets you into the pool of available talent where you can be spotted. Elinor Guggenheimer says, 'It makes such a difference to get into the good schools because that is where the employers look for the people they want.'

Gold-starred not only at the beginning of a woman's career but all through her professional life are the heavyweight areas of economics and finance. For Barbara Ward Jackson the specialist economics route led from a convent in York to a governorship of the BBC, professorships at Harvard and Columbia, world fame with her books *The Rich Nations and the Poor Nations* and *Space Ship Earth*, and finally a seat in the House of Lords. In America, the first woman director of the Stock Exchange and first woman Secretary of Commerce in the US Cabinet, Juanita Kreps, had built up her track record as an economist first. In the realm of practical or applied finance Anne Mueller, Britain's leading woman civil servant, identifies her secondment to the high-prestige Treasury at a formative stage in her career as a significant factor in her advancement. Having knowledge and understanding of these areas does a great deal to counteract the unconscious prejudice against females as lightweights or 'bird brains'. And at the simplest level, as Margery Hurst, phenomenally successful founder of the Brook Street Bureau, advises, 'If you go into business, you must understand figures.' As a child Margery Hurst could add up in thousands, all good practice for subsequently having to add up in millions.

Starting off without the right tools for success means that a woman has to be prepared to turn herself round. Making

127

yourself over can involve not only giving up a steady if unexciting job, but taking on a bank loan to pay for the retraining. This can be daunting but investment banker Helen Matthews has no doubt that it was the right move for her: 'It was just so dim of me not to see the importance of work in your whole life.' Helen actually had a job in advertising that was both exciting and well paid, but could not see, looking ahead, that this career path would deliver what she wanted. Similarly Janet Mead, after years of studying during which she mastered French, Spanish, Italian, Portugese and Arabic, sent herself back to school. She had decided that 'being a linguist was not enough. I wanted management – that was where the action was.' Janet studied three nights a week to obtain the business qualifications that demonstrate capability and commitment in the way that art history or anthropology never can.

In the knowledge that subject areas like the law and business studies deliver the goods in terms of status and credibility, many women are seeking to climb on to the bandwagon. The numbers of women applying for MBA and the proportion of women in business studies, especially at post-graduate level, has risen sharply in the last five years from less than a fifth of total intake to a figure approaching or in some places exceeding 40 per cent. These figures from Britain and America are not so encouraging as they appear on the surface. First, there is a wide gap in all professional subjects between the numbers of females *studying* it, and those actually making a living *practising* it, so that although almost 40 per cent of law students in Britain now are female, under 10 per cent and 8 per cent of solicitors and barristers are women. The time for hats in the air is when all these women are out in the world and cheerfully tucked up in good jobs which they would not have obtained without the extra work qualification.

In addition, the recent glamorisation of the 'fast track' presents too narrow a formula for success. It is in danger of becoming a modish update of the harmful cliché that only an exceptional or brilliant woman really stands any chance of getting anywhere. It implies that the female high-achiever springs into the stratosphere fully tooled up from the very start. Some do. Barbara Thomas emerged from New York University Law School with the highest profile of any woman in a very long time and her career has been commensurate with this. Management consultant Orna Ni Chionna did not have her first long-term career job until the age of twenty-seven, but began then in the top 5 per cent of UK salary earners, and confidently expects to hit £40,000 long before she makes forty in years. But the majority of women take a longer, slower path with a gentler curve. It is important that all women should have the confidence to find the right one for them. No one should be made to feel that they have missed their chance of success if they have not achieved one of these 'top woman' seals of approval at the very outset.

For there are as many ways into the wood or up the mountain as there are women to tread them. The only imperative is to find your avenue, for only in very rare cases will it find you. For some women this may mean turning your back on the paper qualifications which can seem so vital to those women who do not have them. Alison Newell moved out of the academic world, leaving her university degree course in science and technology after only a year, and discovered her fast-tracking route; she trained as a computer programmer instead and became managing director of the computer software house F International Ltd and president of the Computing Services Association before she was forty.

In finding the path for you, give some thought to the question of situating yourself for success. Certain areas are more promising than others for women thinking in career terms; in publishing on both sides of the Atlantic, for instance, the numbers of women employed mean that as a beginner you will have company and solidarity, and never be in the exposed position of the lone woman pioneer that can be so demoralising. High numbers of women at all levels also means a better-trained bunch of male colleagues who are used to working with women, promoting them and serving under them when they rise, as women are now doing more and more, to the very top. The higher ranks of this once gentlemanly but now womanly occupation may not offer such spectacular financial killings as some others, although Patricia Soliman, associate publisher and vice-president of Simon and Schuster Inc., owns up to being 'a six-figure woman'. But the area as a whole offers great creative power to innovate and control.

129

Finding the path will not always be as quick and easy as it can seem from the dazzling careers of others. For politicians, it is essential to be out of the starting-gate like a whippet, since it takes so long to win public office. This difficulty is compounded for women by the selection boards' habit of using women as sacrificial victims so they can inspect the entrails of an unwinnable seat. Margaret Thatcher embarked on her political career at Oxford University, where she became the first-ever woman president of the influential Conservative Association. She did not get into parliament until the age of thirty-four, over thirteen years later. Similarly Ella T. Grasso, the first woman to become an American Governor in her own right, ran for her first primary when her youngest child was eighteen months old, and had had over thirty years as a career politician before she was elected Governor.

But the experience of politics is unusual, possibly because it has to be seen as a vocation rather than a straight choice of job. Sucessful political women are mono-motivated, frequently from very early experiences in a political family. For other women it is often not so much a question of deciding on a given power route, and then unswervingly pursuing it, but of trying a variety of things and going where the path opens. None of the top women interviewed for this study had mapped out their ascent. All had taken things a step at a time, allowing life to surprise them and equally often surprising themselves. What they had listened to and answered was not the siren call of the bitch goddess success, but the still small inner voice dictating one course or preference over another. So Sheila Needham, founder and managing director of Needham Printers, only 'knew she was a printer' when offered a managing directorship that would have taken her out of printing.

Sheila's career is a fascinating example of the mysterious ways in which women come to positions of authority rather than carve their way singlemindedly towards them as in the stereotype of the high-achieving woman. After rebelling against going to university, she was working as a secretary when her boss asked her to set up a new instant print method for one aspect of the firm's business. When the printing operation had expanded to employ fifteen full-timers, he gave her the choice between concentrating on the printing side or remaining as his

130

secretary. She chose the printing business. 'He was *furious*,' she remembers. 'He thought I'd choose him! And ironically, only a month before I had been saying to friends that I was one of those lucky women who was perfectly happy as a secretary.'

Taking the Risk

Sheila's path eventually led her to realise herself as founder of her own company. Her story illustrates one vital aspect of the quest for success by women; the individual must be ready to go on the journey of self-discovery, to risk change, and eventually to go it alone. At the simplest level, you should leave jobs while you still like them, counsels Donna Shalala: 'Don't stay in jobs too long. This is a big problem for women, it makes their resumés too short. Use jobs to learn, and to get experience, and then move on.'

The ability to take risks, to back a hunch, and to face the chance of failure, is in fact a distinguishing characteristic of top women. So is the ability to have the kind of hunch worth backing. Audrey Slaughter conceived, launched and edited the magazine *Over 21* on a shoestring. Within eighteen months four major companies vied to buy it and the successful bidder paid Audrey £16 for every £1 share she owned. 'Launching a magazine is not a rest cure,' she says with wry understatement. But that has not deterred her from putting together the finance to bring out another Slaughter brainwave, *Working Woman*, again with her own money and reputation on the line. Similarly Carmen Callil put together what was to become, as Virago, the publishing success of the 1970s, around her own dining table, 'working twenty-four hour days on a non-existent salary'.

Taking the risk is inseparable from high achievement – indeed, high achievement is *in itself* a risk, since it singles a woman out from the group, may detach her from family and friends, and propels her towards those high places where the powerful and eminent live alone. So Ambassador Kirkpatrick describes her entry into government as a 'totally unplanned move'. 'I said yes, but with enormous misgivings,' she recalls. 'It meant a colossal change in life, in life-style, role, and everything – I'm still fundamentally an academic and intellectual.' Other

131

factors too made this a very hard decision: 'It's a dreadful job, peculiarly difficult and demanding because of the psychic wear and tear.' And as a scholar by nature and training, the ambassador does not much like public life: 'One loses one's freedom. The conditions of public life in the US today are very onerous. You become the target for so much free-floating hostility and harsh criticism.' But then, she did not choose the job; it chose her.

Many women expressed in conversation a sense of events taking over, of fate lending a hand in the formation of their careers. Anne Joy, managing director of Challoners Recruitment, described in fits of laughter 'one zany episode, totally farcical!' She had answered an advertisement from an employment agency to find the office obviously closed, with the phone going like mad inside. As she stood there, a gypsy fortune teller burst out of the next door, screeching '*Will* you silence that phone?' and threw herself against the office door in a rage. It burst open, and Anne obediently went in to silence the phone. By the time the owner arrived, she was running the office. After his initial surprise ('Who the hell are *you*?') he hired her till the end of the week. Within six months she had two juniors and had expanded the business so much that her boss had to open another branch.

Although successful women very often attribute their rise to luck, fate or chance, it is clear that their sense of adventure means that opportunity does not have to knock twice on their door. Many such examples in the lives of these women of rising to the occasion as Anne Joy did tend to confirm the accuracy of Mrs Thatcher's crisp and useful dictum: 'Luck is opportunity meeting readiness.'

Their sense of adventure also gives top women another attribute which enlarges their experience and contributes to their success. It is remarkable how many women of power have at an early stage of life travelled abroad, to work or study overseas. This is not simply a question of heaping up further degrees from high-status foreign universities, although the Sorbonne, Harvard and Oxford do tend to crop up on top women's *curricula vitae*. It is more an openness to life and desire to explore, to experience and to know that leads these women all over the globe, in the footsteps and tradition of the great women travellers of the nineteenth century. So Barbara Hosking did not hesitate when the chance came up to work on a gold and silver mine in Tanzania and spent three years there, while Jane Deknatel and Donna Shalala went with the Voluntary Service Overseas and Peace Corps respectively to Malaysia and Iran. Others, like Janet Mead who criss crossed Europe and South America, travelled for the sheer joy of travel and thoroughly disproved the old adage that a rolling stone gathers no moss. It is also critically important that women of ability do not get so hooked into upward ascent that they lose sight of all the other joys of life. So when your daughter expresses a desire to go off and bum around India, the correct response is not 'What ever do you want to do that for?' but '*When do you leave?*'

> Take the risk. Make the journey. The pain of change is the price you pay for growth.

Solo Flight

Peter Pan thought that to die must be an awfully big adventure. Setting up your own business comes into the same category. It offers a unique pathway to power and control, and yet demands that whoever chooses this must be ready to hazard all they have. 'It's very scary,' said one woman who launched her company a year ago. 'I go home at night and think weird thoughts like "bankruptcy – the final frontier!" Mind you, that concentrates my mind wonderfully for the next day!' How do women come to make this election for sole charge and sleepless nights, top rewards and top responsibilities, in the full knowledge of the stark warning on Detta O'Cathain's wall, 'NOBODY HAS A RIGHT TO COMMERCIAL SURVIVAL'?

Many top women find their way forward and build a business on the basis of a great idea whose time they make sure has come. Sarah Breedlove Walker's authentic Cinderella story began when she was taking in washing at $1.50 an hour simply to survive. She hit on the idea of a special hair treatment for black women, and so successfully developed both her product and her operation with her well-trained Walker Agents, that she became the first black woman millionaire and lived in what she proudly called 'a coloured woman's palace' on the Hudson River. The golden age of cosmetics, when women like Elizabeth Arden and Helena Rubenstein could make a career out of cold cream and a fortune from face powder, is over, but this remains a promising pathway for women, as it is one of the very few specialist areas where being a female is an advantage not a drawback: Janet Lloyd has become managing director of Yardley of London, Loretta Balfour, 1984 finalist for the Veuve Cliquot Businesswoman of the Year award, is managing director of Estee Lauder UK, while Anita Roddick, the 1985 winner of this high-prestige away, has revolutionised the sale of beauty products with her brilliant Body Shop concept.

Other women too have succeeded in turning their womanhood to advantage, often by being in touch with things that men are quite ignorant of. Eve Mahlab, recently Australia's Businesswoman of the Year, discovered a whole new province in the large numbers of qualified women lawyers who had given up their careers for their family commitments. 'It was a huge untapped resource,' she says. 'All these women sitting around doing nothing.' Her initiative in organising the 'married woman market' for legal work part-time not only proved the foundation for a highly successful business – it enabled Eva Mahlab to live her Liberal-feminist belief that 'women are Australia's most under-utilised resource'. It is not hard to imagine, either, what this chance to keep their professional skills active during time out to raise their families would mean to the women lawyers given this employment, income and recognition of their worth. In this light, Mahlab's operation looks less like a business than a rescue mission. The much admired Steve Shirley, founder of F International, has performed a similar service for the housebound women of Britain.

Top businesswomen do not necessarily draw on their traditional skills of womanhood in order to make their way. 'Go for your gap wherever you see it,' says one, advice clearly not needed by the redoubtable Pamela Murphy. As a dairy farmer (she was the first woman on the council of the Royal Association of British Dairy Farmers) Pamela concluded that 'the animal ordure that is wasted in this country is a disgrace!' She not only developed her cows' other product into a highly marketable fertiliser called Cowpact, she sent herself to the

London Business School at the age of fifty-seven to learn how to develop the machines that performed this valuable transformation. The Murphy Separator, patented and on the market, won an award from the National College of Agricultural Engineering. Where there's muck, there's brass, and waste is too good to waste. Pamela Murphy subsequently gave her attention to marketing the liquid left when the solid had been extracted, under the sprightly name of Cowliq.

Having your bright idea, however, is only the start. Press coverage of top women tends to suggest that one day comes the bright idea, next thing the successful business, just like that! A substantial number of women who have set up on their own see themselves as having been forced into it. 'I couldn't please my mother, I couldn't please my boss, the only person left to try to please was myself,' was the comment of one woman entrepreneur. And in view of the obvious ability of these high achievers, it was surprising to hear the self-denigrating 'Who else would have employed me?' so often stated as a reason for going it alone.

Possibly what these women really mean is, 'Who else would I be prepared to work for?' Many women in business tell of experiencing the situation summed up succinctly by Detta O'Cathain: 'I look at some oaf doing it and know I could do it better!' Carmen Callil too knows how to do it better. But she was only able to when she went on her own with Virago, and later became one of the tiny handful of women ever to be managing director of a major British publishing house, Chatto and Windus. 'I just wasn't happy working for others,' she says, 'I found it so *boring*!'

'Success stories' also take little account of what establishing a business can cost. Clearly if the enterprise in which you have invested every mortal groat along with your reputation and self-esteem cracks, then it will be no surprise if you crack up with it. What is less often acknowledged is the 'psychic wear and tear', in Ambassador Kirkpatrick's phrase, of running a successful operation too. Margery Hurst's career described a classic 'rags to riches curve' when beginning with nothing but her own secretarial skills she developed the business that within ten years made her a millionaire. Her brilliant flair for the market and tremendous energy led to further successes when her company went public and with over 200 branches she now runs the largest secretarial services business in the world. But her honesty leads her to dispel any suggestion that hers was a Cinderella-type fairy-tale, as the title of her autobiography, *No Glass Slipper*, indicates. She became a casualty of inner conflicts and external pressures, suffering a nervous breakdown: 'I was in my early forties, and could only see suicide ahead. I recovered, but it took me more than a year to get over it.'

With the courage that gave Margery Hurst the will to fight back when her first husband abandoned her with a three-week-old baby, and which has earned her the accolade of Britain's most successful businesswoman, Margery Hurst published the story of her breakdown thirteen years ago. The fact that she is still getting letters from other sufferers shows that this is not an isolated problem. Margery Hurst has drawn attention to the kind of danger area usually left unacknowledged by the bank managers, accountants and consultants who advise on every other aspect of setting up a new business, the need for enormous resilience: 'If you can pick yourself up from the floor in a condition of agony and despair, and simply obliterate the memory of why you were down there, then you have a good chance of succeeding.' But the pain of the struggle cannot be minimised, nor the cost of the effort. You cannot know your psychic strength and capacity for endurance until you try it. But as you will be your own principal business asset, you owe it to yourself to evaluate this capacity at least as ruthlessly as you are scrutinising every other angle. And if you are a mental and emotional seven-stone weakling, you need to undergo a crash course in what the poet Coleridge called 'creative self-modification', or forget the whole thing!

Yet for all this, forming your own business is still one of the most attractive and accessible pathways to power for many women. Dr Leah Hertz, lecturer in business studies and a successful businesswoman herself, emphasises, 'Women have the greatest chance in self-employment.' She has just completed a study of 110 women heading up their own organisations in Britain and America, excluding those not holding the lion's share of their own business: 'You may have a big name, Laura Ashley, Mary Quant, but if you don't have 50 per cent, where is the power, you can be sacked!' As she explains:

Minorities and marginals have always succeeded in business.

Jews, Asians, you don't have to integrate, just get on with it. Women, although a majority, in fact are a minority, hassled every day and their confidence disappears. Executive women get stuck. Men make it tough and the recession makes it tougher. Women executives are said to be bitches. Is that surprising? They don't have a choice, men make them into bitches. If men had to carry the same burdens they'd be in a mental home.

Women owners create their own environment and don't compete with men. Problems with children disappear too. I was never harassed or frustrated in my own business. I had my children only when I had enough money and could pay for nurse, nanny, the lot, while my secretary went home and had to do housework till 2 in the morning!

No one business area is better than another for women, Leah Hertz feels. The one golden rule is simply, control the thing yourself. Since for so many women the aspiration to power is essentially a reaching for control, a way of striking out against and mastering feelings of powerlessness, starting your own business has obvious attractions. The one irreversible negative for women is that if you fail, you can't start up again in your wife's name!

Who Needs a Mentor?

In strong contrast with the freedom of running your own business and life is the system by which males in business sponsor a younger person and develop their career that has come to be known as 'mentoring'. The highly placed businessman takes another under his wing, advises and guides him, sees that he is placed to receive the right experience at the right time, and in the classic mentor-protégé relationship, grooms him to be his successor. This system, whether semi-official or discreet and unacknowledged, does not only work in business but in any area where males hold power, including the power carefully to select who else will be allowed to hold it.

Like so many other male power systems, the mentor process has so far failed to adapt to women. Generally, even today, they simply get left out. Social psychologist Dr Martha White suggests some of the reasons:

137

A man may be hesitant about encouraging a woman as a protégé. He may be delighted to have her as an assistant, but not see her as a colleague. He may believe that she is less likely to be a good gamble, that she is financially less dependent on a job. Because of subtle pressure from his wife, he may temper his publicly expressed enthusiasm or interest. Furthermore he may fail to introduce her to colleagues or sponsor her for jobs.

So while the high-achieving male may feel his status enhanced by having a high-achieving female as his 'right hand', he does not see her as mentorable material. For the point of the system is that the protégé outgrows the mentor, becoming at least equal in the hierarchy if not superior, in a process of informal control by the power-holders over the rights of succession. Consequently while men may take women's 'junior partner' support, or even assist them to move up and away on a different career path, they will not groom women to succeed them. Nothing diminishes the power and prestige of their job like the idea that it could be held down by a woman!

With the identification of mentoring as a system, and as a critical path by which high-rising males make it to the top, has come the idea that women must be sure to get a piece of this pie. Like all outsiders who have spent centuries trying to get in, and have only recently been admitted to the status of insiders looking for the way up, women have been feverishly studying the mechanisms and trying to make them work. The importance of securing a mentor is now taught to female students in business schools with the fervour with which women used to be taught the importance of catching a good husband. The reality is more reassuring. Very few of today's top women ever received the assistance of a mentor. The only steam they came up under was their own.

Of the interesting exceptions to this rule, Anne Mueller was lucky enough to have had two. Her first mentor, in her second year in the job, 'taught her a lot': 'I always say he helped me to be a civil servant.' To the second she owed her posting to the Treasury on secondment – 'a mark of great appreciation and a real distinction', or perhaps a recognition of the quality which has brought her to the top ranks of the service in later years. Anne's experience is not typical of that of other women. The civil service has always been a career service, and prides itself on developing individuals at their own pace. Among the numbers of other women surveyed in this present study, only three had had the experience of being mentored in the way that the system is operated on behalf of men.

Investment banker Mary Lou Carrington had the good fortune to be at university in Ohio when a new president arrived from Harvard Business School, bringing a small group of men with him. At the age of nineteen Mary Lou said to one of these that she was thinking of going on to Harvard Business School. He immediately said, 'You should meet ——,' and that 'opened the door to the inner sanctum'. Mary Lou became one of a special set, received direction and encouragement, and went to dinner at the White House. 'He pushed me like mad,' she remembers. 'He used to say "You could be doing a lot more than you are, the whole world is out there – break into it!"' Mary Lou did not in fact go to Harvard Business School in the end, but to the prestigious European Business School insead. But the declaration of her serious career intentions had been enough to stimulate the interest of an important man at an important time. 'He widened my horizons and provided introductions,' she said. 'He helped me tremendously.' Donna Shalala likewise had had the benefit of what she describes as 'a classic mentor' at graduate school, who helped not only her but a number of women 'from conviction'.

Mary Lou's mentor was perhaps able to help her so freely because whatever job he was helping her towards, it wouldn't be his. Clearly a distinction must be drawn between mentors operating in the educational and the business world. Of all the women I spoke to in Britain and America, only Jill Currie had had the benefit of the classic mentor-protégé relationship, which paid off for her with a seat on the operating board of a major brewery (the only woman in Britain to hold such a position) at the age of thirty-five. She was noticed ten years earlier by a top man in the regional management of her industry who 'obviously had a future with the company'. He asked her what she knew about performance reviews, was impressed with her answer, and afterwards requested information and briefing from her on various subjects in his area of responsibility. 'It was him developing me and I supporting him,' Jill says. 'It was a two-way trust. He never doubted I'd sent him off properly prepared for his management work.'

Protégé status is not a soft option. 'I worked like a black for him,' is Jill's memory of those days, 'doing all his thinking and writing for him. He'd be there early, but I'd be there an hour before.' But unlike most managers who take such female devotion for granted, Jill's mentor, on his next promotion, asked her to apply for a big step up. Once there, in the company's heartland, where she was the first senior woman they had ever had, he continued to support her, saying, 'She's here, she's trained, use her.' If anyone went behind her back, he would say, 'I haven't a clue about that, ask Jill.' And when the time came he allowed her to outgrow her current job and move on. As Jill looks back, she feels that he was the only man in the company who would nurture a female executive: 'He's secure in his own ability, he's strong and able, and has no problems with his identity.' In terms of his own career, too, he could see the benefit of this unorthodox course: 'He broke all the traditions in one go. It set him apart and elevated his status.'

In the absence of a regular mentor, other high-achieving women find their own. 'I married one!' commented Ambassador Kirkpatrick. 'A university professor, fifteen years older than I am, established and accomplished at the top levels of political science when we met and married. He became my professional mentor and remains such to this day.' Other women too named their husbands as mentors. Some husbands brought the mentors into the family with them: Anne Joy derived a good deal from her father-in-law, a 'very spiritual man, very erudite', and Elinor Guggenheimer was inspired by 'a dynamic mother-in-law with a great contempt for women who didn't do anything'.

As the vast majority of these women had no professional mentor at all, it is hard to escape the conclusion that 'being mentored' may not be so important as it has been cracked up to be. Women should consider too the disadvantages that may accrue from such a relationship of power imbalance and deep dependency. Mary Cunningham chose to go to Bendix to work because her professors thought it offered an unprecedented chance for her: 'Mentorship was a favourite route to the top around Harvard, and who could be a better mentor than Bill Agee? The system's leading advocate, he was one of its youngest, most successful products as well.' Later she came to see 'the inherent problem of being mentored':

I had only one major priority, and that was to prove myself to Bill Agee ... How many times did I go into a meeting with Bill and, because my job was to make the chairman look good, not raise my hand when I had a good idea, I'd wait until after the meeting and offer my suggestions to Bill. Then at the next meeting, when he'd make them, everyone would say "Brilliant!" People would praise Bill and Bill would praise me. That's how it worked. The problem with such a system was that it didn't let other people at Bendix know just how much work I did. In the end, when I most needed outside support, I didn't have it.

Put like this, the mentoring system smells suspiciously like all the other kinds of male power only ever offered to women on loan, to be withdrawn on a masculine whim. As Cunningham herself discovered, the female has no power of her own through this, and wins no control over her own fortunes. As she ruefully writes, 'That was the flip side of mentoring they never told you about in business school. Once you were mentored, how did you get unmentored?

The answer is, in every case, the hard way. For the final irony of the whole mentor myth, and the single fact that should warn women to treat a would-be mentor like a boa constrictor, is the fact that *it doesn't work for men, either*. Agee himself, a chief proponent of the system, was finally the victim of a former mentor gone sour. In America, psychologist Srully Blotnick has interviewed 3000 mentor-protégé pairs over a period of twenty-five years. *Only 1 per cent* expressed satisfaction with the relationship – and nearly 40 per cent of mentoring bosses ended up firing their hand-reared protégé!

The whole question of mentoring throws into relief the wider problem for women of finding appropriate ways of working their way to the top. As newcomers, many women subconsciously feel that they need to be accepted, recognised, validated by men – hence the almost religious faith in getting mentored among some of the products of today's business schools. This not only throws women back into the immature state of passive dependency (Daddy will take care of me); it also condemns women to operating in the reactive not the active mode, forced to wait and see what your Big Daddy is going to make happen for you, instead of being able to make it happen yourself. Women in power repeatedly counsel female aspirants to beware of this. 'It's no use breaking free of domestic or personal dependency if you become professionally dependent on your office uncle or father,' was one comment. 'Don't lean on men – not *one* – not *ever!*' was a more emphatic warning.

Instead, it is vital for women to become strategy-orientated. Work to a plan, including long, short and medium-term goals, not necessarily patterned on a man's life plan, but certainly commensurate with your talents. Then work out what you have to do to make it work. In the words of Meredith Fernstrom, senior vice-president of American Express:

> A lot of women overlook the extra things that they have to do. Many believe that if they just work hard and perform well, they will be elevated or have other opportunities. I have found that you have to understand the politics of an organisation, and learn how to be an effective player in that environment. It's just not enough to know how to do your job well but you also have to know how to promote what you do and how to play the organisational politics when you have to.

How far you can go with office politicking is a particularly vexed issue for women. All organisations use as much legal deceit (and frequently illegal, too) as they think they can get away with – '*what you can get away with*' is, after all, one of the definitions of power. As psychological profiles show that women generally have far higher ideals and are more moral than men, the ascent up the ladder can bring a serious crisis or conflict of interests between personal and professional values – how far would you go for or against an opposing colleague or dubious company policy?

Opinion among women is strongly divided on these issues. Some say that the only way to survive and get on is to 'be an artful dodger'. 'I'm in the business business, not the ethics business,' said one top executive in an import-export concern. 'I don't go for the "lady trader" routine.' Wise up on the dirty tricks and how to use them, is the message – if you don't, be sure that they'll be used against you. It's a man's world; it's dog eat dog; and if you can't stand the heat, get out of the kitchen.

Other top women, though, feel equally strongly that these are the very clichés that women must resist. For them the supreme opportunity of professional life is not only personal success, but

142

the chance to redefine the systems and processes, to change the nature of power. On this argument, the young woman on her way up does *not* pattern herself on the men's ways of doing things. 'Learn the rules,' was one summary of this, 'then *adapt them to your personal style*. It's no use trying to be a Johnny Brightsparks clone – they've got plenty of those already. We need to do it woman-style.'

Doing It Woman-style

First and foremost woman-style means totally avoiding any kind of heavy butch behaviour that can make a woman on the way up seem 'all tongue and toe-caps', as one man feelingly commented. Tales of female supertoughs who swear, smoke cigars and pursue quivering male colleagues into the lavatories rather than lose an argument circulate freely; they sound mythical and manufactured, but can be read as warning or distress signals from men who have not come up against women as colleagues in any earlier stage of their professional lives, and are finding it very troubling. Women have a major task of re-education on their hands here, and have to face it from the moment they set out. It is not a task that can be deferred until you reach the top, for by then you will have made too many compromises with the masculine style and system to be able to separate out from it again.

So, rising woman-style means gently but firmly refusing from the first to be consigned to the 'gender ghetto' on the basis of your sex. It is a common experience for a woman at a meeting to be asked to speak 'from the woman's point of view', while male colleagues speak for themselves as individuals. But being tacitly elected spokeswoman for your sex not only wipes out your individuality, it greatly increases your chance of failure – how are you to know how *all women* would react to a given proposal or product that is being mooted?

Sexual reduction works constantly and insidiously at many levels. The jargon of the power world is male, a blend of three strands drawn from the military, sport, and sex. As language in general has had to be purged of offensive racist terms (who now misses 'kike' or 'wop'?), and as man-made language is being overhauled by Dale Spender and others, so the language of power requires stringent revision to make it acceptable to women. It is impossible for women to feel comfortable either hearing or using terms drawn from alien worlds and power bases ('this one's come straight out of left field', for example, or 'now we've really got their tits in the wringer!') let alone the choicer phrases of the 'expletive deleted' variety – especially when these are followed, as they so often are, by elaborate excuses designed to direct attention to the woman as outsider.

In its ability to designate in-group status, language *is* power. With it, male power-holders can fight as dirty as the next docker or deckhand. Countless women report attempts to undermine them at meetings with lines like, 'What you're groping towards is ... ' or 'You'll find you're going to have to prove that to me, sweetheart.' A sure sign that something nasty is stirring in the woodshed is when males start showering female colleagues with endearments: duckie, dear one, my little flower, bright eyes.

Body language also speaks volumes. Highly qualified women report that their degrees, their specialisms, their high performance do not protect them from male colleagues introducing them with a proprietary arm thrown round their shoulders and a line about how he knows that they are just going to give a terrific welcome to this great little person. Barbara Thomas was introduced to one board with an effusive compliment to her 'beautiful big brown eyes' and a British woman banker was introduced with a crack about her 'visible assets'! Women need to be on guard constantly against this kind of downgrading, and need to perfect ways of asserting their resistance to it, if possible non-aggressively. Above all, *never* let men get away with suggesting that they cannot talk properly with or in front of you – to accept that is to collude with a serious attempt to out-manoeuvre or exclude you and manipulate you into a subservient role.

The Marriage Settlement

No woman should ever have to trade off her self-worth and her womanhood for success. But the decision to tread your pathway to power inevitably involves other decisions, among which those

144

concerning your private life critically shape your professional future. The difficulty is that the formative decision-making stage – between, say, twenty and thirty-five – is the same for life *and* work, and the problem of trying to do justice to yourself in both areas is the greatest single preoccupation of ambitious women.

It is clear that the wise virgin exercises far more control over her personal life than is either traditional for a female or consonant with the romantic myth that you do not *choose* love, love chooses *you*. 'I wouldn't consider marrying before twenty-six,' said Janet Mead. 'I wanted to prove something to myself, make something of myself. I knew I'd have a sense of frustration otherwise.' As Shirley Conran has said, *of course* you can have your brilliant career, happy marriage, a close relationship with two wonderful children and a lovely home – *but not all at once*. Making the bid for the top does things to your life curve, to your life itself. Everything, including all the old certainties, must go into the melting-pot, and what you come up with in the end will be a far cry from the 'roses round the door, happy ever after' dream that we all carry round with us in some dusty attic of our consciousness.

Marriage for women who are serious about their careers is a classic 'damned if you do, damned if you don't' situation. If you do, you run the risk:

* of being taken less seriously from that moment on ('I understand you are a married woman, Dr Hicks,' said one interviewer, 'Then you can't intend to be a serious bio-chemist')
* of the unspoken assumption that your husband is the major breadwinner, so you don't need your salary, but may hop off at any time to follow him and will put his career needs first
* of being harassed with questions or unspoken assumptions about your reproductive life and plans

If you *don't*, the risks are:

* of being thought unnatural, unfeminine, deviant
* of being open to the blanket masculine insult of 'lesbian'
* of being thought *over*-serious and neurotically dedicated to career and self-advancement
* of being bitterly envied behind your back by male and

female colleagues alike for what they take to be your free, self-pleasing life-style

How can you thread your way through this minefield of malice and misinformation?

First, try to consider marriage as an option rather than an essential to happiness and fulfilment; nobody is more wretched or starved of self-esteem than an unhappily married woman. Try to develop some forward thinking about marriage and career compatibility in general, rather than postponing it until a magic man appears, so that it's not marriage itself you're having to think about, but marriage *with* John or James; nobody can think straight when they're in love. Remember that various research studies have established that marriage is more harmful to your career than working is to your marriage! And on the basis of the divorce statistics, if you are ambitious for high achievement and high earnings, it may be better for you both if you decide not to marry him than if you have to dump him when his ego can't take your success or when he can't adjust to the rhythms and demands of a commuting marriage, or alternatively if you have to allow him to hold you back at a level that is comfortable for him.

Not to marry at all is a decision that in fact a substantial proportion of top women come to early on. In this survey, over a quarter (27 per cent) had never married, while research by Suzanne Lainson for her study *The Instant MBA* showed that 52 per cent of top women executives were single. Top women's not being married is often taken to be a sacrifice of some great good, a denial or loss. There is an assumption very flattering to the male of the species buried in there somewhere, and it ain't necessarily so!

If you are thinking of marriage, these are the most advantageous conditions for you:

* *Marry late.* Researchers Hennig and Jardim found that late marriage increases a woman's sense of self-esteem and well-being, in contrast with early marriage which subsumes selfhood and undermines independent identity;
* *Marry a special type of man.* Select with care the rare male who does not want an adoring supportive wifey-poo, a

hostess, a junior partner in his career, a housekeeper or a mother substitute. He must accept that like him, you are moving for yourself; he must not feel threatened by your success but embrace the possibility to the extent of asking himself how he'll feel when you are running the company; and he must *not* want a large family.

If this sounds too schematised, it is reassuring to realise that these decisions tend to take themselves, and in the view of the women concerned, turn out for the best anyway. In this present survey, 60 per cent of the women who had married did so after the age of twenty-five, when the vast majority of the female population does so before that time; only just over a quarter (27 per cent) had married in the 20–24 age group, when the highest numbers of weddings occur for females. For some women, the failure of the conventional marriage expectations at an early stage helped to launch them or concentrate them upon their career. 'I had an unhappy broken romance, and took my law degree to get over to it,' says Judge Jean Graham Hall. 'I'm *most* grateful to the man now!' Similarly, Margaret Pereira might not have become controller of forensic services at the Home Office if she had not looked at her first love and realised that his devout Catholic faith would be a cross for her to bear: 'I could see myself with ten little Desmonds, and it would drive me mad!'

Marriage is in fact a far greater problem area for top women than children – you can control your reproduction far more easily than you can allow for a husband. You can also plan your childbearing in a way that male colleagues cannot plan their ulcers and their heart attacks, a fact worth reminding offspring-obsessed employers. This is not to underestimate the importance of this issue to women both as people and as professionals. Dorothy Sherman Severin, first woman holder of the oldest and most prestigious professorship in her subject, the Gilmour Chair of Spanish at the University of Liverpool, has commented, 'One can never minimise the difficulties of combining a career with motherhood.' Mary Moore, principal of St Hilda's College, Oxford, agrees:

Everything is all right until you start having children. Society

147

gives no help at all, and every couple has to work it out for themselves. Women have in the past shouldered the double burden unquestioningly, but the next generation is starting to think in these terms – will he get up at 3 a.m. and feed the baby if she has got a meeting the next morning? The struggle is inside yourself, and you're entirely alone when you're up against someone you're in love with.

The 'combining a baby with a career' question is usually discussed principally in terms of its logistics – when, how, how many, organising the right care. You also need to allow for the possibility that the experience of giving birth can change you in ways that you never thought possible. 'Some women become totally absorbed in their baby and move into that world,' comments Mary Moore. 'Then they want to give up work and feel totally fulfilled.' One top London accountant had planned her career, planned the birth of her daughter, the baby-care and the return to work. When the moment came she experienced an emotional revulsion at the idea of leaving her baby, and resigned her job to stay at home with her. Mary Moore sees this as one perfectly natural reaction. But as she says:

> These women are lost when the child goes to school. I always say, think ahead five, even two years – what will you be doing then? There *is* a shift of perspective when you have your first child – job, everything moves into second place. Any other job can be done by others, but only you can do what you do for your child. But then the situation changes again, and women must be flexible enough to change with it.

Ultimately, of course, the career disruption which seems so threatening to ambitious women is not necessarily so in the long run. Two of the most powerful women in America, Ambassador Kirkpatrick and Judge Sandra Day O'Connor, the first woman to be appointed to the Supreme Court, are both mothers of three sons, and spent eight and five years respectively as full-time home-makers caring for them. It is hard to feel that either they, their careers, or (not least in importance) their sons, have suffered from this decision.

In seeking their individual route to success, when for so very long they have been held back, women are rightly encouraged to be ambitious and forward-moving. But the path to the top takes one other vital quality, too, what D.H. Lawrence called 'patience, and the long pause'. Give yourself time to move in a number of directions, to explore them and yourself, and above all to grow. A fretful haste to get going often leads to a premature and unwise decision which closes other options for you. Work out your goal before you puzzle over the available avenues, or agree to travel hopefully wherever your road leads. For there are more ways than one to the wood, and the only one worth travelling is your own.

I understand that you are having trouble about married women working. I am in favour of all women doing what they want to do.

> HM Queen Elizabeth the Queen Mother to Mary Anderson, first director of the Women's Bureau of the Department of Labor, on a visit to America

CHAPTER 7

Mine is the Kingdom

Elizabeth Garrett Anderson, the first English woman doctor, was asked by one of the men who had refused her admission to medical school why she wanted to be a doctor, not a nurse. She answered: 'I should naturally prefer £1000 to £20 a year.'

The rewards of high office have no gender. Power, money, success and esteem can be enjoyed by males and females alike, as women are now discovering in increasing numbers for the first time in history. 'More and more women are now making their way into the inner sancta and top-level power processes,' says Ambassador Jeane Kirkpatrick. Naturally enough, males like to cling to the idea that power is still securely in the hands of men, and that a top woman is still exceptional, a one-off, a real *rara avis*: 'The sight of one in the managing director's chair is as exotic as a pair of nesting ospreys,' warbles *Director* magazine in a recent issue. In fact, unknown and unobserved of many, women have made their way into top positions in almost every area of life: politics, business, industry and government service. How do they handle the power they have? What are the problems they face and the rewards that come their way? What is life at the top like for a woman?

What we are looking at now is a range of women worldwide who are displaying their grasp of power, and rejoicing in its glow. Dianne Feinstein, mayor of San Francisco and 1984 US Vice-Presidential possible along with Geraldine Ferraro, has proved herself in what Ambassador Kirkpatrick identifies as the most demanding area for power-holders, 'the rough-and-tumble of decision-making'. As the ambassador comments: 'To be the mayor of San Francisco is not easy. The city is socially very diverse, politically heterogeneous, exceptionally difficult.' In the opinion of the chief of the *Time* bureau in San Francisco, Michael Moritz, 'Feinstein has had to work harder, leap higher barriers and endure more political setbacks than most of the men who came before her, and the city is working better than it has in twenty years.' Feinstein has not only had to pull together a city with problems such as a high incidence of crime and unusual characteristics such as a very large homosexual population, but to fight for her political survival as well. Her attempt to ban handguns provoked an obscure fringe group called the White Panthers to mount a campaign for her dismissal by the unprecedented device of calling a city referendum. With a majority of over 80 per cent of the votes cast in her favour, Dianne Feinstein swept them into the sea. Her prowess has been noted in the highest circles: Ambassador Kirkpatrick describes her as a 'highly competent woman, demonstrating *very* substantial skills, all the key political skills'.

Dianne Feinstein has both the ability and the ambition for high national office. When she was auditioned as a potential Vice-Presidential running-mate by Walter Mondale for the campaign of 1984, he described her as 'a spectacular person'. In the event Feinstein's combination of 'strikes against' – being a woman, Jewish, and tarred with the Sodom and Gomorrah tag of her gay community – meant that she lost out to Geraldine Ferraro's apparently more wholesome appeal. But it is inconceivable that this woman, so able and so effective that she can reduce her city's violent crime by 10 per cent a year and convert a $127m budget deficit into a $122m surplus, and still at fifty-one so young, will not make her mark on a wider platform.

Women Fight Uphill

Feinstein's career to date illustrates the truth of Ambassador Kirkpatrick's warning, 'There is still a good deal of resistance to women at the top levels. I know there is, I've been there!'

Women who are at the top now are those who have fought discrimination in its most open and brutal forms, and are still engaged in the work of rooting the tyrants out of the citadel. Margaret Pereira failed to gain entry to medical school as her application coincided with the post-war period when 90 per cent of university places were reserved for ex-servicemen. Later, she was turned down for a blood-grouping course that she was very keen to go on, as her director did not regard her as a permanent member of his staff. He sent instead a male colleague whom she knew was actively looking for another job! Finally she had a 'great disappointment' when after a good honours degree, postgraduate work and years of experience, she was turned down for promotion to a grade in which she would have had to act as an expert witness, on the grounds that as a woman she would cry or crack up under cross-examining, or be too embarrassed to talk about sex crimes. She then suffered the classic indignity of teaching a man who was made her boss. 'That was a rather embittered stage,' she says, with what seems under the circumstances a positively sainted mildness.

Like Margaret, other women too contrived to remain active and positive in the face of reflex and institutionalised discrimination. Detta O'Cathain was so incensed to see an advertisement for an interesting post in the motor trade declaring, 'the *man* appointed ... ' that she wrote direct to Lord Rootes to say, 'I've got all the qualifications except the sexual one' – and thereby *became* 'the man appointed'. Judith Hope remembers that in her year group at Harvard Law School, there were only a dozen women to 500 men. The women all had to sit in the front, where they would be picked on one week and ignored the next. 'It was a real hazing,' she says. But all the women of her year have had the last laugh by doing extremely well. 'If you could make it through, in an era when they said, "Why should we admit you, when we could have a man who would *use* this education?", you'd gone through fire to get it!' was her cheerful summary. Another victim of *'men's rea'* in this area was Sandra Day O'Connor – when she passed out of law school in the top 10 per cent of her class, she could not even *gain employment* as a lawyer in a law firm. The highest and only post she was offered was that of legal secretary.

Many people today (especially *men* people) like to comfort

themselves with the belief that discriminatory attitudes and practices are a thing of the past. This is not the case. Many top managers are carrying on business as usual in a state of ignorance uncompromised by any knowledge of the fact that their actions are not only harmful but in the wake of 1970s legislation may even be *illegal*. Britain lags embarrassingly behind the USA in this regard. From her unique perspective of high-level occupation on both sides of the Atlantic, Barbara Thomas comments: 'There are less people whose consciousness is raised here in Britain.' Men unthinkingly perpetuate old rituals, and women are not sufficiently aware of the infringements they suffer as a result to question them. Part of the problem as Barbara perceives it is rooted in the divisive British education system: 'There are more men here who haven't grown up with women, gone to school with women and got used to treating them as equals.' She attributes her entrée into British banking to the fact that the chairman and chief executive of Samuel Montagu, Staffan Gadd, who invited her to join the board of the bank, is Swedish: 'He's not hidebound,' she says. 'He's very forward-looking, with a positive vision of the future, and a great leader. I had faith in him that he wasn't chauvinistic. He really wanted me to join and he understood my position. It wasn't the most attractive offer I had, but it was the one I wanted to try.' 'Bloody old Gadd,' growled a prominent British banker over a double gin. 'He got her while we were all still thinking about it!'

On present performance, the money-men of Britain have a lot of thinking still to do. Even before graduating from business school, Helen Matthews had already resolved not to work for a British bank: 'They don't give you a fair crack of the whip.' Highly successful businesswoman Jennifer D'Abo, owner and managing director of Rymans the stationers, with a clutch of other directorships to her credit, pinpoints the continuing difficulties that women labour under:

> I still feel I'm patronised by men, and if I put up a feasibility study for a business project, it's read by ten analysts as opposed to two, simply because I'm a woman. The City is still terribly cautious about women. I went to a lunch at a certain bank and I said, rather facetiously, to the loans manager, 'How high can a woman get in this bank?' and he replied, 'Quite high enough.'

153

The City is not the only country where the dinosaurs roam free. One woman in the civil service reported having to do a completely unnecessary PhD in order to gain promotion; another was deemed bright enough to become the first woman sales training manager in any part of her organisation throughout the world when her boss left, but had to put in six months on the lower grade, to see if anyone noticed or complained; and Bridget Skipworth, who became marketing director of Unigate before she went to America to become a VP, attained her first management post only to have 'marketing services' on her card, because 'they couldn't bear to call her a marketing manager', according to a friend. But all this pales besides the experience of Julia Cleverdon, director of education for the Industrial Society. On a trip to Australia she was refused permission to attend a business meeting to which her male colleague was invited, and when she protested, was told she might be able to sit 'out of sight in the catering area: we might be able to find you a screen to sit behind'. And a bell to ring 'unclean, unclean' perhaps?

To succeed as a woman you must be an india-rubber ball. The harder you're bounced, the higher you come back.
Professor Marian Hicks

Life at the Top

Apart from working with and around the male of the species, the preoccupations of women in power positions are remarkably similar from one woman to another, and even from one country to another. Top women give a considerable amount of thought to getting their act right. The question of personal presentation is felt to be an important one in every way, and far more critical to a woman than to a man. On the superficial level, you should make sure that you are looking the way you want to be, the way that you feel comfortable with, so that you can then forget about your appearance and concentrate on the work. The advice is to cut out completely tight-waisted clothes or high heels: 'Women's clothes are the very emblem of their subjugation,' says Suzanne Hunter, British Oxygen's only woman branch manager.

154

But far more central than their own comfort in the thinking of top women is the comfort of the men they are dealing with. Men are easily rattled, it seems, and all high-achieving women have learned the importance of minimising their own disruptive effect. 'Being attractive is a plus and a minus,' says Barbara Thomas. 'You get attention, and you get remembered, but it can distract them.' So the only sensible tactic is to avoid *anything* that draws attention to your appearance. In one case known to Anne Joy, a woman turned up for an interview as a financial analyst in a man's suit, with waistcoat, shirt and tie. 'Men can't relate to women like this,' Anne comments. 'It makes them jumpy and then they can't see the woman's qualities.' Several women pointed out that a slit skirt in a pin-striped business suit is far more sexually provocative than in a lurex evening gown, and as Jill Currie crisply stressed, 'You don't want the attention of the leering male, you want the respect of the chairman of the board!' In Mary Baker's summary of this issue, 'You worry men if sexuality intrudes. You're throwing in another item. You may wish to do it deliberately, but *don't do it by mistake!*'

Getting the look right is only part of the wider question of finding the way to behave as a woman in a position of authority. 'Women in top posts are on the frontiers, pioneering,' says film producer Jane Deknatel. 'Territorial delineation, the dynamics of mothers and sisters – these are the issues for successful women.' There is a fundamental conflict between the nurturing supportive mode expected of women and ingrained into us, and the individual achieving mode. So even if you are the chief executive, employees may still feel free to invade your space, bringing personal problems and extra pressures as they never would to a male boss.

'A woman power figure always represents Mother, if only subconsciously,' said one managing director, 'just as a man boss represents Daddy. The difference is that people more willingly accept Daddy's dominance, and often are thrown back by a woman boss into a morass of childhood resentments.' In one case, a woman boss interviewing a woman for a job realised that the candidate did not realise that the interviewer *was* the boss, but thought she was interviewing for some absent male. When the truth was made clear, the candidate burst out, 'I can't work for you, it would be like working for my mother!' In any

155

situation where you hold authority, you will be constantly under subtle pressure to handle your power in a mothering way. Employees expect not only that you will give more time to their problems, but that you will be able to make things 'come right' and that they will go away feeling better.

Be realistic about the extent of your own energy and power, is the advice from the women who have handled this; you can't keep giving and giving, and you can't just kiss it better or solve their difficulties by magic. Employees will also often try to make you feel bad for reproving them or criticising their work. They would take it without fuss from a man, but as a woman you're supposed to be ego-boosting all the time. 'Don't play nursery games,' said one woman financial manager.

> It's nice to be liked, but you're there to get a job done. So are they! Don't let them put all this stuff on you. Say straight out, "I see that you are having a problem with this, and I think we should talk about it right now." Get your message across: "You may not like working for a woman, but that's *your* problem, and you have two choices – shape up or ship out!"

Queen Bee

The greatest single difficulty faced by many high-achieving women in their work relationships lies in dealing with the type of female colleague known as the 'Queen Bee'. Numbers of older women in high places, especially in Britain, do not see being a woman as an issue of importance, and will brush aside questions on the subject, insisting strenuously that they have never been treated any differently from a man. These women see themselves as exceptional individuals who have made it to the top in what they have no problem with thinking about as 'a man's world'. Each Queen Bee is alone on her peak of eminence, out of touch with other women from a very early point in her career when she left all the others behind. Her ability to accept and act upon masculine values of competition and achievement has been a pre-condition of her success. She has swallowed the dominant male ideology whole, and with it the traditional concepts of womanhood, however inapplicable to her personally.

The Queen Bee truly believes that because she has reached

the top as an individual, on her own, any woman who really wants to could do so too. This view allows her to go on thinking of herself as exceptional and other women as somehow weak or uncommitted, less talented or hard-working. So she feels justified in putting other women down, or giving them an exceptionally hard time, because she feels that they should have to prove themselves as she did. She is also quite naturally motivated to defend her privileged position in the 'man's world'.

For Queen Bees are reinforced and rewarded at every turn by the male system of business and politics. Their value to the power-holding male élite is enormous – while this one woman is highly visible in some top position, tokening away, they don't even need to think about 'the woman question' – she dismisses it for them. On her side, she will actively oppose any special programmes for women, positive action or women's management courses, feeling quite satisfied with a system that has let *her* through. These women are the Uncle Toms of the sex conflict. The supreme compliment to one of them is, 'You think/act just like a man.' Yet each is careful never to threaten men by aping them but preserves instead a rather exaggerated 'femininity' by dint of soft hairdos, brooches and bows.

The Queen Bee is problematic for other women achievers in a variety of ways. She is likely to feel resentful of other women coming up to the top, because they take away her own special status and because she thinks that the path has been smoothed for them in ways that it never was for her. She also has set the only standard for a female colleague that the men around her have known, so the incoming woman is constantly faced with 'Betty always used to … ' when trying to determine her own programmes and processes. She may also have set a very disadvantageous financial standard too. Although not thinking of herself *as* a woman, she nevertheless feels she has done well *for* a woman, and not perceiving the extent to which she, as a lone female, has been competitively disadvantaged by men, is likely to have accepted a lower salary than the job entitles her to.

'Equal pay for equal work' is a slogan just as enthusiastically subverted by male employers at the top of the tree as at the bottom. One woman in the US media industry was ecstatic to get a job offered at $75,000, an advance of $25,000 on her current salary – until she discovered that the man she was replacing had started on $100,000. The Queen Bee would have taken that, on the 'be grateful, don't make trouble' principle. She didn't. Even though threatened with the withdrawal of the job offer, she fought for and won the $100,000. 'Women must rise *with* their sex, not above it,' she says.

What's the women's movement ever done for me?

Margaret Thatcher

The Down Side

Women who have succeeded in business, politics or top management do not play down the weight of the load that a woman takes up along with the salary, the status, and the razzle-dazzle. Janet Mead pinpoints 'the tough patch when you go from management to responsibility for the profitability of the organisation', and advises giving yourself six months when you simply hang in there and feel your way around the job. Anne Joy adds a warning:

> There are many women who despite their brave words do not want to accept responsibility. It's not the glamour of the words 'managing director', it's the grind of the action. Many women do not want this in the final analysis.
>
> Women who want it must not duck out. At top management, the buck stops there. It's sometimes so god-awful that you have to take a decision. There are warring factors and you have to decide. So take the decision, and *take the consequences*!

However successful the decisions are professionally, personally they can cost women a good deal of strain, discomfort or distress. Sometimes even ordinary things are too much. Pat Lovell, producer of *Picnic At Hanging Rock*, admits, 'I had and still have a terror of going into a room full of people. I feel quite ill, and can't face it.' 'I still get diarrhoea and nerves the night before a lecture I really care about,' says Professor Marian Hicks, and Shirley Porter, leader of Westminster City Council, reports, 'I'm physically ill before every big step. I'm a worrier, I have a sensitive stomach and feel it in my diaphragm.' Other women describe going through phases either of massive overweight or anorexia, depression or other emotional crises.

Even in the good times the life of a power-holder is peculiarly demanding. 'There are so many down days,' says Barbara Thomas. 'I want you to tell them that it is not all rosy. At times you are battering your head against the wall with problems, worrying, agonising. Women have two sets of problems, their regular business problems, and then their problems as a woman in business. Then they have to run their homes – there's a third set of problems. And men have wives to help them!' Her comment is illustrated by Jill Currie: 'Mine [the brewing industry] is a terrible industry for failed females. They take newcomers out, it's a baptism of fire, and get them sloshed. The males can throw up in the car on the way back, but not the females, even though it's the same man doing it.'

But these stresses are generally more severe in the early stages of a woman's career than when she finally makes it. A top woman is spared all the routine daily jockeying and hassling which produces the stress and distress symptoms in women managers researched by Professor Cary Cooper of the University of Manchester School of Management Studies and others: ulcers, hypertension, sleeplessness, and so on. It is also reassuring that it all gets easier the more experience you have of it. As Elinor Guggenheimer drily observed, 'My husband says, "You used to get sick if they asked you to make a speech, now you get sick if they don't!" ' And finally, it is worth emphasising that large numbers of the female populations of all advanced countries suffer all these symptoms, often all together and to an acute degree, without any of the rewards of high achievement to counterbalance them!

One final problem is peculiar to women at the top, in that it is created entirely by *being* at the top, and that is, where do I go from here? In the past, a woman's ascent would be gradual, restricted, conditional. To set sights upon a top position, or even the next step up the ladder, was not a realistic proposition when access for women was so severely controlled and strictly limited. How high was too high to aim? A woman had no way of knowing but could only keep travelling and see how far she would be allowed to go. In those circumstances, every promotion was a bonus.

Now every office, every structure theoretically lies open to women, and many of today's high achievers are already in impressive positions of power at thirty-seven or forty-two years of age. With a good twenty years or more ahead, where do they go? 'That's the question I keep asking myself!' says Shirley Porter. 'What next? Where now?' It pyramids steeply at the top,' as many women who get there discover. 'Your choices are very few and your career slows at this point,' adds Donna Shalala. On the other hand, by the time that you reach this stage, the question of your further advancement has substantially passed beyond your control. 'You can't determine it,' Barbara Thomas says. Donna Shalala amplifies this: 'Will I get a chance of a Cabinet post? I'll be on everyone's list but there is nothing I can do any longer to influence that. I'll just have to keep on doing what I am doing, well!' she concluded cheerfully.

Doing What You're Doing Your Way

Whatever problems they face either of a particular or a general nature, women of power remain confident that their womanhood has made a positive contribution to their success. 'Don't lose sight of the advantages you have,' advises Judith Hope. Many argue that women have a much wider range of permissible behaviour than men; that women can ask a question and look as if they are asking it in the spirit of enquiry, for instance, while men may lose status for seeming ignorant. Men's fear of losing face in front of colleagues and superiors often works to women's benefit: 'Women tend not to suffer from pomposity,' comments the extremely unpompous Anne Mueller. 'I find that at meetings I can sometimes ask a question that a man might hesitate to.' '*Never* underestimate a woman's power of the obvious,' says June Robertson, mayor of Richmond,' and bring up all the commonsense points that men haven't thought of or wouldn't dare to.'

As newcomers to power, women can afford to be unorthodox in many matters. They have not been conditioned to swallow the man's way of doing things and will often challenge it, either deliberately or out of ignorance of the prevailing conventions. One woman director said:

When I first came on the board, I simply didn't know that it was

160

the golden rule that the chairman kicked off, everyone put in their pennyworth, and then when —— [the chairman's protégé] started to speak, he was summing up, and that was supposed to terminate the discussion. So I piped up after he'd finished, which started it all off again, and in the end the decision went against what the chairman wanted. Afterwards, all the sycophants came to tell me I'd blotted my copy-book, etc. But at the next meeting, I did it deliberately – I just didn't see that the chairman and his sidekick ought to be allowed to nutcracker the rest of us. There's been plenty of flack, but I'm still here!'

Women have been brought up not to interrupt, shout people down or cut them off. Mrs Thatcher will have none of that. She doesn't know how to behave. It may well be that she'd never have got where she was if she did know how to behave.

Baroness Warnock

One way in which top women are determined to be different from their male equivalents concerns the vital area of status symbols, the measurable tokens of success. Trinkets and trappings are very important to males, not only as external and visible marks of their progress up the ladder, but at a deeper level, according to numerous research studies, as lending them the feeling of power; they are, literally, empowered by a big car, office or desk, while women find all that a fatuous charade. 'In the thirty-four years I've been in business I've used a desk only twice,' says Marilyn Lewis, chairman of the Hamburger Hamlet restaurant chain. 'It's a barrier, a stage set. You know, "Where are the cigars?"'

Many women were keen to dissociate themselves from what they variously dubbed 'the pomp and circumstance' or the 'toys for boys syndrome'. They could be scathing about the male boss who played 'little Hitler' or 'the great I am'. One top dog was known behind his back as 'Rover' because of his childish pride in getting one of these cars. For women, in contrast, the pay-off of a power position lies in the substance, not the shadow. 'I'm not one of the glory boys,' says Anne Joy. 'It's the action I'm in it for.' Men who are in it for the title are not really up to the job. They will be continually protecting their rear, and will use any weapon against a woman who threatens to see through them or call their bluff. 'Always look out for insecurity, even in the very top people,' Anne continues. 'Often they're men who have just

161

become very adept at varnishing their shell. Women prefer the satisfaction of a good job well done to the feeling of a power complex.'

The truth of this is borne out by the women's responses to the question, 'What do you value most about your success?' In a survey performed on *male* high-achievers, the answers to this focused entirely on material rewards: a corner office, a company car – even, in one gloriously hubristic instance, 'my own private elevator'. In the present survey for this book, not one of the women of power even mentioned such things. They all responded instead in altruistic and personal terms. The most common reaction was 'the people I meet'.

Success was important to these women, too, for the sense of personal fulfilment it brought: the interior, not the exterior validation. Not least of the value that they placed upon their success was the feeling of helping to shape the world we live in, making a contribution in a job of high leverage and significant impact. Anne Mueller's answer encapsulates the themes preoccupying a number of highly placed women:

> The nicest thing is to be recognised for the work achievement and to be in a position to achieve more – with more freedom of choice, more variety, range of contacts, more power possibly, but more influence really – and the ability to do things for juniors.

The task of bringing up juniors in the right way is taken very seriously by women bosses. There is a strong feeling among them of the supreme importance of 'supporting the sisterhood' and bringing on other women. 'My secretaries don't stand a chance, I boot them on to the executive ladder,' says Barbara Hosking gleefully. Many women are now using their power to cultivate the careers of other females. 'My time is to do it,' Jennifer Coutts Clay considers. 'I encourage the women I come across in my work life – I've just appointed one woman manager, but we need more! I do what I can do and work through doing it.' Like Mary Lou Carrington and others, Jennifer also contributes to the career advancement of women setting out on the upward path, by lecturing on management courses for women run by the Industrial Society, where the Women's Campaign is progressing strongly under the

162

enthusiastic management of Elizabeth Willis. Its success has led to the inauguration of a special department for women, the Pepperell Unit, which provides education and encouragement not only for women but for employers, too, in order to tackle the problem of women's low management achievement from both sides.

Today's top women are deeply committed to the cause of women, even when a selfish Queen Bee attitude might suggest the opposite course of action. As Orna Ni Chionna sees it:

> If you're the only one, you're getting attention just for being a woman. So you don't want that threatened. Women must cop on and realise that having another woman in is an enormous asset, an enormous relief, someone you can talk to. Women must realise that another woman being around gives you companionship and makes it easier for men to relate to you and relax with you.

Barbara Thomas says, 'I believe that women have to help each other because in the end nobody else can be counted on to. Very few people in power really give a fig for women!' She herself feels that she has benefited from the sisterhood system: 'When I was appointed commissioner they asked a lot of people and a woman first submitted my name.' So when she came to resign from the commission, she provided with her resignation a carefully drawn up list of twenty women who could take her place. Mary Baker would agree. 'I was approached by Thames Television [to become the first and still the only woman on the board] through a woman suggesting my name. It's simply not true that women don't promote other women.'

There are so many ways now in which women in power are advancing the hopes and prospects of others, from the humblest to the highest. As a judge and state senator, Sandra Day O'Connor has been able to make her concern about sex discrimination felt in a number of legislative initiatives such as the repeal of anachronistic 'protective' labour laws, and the reform of community property laws that privileged the husband's interest over the wife's. As Minister for Education, Baroness Young was able to scrutinise syllabuses and systems for discriminatory practices and root them out. At American Express, senior vice-president Meredith Fernstrom has assisted women to build up a credit rating in their own name to avoid the trauma when death or divorce reveals that their man has been the family's only source of credit-worthiness. These examples of women taking positive action for less privileged women, or even acting on the basis of thinking like a woman instead of 'having a mind like a man's' (wow) could be multiplied a hundredfold.

> We'll all hang separately if we don't hang together.
>   Benjamin Franklin on signing the American
>   Declaration of Independence

'Networks are Power'

So says Jane Deknatel. The importance that top women place on female solidarity and the 'female mafia' is indicated by the fact that in the survey conducted for *Women and Power*, over 70 per cent were members of female networking organisations. The growth of these groups within professions or companies, or across occupational or sectional interests, has been a fascinating and encouraging phenomenon of recent years. 'We're mushrooming,' said one networker with relish, 'probably because as women we've spent so long underground in the dark with people shovelling shit on us!'

Women's networks, in their self-appointed and substantial task of supplying for women what men gain from the 'old boys' net', work in a variety of ways. Some, particularly in areas of 'hard' or heavy industry, are designed to propel women into non-traditional (read 'men's') occupations. One of the largest of this kind is the Women's Employment Network of Seattle, USA. 'We teach women what they need to know about the industrial world of work, and how it differs from the work-places that have traditionally welcomed women,' says Michelle Hirsen, the network's assistant director. Others, like Women in Banking, Women in the City, Women in Media, aim to enable women with common professional interests to pool their experience and push for improvements. According to the secretary of the Medical Women's Federation, 'They formed it because they weren't getting anywhere on their own!'

Other networks operate not so much as pressure groups, but

rather to bring together very senior women in the congenial company of the very few others on their level. They prefer to keep a very low profile, and membership, which is restricted to women chairmen, managing directors, or those heading up a big budget organisation, is by invitation only. One member said:

> We want to relax, and eat and drink with women we can talk to. We're a dining club. We meet every two months and talk. The companies give us dinners, so nobody's had to pay. We try to build up international links – other agreed objectives are to give a hand to young women on the way up, so if you hear of a job going, you'd put in a word for a woman.

Some of the women's networks prefer a subterranean policy out of the conviction that, if men were aware of their activities, they would sabotage them. 'We do *not* want "the man's world" to get on to us,' says one spokeswoman. 'It only makes them paranoid about the "petticoat brigade", "monstrous regiment" and all that rubbish, and they'd undo all the good we do.' Others feel that it should be in the nature of a network to move in a mysterious way, its wonders to perform. For most networks, however, the whole point is to let women and men too know that an organisation exists which is openly committed to bringing women out of purdah to claim their right not only to work, but to succeed.

There can be no doubt that women's networking serves a long-felt need. 'Who is looking out for your interests? Who is helping to create a better climate for your business? Who is offering support for the business-owner who is a woman?' pungently demands the US National Association of Women Business Owners, sister organisation of the British Association of Women Executives and the European Association Mondiale des Femmes Chefs d'Entreprises. It is the clear-sighted recognition that for women in all walks of life the answer to that question is, 'Nobody!' which has made for the launching of all these different remedies for that situation. And these women's networks are taking enormous strides in remedying the disadvantage that women have suffered through not being able to be in touch with everything that the males have held down firmly under *their* net. One woman went to a meeting of a group that she had never attended before and at which she knew no one.

165

She came away with three contacts which have since produced not only new and interesting work for her, but other promising introductions too. 'That's networking!' says Irene Harris, founder of Network, the organisation in question.

It's such a thrill to be able to talk to other women about power.
Elinor Guggenheimer

Enjoying Woman-Power

Popular mythology, fed by the fictions of our meretricious media, paints a picture of the top woman as a neurotic, driven creature, a blend of other crude stereotypes like bitch, witch, or domineering dyke, but above all unhappy and maladjusted. Nothing could be more remote from the real life of successful women. Each one gives a different reason for the pleasure and satisfaction that she derives from her achievement but to an outsider they all look happy in pretty much the same way. 'It's so rewarding at the top,' says Barbara Hosking, 'It's lovely! The other day I was going to the House of Commons to have lunch with Sir Geoffrey Johnson Smith, and the taxi-driver said "Oh, is he taking you out to lunch?", and I could say, "No, I'm taking *him* out!"' Mary Lou Carrington and Jean Denton agree that the key word is 'fun' – 'I wouldn't swop it for anything, it's got a price but it's worth every penny of it,' adds Jean. All these women agree that 'it's very exciting to be at the sharp end', 'immensely satisfying to have direct influence and control' or 'to set your own priorities and achieve them'. Ambassador Kirkpatrick has the experience of 'being rewarded in a variety of ways, with reliable welcomes and large ovations'. It was not hard to believe Judith Hope when, sitting in her spanking smart office in Washington's lovely old quarter, she said with a wonderful smile, 'It's pretty nice. It ain't bad, I tell ya!'

High-achieving women work hard, but not in the way that people imagine. They do not live for work, staggering home with heaps of files to chew over them compulsively all evening, but pursue an impressive range of interests and activities. Faith Legh is secretary-general of the Institute of Sales Promotion and committee member of the British Association of Women

Executives, of which she won the President's Award for services not only to the Association but on behalf of all women in business and management in 1984. She is also a musician, theatre director, champion dog breeder, and Cordon Bleu cook in her spare (?) time. Faith also makes time to be a member of the Fiat Motor Club. With her mother (at seventy-plus) as navigator, Faith won the Ladies' Trophy in her first-ever rally year, and drives in as many rally events as she can manage.

Fast fun cars are a pleasure in the lives of very many of these women. The 'company car', with its implied mark of status and success, meant very little. But they reserve the right to reward themselves for their achievements in their own way. In the present survey 66 per cent reported themselves as 'very keen' on cars, and would wax lyrical and dewy-eyed over red Morgans, fancy roadsters or coupés now departed. In true top-woman style they had no truck with status for its own sake; the car had to perform. As Dame Josephine Barnes briskly reported:

> I loved my TR3. But my first car was a 1928 Fiat, I bought it for £8. I wouldn't have another Rolls-Royce, they're slow, heavy, the devil to park and *ruinous* to service. I've had two Mercedes, they're the best, they're beautiful. I bought the second one for three and a half thousand pounds, and ran it for eleven years.

One or two women admitted being completely oblivious to all the car mystique, like Sheila Needham, whose company driver eventually had to inform her discreetly that if she didn't get a better car, while her director was driving round in a smart new model, the customers would become confused as to who was the boss! But in the main they are both keen and good drivers. Doyenne of them all is Jean Denton, managing director of Herondrive; she did not even learn to drive until her mid twenties, but zoomed straight into the fast track to become a top rally driver, and British Women Racing Driver's Champion. 'If anyone tries to beat me away from the lights on my way to work, it makes my day,' she says with a wicked grin.

With such strong feelings of well-being, it is perhaps not too surprising that almost all of the women interviewed for the present survey considered themselves to be in top physical condition. A massive 94 per cent stated that their health was 'quite outstanding', 'exceptionally good', 'absolutely wonderful' or '200 per cent'. They are careful to look after themselves: 93 per cent said that they consciously followed a healthy diet, avoided salt, sugar and additives, and never touched junk food. 58 per cent took regular exercise, and of the total survey only three women smoked. On closer inspection it seems as if the feeling of health and strength must be psychological perhaps even more than physical; women reporting themselves as 'wonderfully healthy' would when questioned further unselfconsciously come out with reports of serious illnesses like hepatitis and meningitis. Very few had had no illness at all in adult life. But they looked well, and clearly believed that they were well. Perhaps the paradigm of this type of positive thinking is Mrs Thatcher, standing on the steps of the hospital in which she had just undergone surgery, declaring to the assembled reporters and photographers, 'You know me – I'm *never* ill!'

A close acquaintance with a number of highly placed women makes it easy to accept the pronouncement of Nicky Joyce, president of the British Association of Women Executives, that 'work is good for women', and success is even better. They enjoy their lives and conduct them with great style. When Barbara Hosking became one of the first women to be admitted to the august Reform Club, amid rumblings from some of the reluctant males that women wouldn't know how to do the right thing or weren't going to be the right sort of material, her first guest to lunch in the Club was Edward Heath. 'That showed 'em!' she says. When someone sent Australia's Commissioner for Equal Opportunity, Fay Marles, a cartoon showing her as 'the Beast' against the leader of the Women Who Want to Be Women Movement, Babette Francis, as 'the Beauty', she had it framed and hung it on her office wall.

As this shows, women of power do not take themselves too seriously: Jean Denton's answering machine blithely informs callers that 'Wonderwoman is out and will be back after a couple of twirls putting the world to rights.' As Jean changes her message frequently, people must call up just to enjoy a joke if they can't speak with her. These women not only rejoice in their varying senses of humour, from the driest of the dry to bubbling uproarious fun – they use their humour to see them through the sticky patches. Every ambitious young woman should be able to see Patricia Soliman, now associate publisher and vice-president of Simon and Schuster Inc., telling a story that dates from her early days as a chief executive officer at Coward, McCann and Geoghegan. After a particularly bad day, she went home to call her husband, himself a CEO, and enjoy the luxury of a good weep on a comforting shoulder. Scarcely had she got into her stride before she heard his response: 'Patricia,' he said, '*CEOs don't cry.*'

The relish with which Patricia recounted this, and the laughter that went with it, are echoed in so many of the exchanges of these women. Their zest and *joie de vivre* are a tonic. Very evidently, in spite of the opposition of men, the difficulties of some work relationships and the responsibility of high office, the top is a good place to be for a woman. Jennifer D'Abo sums up for all when she says simply: '*I love my life and I love what I do.*'

CHAPTER 8

The Power and the Glory

I am woman, hear me roar,
In numbers too big to ignore,
Now I know too much to go back to pretend,
'Cos I've heard it all before,
I've been down there on the floor,
And no one's ever going to keep me down again.
                                                    Helen Reddy

The success stories of top women are exciting as individual sagas of women's prowess, and important as models for other women interested in following suit. Women today, however, are not simply rising in vertical ascent, but spreading out, diversifying laterally, extending themselves and their power in every conceivable direction. They are pushing forward into non-traditional areas (a double effort of pioneering since power itself is a non-traditional area for women), they are discovering power as pressure, power as strength, and some of the hazards of all this. In doing so they are also, and very significantly, extending the concept of the way women use power. This has previously been severely limited by our culture's lack of information and experience of women of power. We have known more about the behaviour of the laboratory rat than about this orientation in the majority of the human race. Now the excuse that the top women are 'too few to mention' will no longer hold up as women are activating their personal and political potency in all its diversity and glory.

One woman who radicalised the way in which women and power are thought of was Indira Gandhi. Her personal odyssey is in the nature of an object lesson in how the weak may become strong. As a child she was sickly and shy, growing up into a wan, self-effacing, unimpressive girl. Her entry into politics was facilitated by having a father who was Prime Minister, indeed engineered by him, but she suffered painfully from comparison with his brilliance. Even granted his own power, and the fact that Indian public life is more sympathetic than Western to the promotion of family members, Nehru could only launch Indira in a job that no one else wanted to do, the presidency of the Congress Party in 1959–60. Her next post, as chairman of the Citizens' Central Council, was hardly the place to shine, even if Indira, already middle-aged, knew how to. She only became a member of Congress by a classic instance of the process of 'male equivalence' when she was elected to her father's seat after he died in 1964. The men who made her Prime Minister in 1966 did so because they saw in her a perfect front woman. Nobody then dreamed that this has-been who never had been, whose highest political post had been Minister of Information and Broadcasting, could, as a woman and at forty-seven years of age, make a bid for power in her own right.

They were all blind. Like her famous sister stopgap, Golda Meir, before her, Indira Gandhi saw her gap and made for it, saw power opportunities coming by her and took them with a confident hand. In doing so, she demolished for ever the sentimental assumption that women leaders should all behave like Joan of Arc, bringing a new and lofty spiritual dimension to the sordid processes of *realpolitik*. Although known as 'the Steel Butterfly' and 'the Mother of India' to her supporters, according to her enemies she displayed all the spirituality of Sweeney Todd.

The story of Indira Gandhi's political career, known only in patches in the West, is staggering in its intensity and complexity – who after all in our world could serve a term of imprisonment and then emerge to reconquer the electorate and be swept back to supreme office? Commentators like Dom Moraes, privileged both by his background knowledge and his special access to Mrs Gandhi over a period of time, confessed themselves foxed by this strange and subtle woman. But certain factors emerge above the sea of hatred and hysteria that constitute Indian politics.

First Indira Gandhi's progress demonstrates that power can be learned, and learned just as well by women as by men. When she first came into Congress she showed that she had absorbed one important tactic from the silent years in waiting behind her father's throne – she began at once the practice of touring India, speaking to massive crowds at open-air meetings, which Nehru had always done. Initially she travelled as his daughter and inheritor to capitalise on his name, but by doing so built up a huge if volatile personal power base which she subsequently played upon with great skill to achieve her political ends; in 1971, for instance, she countered opposition moves within her own party by calling an election, which she won with an enormous majority.

But Indira Gandhi also showed that she could learn from her mistakes as well as from her triumphs. As she had come to power in 1971 on an 'abolish poverty' ticket, her credibility was badly undermined by the ensuing period of desperate economic difficulty and raging inflation. Public unrest was fanned by the war with Pakistan over Bangladesh, and, faced with huge nationwide riots and demonstrations against her rule, she responded by declaring a state of emergency, suppressing the freedom of the press, and throwing her political opponents into jail – 110,000 people in all were detained without trial. Indian democracy was outraged to its soul. Personal and human rights were casually violated along with political ones; Indira Gandhi's son and heir-apparent had caused a gathering storm by his programme of compulsory sterilisation for males as a means of population control. At the next election in 1977 her enemies had her on the hip. Her party was annihilated at the hustings and she even lost her own seat. Powerless and humiliated, she could no longer fight off charges of electoral malpractice and in 1978 she was expelled from Congress and imprisoned.

From this string of apparently overwhelming disasters, Indira Gandhi contrived the kind of comeback that could give even Richard Nixon ideas. Resuming her tours throughout the length and breadth of her vast country, through gruelling programmes and endless public appearances, she rebuilt her platform of popular support. Her landslide victory in a by-election was the open signal to her opponents that she was on the way back, and in the run-up to the election of 1980 she demonstrated her matured political skills by a brilliant exploitation of their weaknesses and divisions. She also came back into the ring with a refurbished and more effective image. Where before she had stressed her strength and aggression, presenting herself as 'a Durga', a warrior

172

goddess, perhaps to convince herself as much as others that Nehru's awkward silent girl had what it takes to be a power figure, now she played her ace, a card naturally unbeatable by her male opponents, 'the Mother of India'. In this guise she appealed to the backward multitudes in the south of India, 'You don't know what they are doing to me in the north. If they get in, they'll kill my son, they'll kill him.' The spectacle of this frail sixty-three-year-old woman weeping her heart out, embracing all the electorate as her children, offering a mystical fusion between motherhood and the Prime Ministership, proved irresistible. Indira Gandhi once more pulled out the stops of popular support and was carried to a triumphant victory in the 1980 election.

For over twenty years Indira Gandhi demonstrated an ambition for personal power and a political tenacity that would be rare in a man, reaffirming and consolidating her power and status with breathtaking ruthlessness and skill. Her career appears to support Bertrand Russell's pronouncement that power is inherently insatiable; the power-holder becomes sick with this addictive drug and must continue to mainline power to the point of personal destruction. James Margach in *The Anatomy of Power* recalls Churchill's advice to Lloyd George, that 'L.G.' should retire at the height of his power and powers in 1918 after winning World War I. But Churchill himself after his victory in 1945 defied this sound wisdom, and hung on for another decade through a series of enfeebling strokes into a grotesque twilight. 'Power becomes the drug on which they are hooked,' Margach concludes.

The only drawback to this analysis of Mrs Gandhi is that she seemed, right up to the day of her untimely death, to be thriving on power rather than suffering under it. Her energy, like that of all top women, was stupendous: 'I can do about seven things at once,' she told reporter Reg Davis. 'Many times I've worked all night, and in 1978, when we had elections in the south, I must have gone three weeks without going to bed at all. Usually five hours sleep will suffice. I don't ever seem to get exhausted.' For a woman approaching seventy, Indira Gandhi also had an amazing ability to push forward in the face of the negative aspects and disruptive effects of being a top power-holder, especially in India where violence and terror have traditionally accompanied the exercise of power. She was viciously abused – the slogans that

173

have been hung on Mrs Thatcher are compliments in comparison – and her whole family, not merely the overweening Sanjay, subjected to barrages of hostility. She was frequently the target not of eggs or tomatoes as in the genteel British tradition, but of stones and bricks, and was hospitalised with a broken nose and head injuries following such attacks.

The price for Mrs Gandhi also included a painful and long-drawn-out wrangle with her daughter-in-law Maneka. As the widow of the heir-apparent, Sanjay, ironically killed in a plane crash in 1980, the year of his mother's great victory, Maneka seemed bent on taking a leaf out of her mother-in-law's book and striking out for a power base of her own. Maneka's attempts to build a party out of a remnant of Sanjay's supporters who were disaffected from his mother led to hysterical scenes and public rumpuses between the two women. The row spilled over into the newspapers and spread to include the other females of Maneka's family, including her formidable mother. While consistently presenting herself as a mild and kindly old lady cruelly misused by a granny-bashing daughter-in-law, Mrs Gandhi did nothing to minimise the mutual aggravation, but stuck to her guns and fired on both barrels.

In this struggle Gandhi-watchers unhesitatingly backed Indira over Maneka, described as 'a political twit'. But in the event Mrs Gandhi fell victim to a political, not a personal vendetta. Her death at the hands of Sikh extremists in November 1984 had been feared for some time. But, like Mrs Thatcher, who narrowly escaped death from an IRA bomb within the same fortnight, Mrs Gandhi was not deterred, but rather confirmed by opposition in her messianic sense of power, even to the uttermost. She knew the risk, and embraced it with her eyes open. In a strangely prophetic speech two days before she was assassinated, Mrs Gandhi declared, 'Even if I die in the service of the nation, I shall be proud. Even if I die today, every drop of my blood will invigorate my nation.' She knew the price, then, and was prepared to have to pay. She died for that which she had lived for, the sway and exercise of supreme power in a major democracy of the world.

174

In many parts of the country I am called Mother, and I regard India as my family.

Indira Gandhi

Butterflies of Steel

In direct contrast with women like Indira Gandhi or Margaret Thatcher, who gain and retain power through their grasp of the existing political processes, are those who seek or find power through their determination to change those processes and the world we live in. Yet like Mrs Gandhi they too redefine the nature of women's power with their conviction and capacity for endurance. Equally important is the implicit statement of women's power in another mode of operation – power as pressure and action through influence.

Representative of this type of commitment is Joan Ruddock, chairperson of the Campaign for Nuclear Disarmament. As a woman who makes her living as the organiser of a branch of the Citizens' Advice Bureau, Joan is wholly committed to working through pressure both politically and professionally. Her life is divided between a four-day week at the CAB, and her CND activities. She has to go to the CND offices twice or three times a week after work, or else to the House of Commons to see an MP: 'I virtually never have a night off,' she says. Weekends or holidays can be committed to CND meetings as far afield as Hiroshima, and if she wants to have a real break she has to go somewhere without a telephone.

Joan's career illustrates the truth of a comment by Leslie Abdela, founder of the 300 Group: 'Joining a pressure group is a good way to lose your political virginity.' Women leave school and home seriously underprepared for the world outside, let alone the beargarden of public life, and need to plunge into some activity as an athlete goes into training, to build up experience, insight and muscle. The performance that looks so effortless can be learned. 'Public speaking has never come easily to me,' Joan comments. 'I never joined the debating society at school – I was too scared.' How did she become such a calm and persuasive broadcaster, such an effective advocate for her cause? 'I was thrown in at the deep end when I worked for Shelter and I learned all my campaigning skills when I was on the road as regional

175

organiser. I was also parliamentary candidate for Newbury in 1979. I fought for Labour and got used to dealing with hecklers,' she says.

As this shows, the only way for women to catch up on these vital techniques and areas of experience is by making themselves crash through the barrier of fear and inadequacy in order to make a start. Lady Olga Maitland, who has had considerable success (at the opposite end of the political spectrum from Joan Ruddock) with her Woman and Families for Defence campaign, recalls her first speech:

> I spent so much time preparing those six minutes! I thought I was going to faint, but baptism of fire is the only way to do it, and having done it once, I've done it ever since.
>
> My great philosophy in life is to accept first and worry afterwards. The only way to learn anything is to learn on the go – dive in at the deep end. Do it, even if it's not perfect.

Lady Olga highlights here an element which very commonly holds women back from developing or even discovering their own powers, the dread of not being good enough, getting it all horribly wrong. The recommended therapy for fear of failure is to build confidence gradually with small-scale successes. Rosalynn Carter relates in her autobiography, *First Lady from Plains*, that she initially launched on speech-making because 'I was too proud to tell them I was too scared to speak.' On the way to her first engagement she had to stop the car to get out and be sick. But from this inauspicious start Rosalynn Carter developed the poise to become one of the most publicly and politically active First Ladies in the history of the White House. Such honest admissions help other women enormously to know that they are not alone in going through the growing pains of power. It is also helpful, and a lot of fun, to call to mind the roster of mighty male cock-ups from Napoleon to Nixon. *Anyone* can get it wrong! And you can get it right.

[Make the world better.]
    Lucy Stone's last words to her only child, her daughter Alice

Changing the World

The theme of women discovering their personal potency and, by

176

extending their use of power, changing its nature, is nowhere more encouragingly expressed than through the lives of women who have found themselves and a cause in working for other women. This route not only to personal power but to significant social change has a long and honourable pedigree. Those who perceived Betty Friedan, Kate Millett and Germaine Greer as representatives of a new and threatening species, the radical *nouveau biche* the media loved to hate, had forgotten Susan B. Anthony, Elizabeth Cady Stanton, Lucy Stone and Emmeline Pankhurst and her daughters. Frequently these women came to feminism through their work for other groups or causes. But they made no bones about where their primary allegiance lay. 'I was a woman before I was an abolitionist' said Lucy Stone. '*I must speak for the women.*'

In speaking for the women Betty Friedan started from what proved to be an enormous potential platform for political and cultural power, a basis of personal truth. This arose from her both facing and listening to the concrete, mundane facts of her own frustration and that of other women which came together to form 'the problem that had no name', the 'feminine mystique'. Later, the women's movement and its leaders were to be graced with all the benefits of our media age, suffering the grossest exploitation, vulgarisation and distortion that our image-makers and myth-manufacturers have it in their power to bestow. Hysterical over-coverage greeted such factitious productions as the SCUM Manifesto (Society for Cutting Up Men), although its author, Valerie Solanas, like so many women made famous for fifteen minutes, ended by cutting up only herself. The mindless and servile media, mouthpieces for a society desperate to hang on to the existing state of prelapsarian innocence and to prevent its womenfolk from taking a bite of this new apple of the tree of knowledge, mounted a propaganda campaign painting the women's leaders as hysterical hags, viragos bent on the destruction of all good things from the family and mother love to apple pie. In spite of all this the women's movement gathered momentum and swept the world with the irresistible force of historical inevitability. As Betty Friedan recalls in *The Second Stage*:

It happened, not because I or some other feminist witch somehow

177

seduced otherwise happy housewives by our words, but because of evolutionary necessity. Women could no longer live out an eighty-year life span as childbearers, wives and mothers alone. For function, identity, status in society, and their own economic support, women – for the first time in history freed from passive necessary submission to the role as breeders of the race – were forced by the longer span of their lives to take their own place, as individuals in society.

With the kind of type-casting against which feminism fights, Betty Friedan has been labelled 'the mother of the new feminism'. Less a mother than a midwife, Friedan has brought into the world the National Organisation of Women, a powerful articulation of the swelling resentment of millions of American women. She also helped to found the National Women's Political Caucus and the First Women's Bank, led the National Women's Strike for Equality, and conveyed the International Feminist Congress in 1973. Over twenty years after her tentative and exploratory beginnings, Friedan is still active in the struggle for the Equal Rights Amendment, for divorce and abortion reform and for 'the second stage' of feminism. From being a suburban housewife who 'chauffeured, and did the PTA and buffet dinners', she has become a professor at the universities of Columbia and Yale, a nationwide organiser and an international inspiration.

Betty Friedan titled one of her books *It Changed My Life*. The movement which she helped to create not only changed the lives of its leaders and organisers; it changed the quality of the life that would thereafter be available to all other women. The work, the ideas, the dreams, the schemes of these early visionaries have passed through us all like wine through water, and altered the colour of our minds. And woman power breeds woman power. All women have benefited from the dam-busting operations of the pioneers, breaking down the barriers of thought and custom to release the pent-up flood of women's talent and drive. Even one who admitted to being 'a reluctant feminist' like Ella T. Grasso, the first woman to be elected a US State Governor in her own right, conceded: 'The movement has done a great deal in a short time to provide equal opportunity for women, and I feel I've been a beneficiary.'

If Betty Friedan is the mother of feminism, the aptly named Gloria Steinem is its queen. She is widely admired because she has

178

managed to live as well as preach her feminist values, and has done so with an increasing authority, grace and serenity. 'She sets the standard by which we should behave.' says Donna Shalala. This essential work Steinem also carries out through *Ms* magazine, in itself a fantasy story of runaway success; after the launch in 1972, it reached a circulation of 350,000 within a year. She feels confident that the women's movement, which has dynamited the obstructions out of so many women's paths, is now beginning to change men's lives too:

> The idea of equal pay now has majority support among both men and women, which it didn't ten years ago. There is some understanding of shared work at home and shared parenthood. It would be hard to find anyone who didn't have a changed idea of what women expect.

What Steinem and her co-workers on *Ms* magazine have also done for women and the women's movement is to demonstrate a grasp on a fundamental principle of power applied as pressure – that, to work, it must be not only a successful articulation of the key issues, but must also have a sustained and systematic programme and structure. The task is not simply to release the flood of feeling, but to find an ongoing format for its expression. The success of the women's movement in these terms, and of *Ms* magazine in particular, may be gauged from a comparison with the Ulster Peace Movement in the 1970s.

This movement, described at the time as 'the most hopeful of Ireland's movements for peace', originated from the spontaneous initiative of Ulsterwoman Betty Williams. Hearing of the deaths of the three young children of Anne Maguire, killed by a runaway car after its IRA driver had been shot dead by British soldiers, Betty Williams began knocking on doors asking women to join her in the cry for peace. Within a few days she was leading a demonstration of 10,000 women, both Catholic and Protestant, and assisted by Mairead Corrigan, the sister of Anne Maguire, she embarked on organising and raising money for what was to become the most powerful pressure group that Ireland had ever known.

Like the early feminists, Williams and Corrigan tapped straight into a deeper and more passionate vein of feeling than any of the male leaders of society had ever known existed. Within three months over 150 local groups had come into being, and rallies took place not only in Ireland, but in London's Trafalgar Square. With keen interest in their work both from America and Europe, and their award of the Nobel Peace Prize as the youngest-ever recipients, both women became figures of international standing. They rapidly grew in experience and stature, becoming powerful public speakers and effective fund-raisers for the war-torn province. But they were unable, eventually, to harness the enormous emotional power that they had released, or their own growing powers of management, into an organisation that would express and continue their work. Riven with the kind of internal divisions that have made the sorrows of Ireland legendary throughout the world, the Peace Movement fell apart within five years.

> Oh sisters, come you, sing for all you're worth,
>   Arms are made for linking,
> Sisters, we're asking for the earth.
>   Song of the Women's Peace Movement

Women Are Gathering

It would be a final irony among the many that have been visited on their stricken country if the work of Betty Williams and Mairead Corrigan were dismissed as in vain. These two women, a housewife and a secretary, gave a voice to the rage and despair of women which finds its echoes in other groups, other actions and other countries. In the powerful manifesto of the Women's Pentagon Action 1980:

> We are in the hands of men whose power and wealth have separated them from the reality of daily life and from the imagination. We are right to be afraid ... 'We will protect you,' they say, but we have never been so endangered, so close to the end of human time. *We women are gathering because life on the precipice is intolerable.* We want to know what anger in these men, what fear which can only be satisfied by destruction, what coldness of heart and ambition drives their days. We want to know because we do not want that dominance which is so exploitative and murderous in international relations and so

180

dangerous to women and children at home – we do not want that sickness transferred by the violent society through fathers to sons.

Among many women in recent years who have forged such links between feminism and pacifism, foremost is the charismatic Petra Kelly, co-founder and leading light of the West German political party, Die Grünen (the Greens). 'I have hope for the world, although it is ten minutes before Doomsday,' she writes, 'because women all over the world are rising up ... with a vitality and creativity never before seen.' As a woman who has succeeded in putting her own dream of the future into the form of a political reality, with the tiny group of 'Greens' holding the balance of power in the Bundestag, Kelly speaks from experience when she says that women are learning to organise themselves, to assert their power, and to claim the right to make their protests heard. Kelly herself has campaigned to the point of collapse and beyond, throughout Germany, Western Europe, Ireland, America, Australia and not least in Hiroshima for her 'vision of a non-violent, ecological and non-exploitative republic'.

But Petra Kelly is no female mystic with her head full of sunflowers. Like Mrs Gandhi she knows how to draw upon a base of popular regard that gives her something very like pop-star status in West Germany. She has retained her position as the focal point of the Greens by shrewd political skill and nifty footwork when the small and infant party was racked by internal conflicts. In the face of a government policy to return women to the family similar to that of the Conservative government in Britain, with 'reforms' promised by the Minister for the Family to speed up this reactionary process, she has continued positive and active, working both within and outside the parliamentary framework to 'end forever the war of the powerful against the powerless'.

Like so many of the women of power, Petra Kelly draws her strength from a little-acknowledged source. This is indicated by her opening remarks on the occasion of receiving the alternative Nobel Prize at Stockholm in 1982: 'I dedicate this speech and these remarks first and foremost to my seventy-seven-year-old grandmother, who has accompanied me here to Stockholm and who has been my guardian light and inspiration throughout these past thirty-five years.' Kelly also dedicates her life's work to the memory of her ten-year-old sister, who died of a brain tumour in

181

1970. Both her mother and her grandmother lost their husbands and fathers at an early stage, a factor to which Petra Kelly attributes great significance: 'We have all been fatherless women, a whole chain of us, and somehow we have all become very strong because we were alone.' As a link in the chain, Petra Kelly both incarnates and quickens the sense of power in every woman.

Thinking the Unthinkable – and Doing It

'The Greens came out of my head,' says Petra Kelly. Without money or social position, with nothing but faith and the help of friends, she made her ambitious plan come about. In different occupations, in different countries of the world, countless unfamous women are also quietly engaged in the business of proving that *there is nothing that women cannot do*. After centuries of self-deprecation, the women are junking the 'weaker sex' stigma with great determination, and developing the physical and mental confidence to travel farther, and along new roads.

The success of these women points a number of morals that are highly instructive in view of the fact that society is still in a state of relative ignorance of the extent of women's capacities and abilities. Growing numbers of firewomen, for instance, demonstrate that men can no longer expect to hold a monopoly of any job area, especially in a time of unemployment, and when women's unemployment is increasing at *twice* the rate of men's. It reminds us too, that despite all the play upon sex *difference*, the standard male/female comparison is not between a 5', 100 lb woman and a 6', 200 lb man; the majority of men and women inhabit the mid-terrain between these points, where the overlapping and similarity is much more marked than the difference.

As more and more women prove that they can hold down 'a man's job', so the old bogeys of superstition and supposition which have combined to hold women back are laid to rest. Muriel Allen was appointed as the first woman governor of a British prison in 1982, in defiance of received prison service wisdom that a woman could not handle a jailful of 'hard cases', or alternatively that 'hard cases' could not handle her; as in the old nautical nonsense, a woman 'aboard' would be a jinx, her proximity too much to bear for a crowd of sex-starved and incarcerated men. Not surprisingly, Allen has succeeded in running Kingston Prison without either jinxing the establishment or driving the inmates mad with lust.

Muriel Allen's career story incorporates a couple of the classic strands of how progress comes and what it means for a woman. She made this historic breakthrough by the simple expedient of asking for it. After a career in the prison service, during the period when appointments were strictly sex-segregated, she was asked by a Home Office promotions board what she would like to do next. She told them that she wanted the chance of heading a male prison. 'I had had experience of running every branch of female institutions,' she says. 'I wanted to add to my experience of male institutions in order to further my career.' A career in the prison service, given Britain's peculiar problems of an excessively high number of male prisoners and the legacy of monstrous Victorian clinks, feels like a sentence of hard labour. But like other pioneer women, Muriel Allen is fuelled by a deep conviction of purpose, her 'innate belief in a *positive* use of imprisonment', which she describes as a feeling of 'joy' in her work. From this she derives, too, the rewards described by other female achievers: 'I've had horrendous experiences in my time and gone through every emotion there is *except boredom.*'

It is hard to overstress the importance of women's being able to move into top positions in all areas, and *being seen to do so.* This is not just a matter of the media's rather naive scoring of 'the first woman to ... ', although that has a value that should not be dismissed in keeping the tally of women's achievements. What is significant is that these women bank managers, government inspectors or transport managers will be seen by children, by the general public and by the younger female members of their own profession, at work, in ordinary everyday circumstances. This will have an incalculable effect in remodelling the subconscious assumptions of us all that power is an exclusively masculine preserve.

So it can hardly harm the cause of women that one of us moves ahead in a highly unusual and glamorous area. When Dr Monica Kristensen became the first woman to be appointed to lead a polar expedition in 1985, she featured, plus photograph, in all the newspapers, which inevitably displayed more interest in her long blonde hair and blue eyes than in her doctorate in Glaciology from Cambridge University or her long track record of Arctic and Antarctic exploration. But equally significant in a quieter way was the election, for instance, of the first-ever woman vice-chairman of the Association of Optical Practitioners, Amy Isherwood, not least to the rising numbers of young female entrants into her profession. Throughout the world women are notching up uncounted and unsung a vast range of local triumphs. When the first-ever woman controller was appointed at my local sewage works, the earth may not have moved, but she disposed for ever of the myth that women do not know what to do when the stuff hits the fan! With Britain seeing in the last year its first woman professional conductor, its first woman referee of senior rugby league, and its first woman Lord Mayor of London, the message is clear and very exciting – no barriers of time-hardened tradition, no imputation of incapacity, can any longer hold us back.

> My reaction was very similar to what I felt when I heard
> Geraldine Ferraro was nominated – *we really can do anything.*
> Amy Rennert, editor of *Women's Sports and Fitness*
> *Magazine*, commenting on Joan Benoit's 1984
> Marathon victory

The Final Frontier

The traditional parade of the Lord Mayor through the City of London, at which Dame Mary Donaldson greeted the people magnificent in white lace, red velvet, gold chain and black tricorne hat, is a useful reminder of the vital symbolic significance of visible female achievement, even if the direct modelling effect must be nil. The same holds true for the spacewomen of the 1980s, Sally Ride from America and Svetlana Savitskaya of Russia. Progress has been slow and spasmodic since Valentina Tereshkova became the first woman in space over twenty years ago in 1963. But within very recent history Sally Ride has become the first American woman in space, and Svetlana Savitskaya the first woman to walk in space, when she left the Salyut-7 orbital station to test an important new piece of equipment for cutting and welding metal in space.

Cosmonaut Saviskaya scored another important 'first' when she became the only woman ever to have gone into space twice. This is only the latest in a stunning range of achievements of this space researcher and flight engineer. She has flown more than twenty types of planes, set eighteen world records, and was the all-round World Aerobatics Champion. Spacewomen are, in the classic mode of female skills so undervalued by their possessors, performers on multiple fronts. To their flight skills they add specialist skills: Sally Ride holds a PhD in X-ray astrophysics.

But their main significance from the point of view of the continuing fight for women's equality is that no difference is made between a spaceman and a spacewoman. They undergo exactly the same training, measure up to the same expectations, and everything the men do, the women do too. Some women and men too might shirk the kind of equality that gives an equal opportunity in the gruesomely named 'vomit comet', the spinning chair in which astronauts experience blindfold the horrors of weight sickness. But astronauts, male or female, have stronger stomachs. In space, finally, a frontier where both sexes are equal. Let's all make it.

'Brunette Sally Ride ... '

Sally Ride's career highlights in the meantime a more earth-bound problem faced by high-achieving women. The mass media coverage that they receive ranges through all points from the daft to the disgusting, and never once hits either common sense or truth about their experience. 'The media image of women is a major problem,' says Anne Joy. What she means can be illustrated by an account of Sally Ride's meeting with a group of journalists that appeared in the *Guardian* in June of 1983:

> 'How do you feel about being the first American woman in space?' asked a *Ms* magazine photographer, Janice Rubin.
> 'Standard answer No. 3 – thrilled,' she replied sardonically.
> 'Don't you find it difficult being a woman in a man's profession?' asked Jane Pauly, a TV interviewer on NBC/TV.
> 'Seems to me I should be asking you that question,' retorted Sally Ride.

Reporter Rosemarie Whittman Lamb, who witnessed these

exchanges, nevertheless in her own turn asked, 'I suppose it's crazy to ask you if you're excited about going up into space?' 'Yes, it's crazy,' agreed Ride, and walked off. Naturally Ride's behaviour is interpreted as if *she* were the problem – Lamb complained that it is very difficult for reporters to interview her. This is obviously true. It is clearly difficult, apparently almost impossible, for journalists to come up with anything except the stunningly boring, the crashingly obvious, the nudgingly sexist, and the same old questions as before whenever they are confronted with a woman of ability, power or achievement.

Sally Ride's combination of high profile, academic status and spiky wit serves to keep the phrase-makers of Grub Street, albeit resentfully, at arms' length. No such luck for other women, among whom women athletes are undoubtedly at the sharp end. A recent victim of the kind of press coverage that has made Western journalism the laughing-stock of Eastern Europe has been the world champion woman sprinter Jarmila Kratochvilova. This woman's amazing and unprecedented speeds have set what Carlyle called 'the yellow eye of journalism' spinning in its head. Never mind the achievement, go for the sex smear; she must be a man. Never mind either that Kratochvilova has passed every known drug and chromosome test, and holds a certificate from the International Amateur Athletic Federation stating that she has two X chromosomes when some women who have grown up accepted by themselves and all their family as female are shown to have an X/Y pattern.

No section of the British press has been immune from the grubby anti-feminism of this titillating speculation. So an exclusive interview with Kratochvilova in the *Sunday Times* billed her in the best style of breathless subbing as 'THE DYNAMIC ATHLETE FROM CZECHOSLOVAKIA WHOSE STARTLING PHYSIQUE HAS SET THE WORLD ASKING; IS SHE A WOMAN OR A MAN?' Set the world's hacks asking, anyway. *Sunday Times* reporter Rob Hughes manfully avoided the unacceptable face of journalism in his profile, in which he stressed Kratochvilova's ferocious seventeen-year training programme, her weight-lifting and body-building and her total commitment to running and to being 'the best in the world', posing the suggestion: 'Perhaps we need to ask, before too long, whether we are merely becoming unnerved by the appearance of a woman who in musculature and prowess closes the gap on man more than any others?' Or as Martina Navratilova asks, 'If Kratochvilova is masculine, does that mean that Sebastian Coe is feminine?' But the *Sunday Times* sub-editor had no time for such subtleties. With the bold and beautiful clarity that will surely make him an editor one day, he titled the article THE GIRL WITHIN THE BODY OF A MAN. Two sexist insults for this thirty-three-year-old woman in one eight-word phrase – sadly, *not* a record.

Kratochvilova's image problem relates in part to the long difficulty that Western capitalist societies, hung up on size ten models, have with Eastern European women. One outstanding injustice occurred in the case of the Polish sprinter and gold medallist Ewa Klobkowska, who was deemed to fail the womanhood test, and subsequently gave birth to a baby, which must be some kind of a pass. But Western executive women also come up against the crass gropings of every newspaperman on his mettle. So some *Daily Mail* sub plunged into the shallows of his experience to come up with the fragrant cliché that TOP BUSINESS WOMEN ARE DEADLIER THAN THE MALE. In an article of March 1984 which was about six of London's top businesswomen, one was described by reporter David Norris as 'an ash-blonde high-flier' and others as looking like 'kind aunts'. It is a safe bet that Unilever did not make Eileen Cole, one of these women, a managing director for either of these attributes; nor did the National Westminster Bank promote another, Eileen Cullen, to company secretary for these reasons. But again, never mind the achievement, feel the ordinariness: 'she lives with her businessman husband' ... 'she is married to a dental surgeon and has two grown-up children'. Just like the woman round the corner, wouldn't you say?

Press journalism has yet to begin to come to terms with today's new breed of high-achieving women, and with a mixture of stale-mindedness and misogyny persists in trying to force women back into the old moulds. So Sarah Pepper, then a reporter on the *Coventry Evening Telegraph*, was sent to cover a university conference of executive women with the instruction, 'Go easy on the "executive" bit, make them sound like a bunch of housewives.' Even more odious is the approach which stresses the woman's 'femininity' at the expense of her work achievement. An outstanding example of this kind of egregious ogling was a piece by Ross Davies which appeared in the *Sunday Times Business Section* in June of 1984. Profiling Detta O'Cathain, the director and general manager of the Milk Marketing Board, Davies contrived one piece of trivialisation (about Detta's church activities) and one error ('first woman director of a clearing bank') in his first two sentences. He then, as they say, had lift-off:

> Trim, tall, leggy, with blue eyes and long brunette hair worn pinned up, she says looks should have no more place in an article on her than in one about her fellow appointee to the Midland board, Frank V. Cahouet.
>
> On the other hand, Miss O'Cathain was on holiday last week, and for our talk she had changed out of sweater and jeans and into a slightly sensational dusty-pink two-piece suit with cream silk blouse which made the most of all the attributes she says she doesn't want attention drawn to. Women can be so difficult.

The pathetic thing is that male reporters are still so firmly possessed of the notion that women appreciate such tributes of the sweaty-palms, wet-lips school of journalism. Or perhaps not. There are only two logical possibilities, as Plato used to say: Davies is trying either to flatter, or to insult. If the former, he should, as Dr Johnson said, consider if his flattery is worth the having. But arguably he has managed to do both.

No matter how successful a woman may be, it is still an uphill struggle for her to be taken as a serious business proposition by male reporters. The career of Debbie Moore, founder, chairman and managing director of Pineapple Dance Studios, has been the stuff that dreams are made of. Beginning with a dilapidated pineapple warehouse in Covent Garden, where she opened her own dance studios, Debbie has created an international centre for the dance world, and brought trading to a halt on the London stock exchange when her company went public in 1982. Since then, she has expanded her business across the Atlantic and opened her first US dance centre, Pineapple Broadway, in New York in 1984, the year in which she also won the Veuve Cliquot Businesswoman of the Year award. Yet still a US stockbroker can dismiss her as a businesswoman, focusing instead entirely upon her as a sex object with the leering line, 'I'd rather look at her legs than her shares.' Clearly to be so successful, young and glamorous is a lethal combination!

But Debbie can afford to have the last laugh. Her progress has in fact been based on her ability to do things her own way, rather than relying on men's ideas of the way things should be done. 'There is a veil over the business world, but it is not a mystery,' she says. 'It's a lot of fun – we must get this over to other women.' It is important to demystify the business process as a 'man's world', Debbie feels. 'Today we must encourage young girls at school by a different image, show them you don't have to be masculine, or they shy away.' Certainly Debbie's own attractive, fashionable and relaxed image is far more accessible to today's schoolgirls than the pinstripe and briefcase model of the female executive, and many ambitious young females must have been encouraged to discover that it is possible to make yourself a millionaire and still look like a million dollars.

But Debbie's bright appealing image is only one aspect of a very bright woman. Press coverage naturally stresses the Cinderella elements of her story; in fact Debbie had already managed one successful career before she began the dance studio business. This had begun with a bang when she won a national competition which took her to New York at the age of fifteen. Her decision to launch Pineapple Dance Studios in Covent Garden was based on a shrewd assessment of an opening for the venture: 'I had already noticed there was a market, as the dance studio I went to was so overcrowded. I thought it all through.' Debbie displays another classic characteristic of other top business-women too – she is nuts about 'the product'. Her enthusiasm for her different operations, the dance, the clothing, the health sides of her business and now the new dream child, Pineapple Broadway, conveys the sense of yet more to come. 'The future is endless,' she says with infectious conviction, 'there are so many areas in this business.'

Debbie Moore is not only making business history with her phenomenal financial success – a recent survey of a dozen Brits who are US millionaires contained photographs of eleven grim masculine dials, and Debbie. She is also an innovator in the far more interesting area of business style. She has confidently cut through all the standard business frontage of big desks, banks of phones and 'Where's the cigar?', as US businesswomen say. Instead her staff are kind and graceful people who glide along looking like the ex-dancers that they all are. She runs an operation entirely without all the side that businessmen seem to need to see them through. 'Business shouldn't be full of people you dread seeing,' she says, 'the City needn't be like that.' And the slice of it that is Pineapple is showing the way.

The story of the Pineapple ventures, stripped of its dazzling effect, is the even more inspiring story of a woman who worked to learn, learned to work, had a good idea and the determination to do something about it, and above all the strength of purpose to do it her way. 'Men can suppress your intuition if you're not careful,' she warns. 'Instincts and intuitions are the most valuable things that women can have. They can be the missing ingredient if you haven't had formal business training.' In trusting to this, Debbie Moore has both discovered her own potential and created something out of nothing that now gives pleasure and employment to hundreds of thousands of others.

But the achievement of individual women, even success as great as Debbie Moore's, is not an isolated phenomenon. They are all links in the chain of women's self-actualisation which is taking place on a worldwide scale. Women are coming through in every area now to realise their own potency and with it their limitless potential. Women's power in unconventional achievements, our power as pressure or protest, our mental power or power as strength, and finally our power as women to be and do what seems good to us – all these are expressing themselves on the national and international platforms, and in every town and village. Women are broadening the avenues, for themselves and for others coming on. They are making it possible to think the unthinkable, to do the previously undoable. 'Whatever you want, you can do,' is the message from the front. We can do it. We can *do* it! In that lies the power, and the glory.

The journey of a thousand miles begins with the first step.

Chinese proverb

CHAPTER 9

Megastars

I am not a star. I look at pictures of Sophia Loren and Jackie Onassis and those are stars. They're always smiling like ladies.
                                    Barbra Streisand

In the pantheon of powerful women, a special hall of fame is reserved for those who as modern media goddesses seem to secure the kind of power hitherto undreamed of by women, and with it the international acclaim and huge wealth that are the stuff of legend. The whole area of media operation has been very important to women, and will continue to be, because it can offer the most dazzling opportunities to those without degrees or even anything much in the way of education (how many O-levels has Barbra Streisand?). Media work also freely accommodates those with unconventional or irregular backgrounds, and as there is no agreed career structure in the majority of media occupations, you don't have to 'work your way up'. Equally, women don't have to fight to get in. It is a long haul from continuity girl or extra to studio boss or star, but at least no one can fall back on the defence being mounted by the City that they've never had women in the business and don't know how they'd work out.

Media power, in its rewards and scope, is truly the product of the dream machine, and many women and men too live their own dreams vicariously through the favoured few who achieve it. This is indeed what power means for ordinary people, the power to live life in this way rather than as a low-profile top female executive, say, making a brilliant career in metal boxes.

But of all jungles where small, bright-eyed and not too smart little creatures should not walk alone, the media jungle is about the worst. Even those prodigious women who become queens in this jungle find that they have caught a tiger by the tail. Nor is there much greater security in working behind, rather than in front of the camera. In the media business you may never have to retire, but as being fired is such a common occupational hazard, you may never get a chance to.

Like every other area, the conglomeration of industries that comprise the media business, films, television and journalism, have seen women rising in greater numbers than ever before to positions of power. More important, they are using their power in a new way. There have always been leading ladies – now they are not only writing the scripts and directing the movies, they are running the studios as well. Sam Goldwyn would have had two words for it – 'im possible!' But it's happened. Women have made themselves mistresses of the media machines and used them to carve out their own kingdoms. They see a number of good reasons not to leave the conduct of their careers in the hands of men.

These good reasons have names like Frances Field, Judy Garland and Marilyn Monroe. The female film stars of the past were granted great fame, success and high earnings – they became the darlings of the populace and looked as if they had only to crook a little finger to satisfy every heart's desire. Stars like Elizabeth Taylor did what they liked, egged on by the unconditional adoration of a public not only ready for, but needing the larger-than-life personality to live out the behaviour forbidden to ordinary people. Stars have always enjoyed, too, an enormous cultural power. World popularity makes them the women that every other woman wants to emulate, or at a deeper level, almost to become – so Veronica Lake, Rita Hayworth and Marilyn Monroe were not so much admired as cannibalised, their special attributes of hair, mouth or twin-cornet bust taken over by women in search of the magic of identification. When you only have to put a bow in your hair to produce a world epidemic of imitation, it must feel like the kind of power that men have never even dreamed of.

This kind of power only comes to a woman when all the world is in love with her. So the Hollywood film stars were dubbed the 'love goddesses' not in hyperbole but in an accurate assessment of the relation they stood in to the rest of the world. The power of this love, both cultural and commercial, is great enough to convey not only divinity but a modern kind of royalty. As inheritors of a land innocent of kings, or power-holding priests, Americans are constantly engaged in the necessary work of supplying these resonances. In this task of cultural production, the provision of an indigenous monarchy looms large. The 'love goddesses' were invented as America's queens. Stardom was also the only route to queenhood for those not born into a real royal family – the applicant did not have to be an American but had simply to go where the queenhood was going, as Elizabeth Taylor did. And when counts, khans and kinglets married these women and an apple-pie American Kelly became Princess Grace, this was enthusiastically embraced as validation of America's 'monarchy' and a symbol of the marriage between the royalties of the old world and the new.

Two women in recent times who have enjoyed 'love goddess' status and the symbolic queenhood that it confers are Jacqueline Kennedy Onassis and HRH the Princess of Wales. By its heroines a nation is known. These women have held an extraordinary sway over the hearts and minds of the people of every nation, every corner of the globe where a newspaper or television signal finds its way. Jacqueline Onassis has been described by Gloria Steinem as 'the world's most famous woman', a title that any woman who has appeared on the cover of thirty-eight of the world's top glossies inside one year, as the Princess of Wales has, could certainly challenge. Jacqueline Kennedy had to marry Onassis on a private island guarded by a private army to keep the world's press from storming the altar; a British couple reported returning to their hotel in inland Sarawak to find the entire clientele and staff *on their knees* in front of a tiny black and white television set emitting flickering images of the wedding of the Prince and Princess of Wales. Both women are modern megastars; Jacqueline Kennedy Onassis has been a queen, and HRH the Princess of Wales will become one.

With their frequent appearances in magazine articles and lists of the 'World's Best and Most', these women carry the most enormous cultural clout. As First Lady, Jacqueline Kennedy set standards of taste throughout America, and the Princess of Wales only has to wear a pie-frill for pie-frills to sprout throughout the nation. Yet they are far more than just image-makers or fashion leaders. They seem to embody all the hopes and aspirations of a large segment of womanhood in society and their actions influence the contemporary definition and self-definition of women everywhere. They become not only living myths, but mythic incarnations of all that is conventionally desired in and expected of women, in a line that goes all the way back to Joan of Arc. As her story shows, there's no power like heroine power.

But in these modern instances the power of these two women comes from the heroes they married rather than from any action of their own as people, and the result has been to wipe them out as individuals. As Gloria Steinem has pointed out, the woman born Jacqueline Bouvier became entirely subsumed in the powerful Kennedy myth in the public mind (though not, as it proved, in her own). That became even more important after Kennedy's death when she was one of the important pieces of the broken dream still left to America, and it was assumed that she would live the rest of her life as JFK's relict, holy relic even. Her husband had hardly been laid to rest before US power brokers were mapping out her future as consort to another presidential hopeful, as congresswoman, ambassador or 'a kind of glamorous Eleanor Roosevelt'.

Heroines, Princesses, Prisoners

Jacqueline Kennedy's decision to live her own life illustrates with great clarity the real limitation of symbolic power. Heroines are deeply cherished, venerated even – as long as they stay within their prescribed parameters. But the images with which they are saddled are constructed to meet the needs of their society, not of themselves. And they are static, not dynamic. The woman who is invested with this kind of mythic potency becomes an icon or totem as time goes by. And woe betide the woman who, worshipped in one incarnation, seeks to reincarnate in another form. When the noble Kennedy widow moved out of the mausoleum and married a man who after her former prince looked like a toad, her popularity slumped till she figured on 'least admired' and 'most hated' lists, and her action was described as 'the biggest insult to American manhood since Pearl Harbor'. Not only the Presidential years but Jacqueline Kennedy's entire future were expected to conform to society's sentimental myth of her, and her total definition as a person was taken as being determined by the man she chose as a partner; 'a problem', in the summary of Gloria Steinem, 'understood by any woman who has had the experience of being treated like a totally different person, even though the only change is the identity of the man standing next to her'.

As this shows, the role of heroine with all its associated power normally denies any active or sexual performance. A heroine is not supposed to be a hot number. A heroine is the repository of the ideal values of masculine ideology – pure virtue, selfless devotion, unstinting love. So the Princess of Wales proceeded, like Grace Kelly before her, straight from the beatification of 'shy Di', the unsullied virgin, to the sanctity of dutiful motherhood, without ever achieving a woman's full and free sexuality in between.

The media's favourite description of the Princess of Wales, 'fairy-tale princess', cruelly exposes the naive, sentimental and factitious nature of her myth. It also demonstrates the true quality of 'fairy-princess' power. For the enchantment of being a fairy princess suffers from the same drawback as everything else about the world of faery – touch it, and it vanishes. Marrying a prince, either literal or figurative, is one of the oldest fantasy solutions for women's powerlessness in the world. But women in these situations do not get their hands on that real power, men's power. And the price of riding in the glass coach is living the rest of your life in the goldfish bowl, the constant prey of gawpers and greeters, wavers and waiters.

Even here the amateurs are not as bad as the professionals. The British royal family, for instance, is happy to belong at least on one level to its loyal people. But who could be happy to accept as a corollary the life-and-soul invasion of the media, ever hungry for gobbets of gossip with which to flesh out their

195

candyfloss fictions and fatuous fantasies? Fairy princesses, so far from being able to wave a magic wand to make their dreams (or anyone else's) come true, are condemned to the ceaseless task of spinning out their lives into the stuff of wish-fulfilment daydreams and low-grade romance.

Heroine power in fact enfeebles rather than empowers. It limits and constricts, denying freedom, individuality, sexuality, or any kind of assertion. A heroine does not threaten men. How could she? – she isn't made that way. A heroine has never bust a ball in her life. How could she? – a true heroine wouldn't recognise one if it popped up and sang 'God Save the Queen' in front of her. A heroine knows her place and the behaviour appropriate to it. Heroine power is to be seen as one of the biggest confidence tricks ever to be pulled on the female race. It is the old pedestal routine once again, the 'elevation' of women to positions of apparent significance, as far away as possible from action, control or power. It works, too; the woman stuck up on the prow of a ship as its figurehead will surely not be able to get her hand to the tiller.

The whole of the female sex is flattered by the choice of certain women to be empowered as heroines, and these women are then flattered by the imitation of lesser women. But flattery *is* imitation, not the real thing. To grant women a symbolic power or centrality means that males can enjoy the luxury of feeling that they are doing justice to the female principle without having to let the reins of real power ever pass out of their own hands. Women are fobbed off with the shadow, not the substance, the trappings, not the reality, psyched out of access to true power with the symbolic queenhood which is itself a trap.

Heroine power is in essence what film stars are offered, and it is all that they get. On rare occasions, the rare woman either translates this, or is translated, into real power, where the big boys are. The remarkable Shirley Temple Black recovered from her mother's determination that she should be a star, outgrew too a film career which pegged her at a level indicated by the titles of her famous films, *Curly Top, Dimples, Wee Willie Winkie* and *Rebecca of Sunnybrook Farm,* to begin a new career in politics, serving as US ambassador to Ghana among other things. Princess Grace of Monaco became the first woman on the board of Twentieth-Century Fox, something she was very

196

proud of. But in general, not only do female stars fail to move forward or out to any other career, they do not even have control of the one they have.

The Issue of Control

The central issue of control, without which there is no power, is highlighted by the film career of Bette Davis. Perhaps because she saw herself as an actress rather than as a star, or as a person before either, Bette Davis found the strength of a horse and the stubbornness of a mule needed by any woman trying to fight the studio system of her day. Almost from the moment of her entry into the film business, she was engaged in a series of battles to try to establish her stature as a leading lady, and to escape being cast in supporting roles in thrillers and sentimental dramas which her contract obliged her to accept. Many actresses were reduced to misery and despair by this system, in which the decisions about their futures and careers were never taken on artistic grounds, and *never by them.*

But Bette Davis stood up against the big bosses, whose bossing and bullying raise the question of how women ever came to be the sex solely honoured with the description 'bossy'. She refused to accept the roles she was given, was suspended, and lost a ruinous court case. At a deeper level, however, she won. Her roles improved in quality, and her standing as a serious actress was assured. When in 1977 she became the first woman to win the American Film Institute's Life Achievement Award, it was as much in celebration of her enormously courageous stand on behalf of herself and all film actresses as in recognition of her film successes.

The Life Achievement Award also honoured Bette Davis as a great original, and as a survivor. Surviving as a woman at all is an original achievement in a business which has been notorious for treating all females on the Kleenex principle of use and disposal, or as indistinguishable and interchangeable sex objects ('Let's fill the screen with tits'). Others did not have Bette Davis's combination of insight, tenacity and bed-rock sense of self-worth. So Marilyn Monroe was adored as a 'love goddess' and worshipped as 'the Body Beautiful', but suffered from this with what a more sophisticated age sees as a 'first profile problem' – in Marilyn's case, being perceived originally as pure 'Body' made it ludicrous when she attempted to exercise her brain.

She was in fact so tightly constricted by her created persona of brainless sexiness that her efforts to establish any intellectual capacity were foredoomed from the start. Her attempts to build some professional credibility as an actress, to learn and to develop through her membership of the Actors' Studio, were greeted with derision – what did she need to learn to act for? Who needed acting? With a body like that, a film acts itself. Under this construction Marilyn's acting exercises, her voice coach, her desire to have more control over scripts and parts, could only be seen as sheer perversity on her part.

Marilyn Monroe became a problem to be resolved. This diagnosis then seemed to be confirmed by her increasing unreliability and instability, her legendary lateness and forgetfulness, her reliance on drugs. Marilyn Monroe's life story has been sensationalised as a bio-pic, pushed around as a parable of our times, and exploited for its martyr quotient as is the death of every female victim from Joan of Arc to WPC Yvonne Fletcher, victim of the shooting at the Libyan Embassy. In at least one of its variants it looks most like the story of a desperately confused and massively deprived woman seeking and being denied that level of control without which there is no life worth living.

> Control is what I'm after. Control is the whole kookie secret.
> Jane Fonda

The Real Thing

Nothing can make media work a safe area for women – it has never been safe for men. The individual who needs security and stability goes to work in a bank, rather than in television, films or journalism. No other occupation offers the chance of such spectacular and public failure; there is a medieval, wheel-of-fortune quality about such events as the 1983 sacking of the golden girls of TV-AM, Anna Ford and Angela Rippon. The previous success of these two women both as newscasters and as personalities was unprecedented – the fact that they were treated seriously as TV professionals is indicated by the fact that they were deemed weighty enough members of the 'Famous Five' to receive the franchise for breakfast TV from the Independent Broadcasting Authority against top-class competition. None of this saved them when early audience figures came in well below the point of viability. Their heads rolled in a public *dégringolade* that Angela Rippon described as 'heart-breaking'.

Yet even in this world some women today are achieving more power and control, and demonstrating the staying-power to hold on to it. The really good place for a woman to be in this context is on the bridge rather than at the mast-head, behind the camera rather than in front of it (unless you are the person who can do both, like Barbra Streisand). For women rising to high executive positions in the media industries, the promise of power is twofold: corporate power to control the machine, and creative power to initiate projects and to change things.

Of three top women in Britain's media industries, none had an easy or effortless beginning. Jo Sandilands, programme director for London's Capital Radio, was fired from her first job as a secretary because her boss's daughter was leaving school and didn't have a job. Andrea Wonfor is now Tyne Tees director of programmes, a board member and the highest-ranking woman in ITV. But despite a privileged start in television, as a production trainee for Granada, she left to get married and later became a house-mistress in a private school. And who would recognise in Verity Lambert, production director of Thorn-EMI Screen Entertainment, tagged by the press as 'Britain's only female movie mogul', 'the most high-powered woman in her profession', 'one of the most powerful women in the land' and 'Cinema Verity', the beginner who fouled up so copiously in her first secretarial job with Granada that she got the sack?

Like other high-achieving women, these three also avoid 'I am the great I am' behaviour. Jo Sandilands comments: 'I believe in myself but I don't have the kind of conviction that makes me feel I am exceptional. I'm good because I work hard, but there are times when I look at my career and feel a fraud. I think why me? Why not all those other able people out there?' Andrea Wonfor similarly refuses to take herself too seriously. As she

199

told reporter Chris Tighe, 'I have never had a view of myself as a career woman. I have always operated on the basis of enjoying yourself and what you do and trying to assess what you want out of life as you go.' At Thorn-EMI no visitor is going to mistake the striking and well-dressed Verity Lambert for anything except a Top Woman, but her manner is open, friendly and unpretentious. What counts for her, as she says, is the satisfaction of the creative input, with an accurate forecast of the key factors – in a word, 'control'.

Control, however, does not mean playing safe. All three women are, on their own admission, risk-takers in a risky business. Andrea Wonfor's innovatory music programme *The Tube*, transmitted for nearly two hours, live, with unknown presenters, was damned out of hand before it even went on the air by critics who all U-turned as to the manner born when it went on to win ecstatic audiences and a clutch of awards. The start of Jo Sandilands's reign at Capital was distinguished by a brisk batch of changes and the odd hatchet job; she said at the time that she had 'taken risks in order to inject excitement into the programmes, to make them sexy'. The risks are part of the business, and part of the risk is the possibility of an adverse reaction, either from individual fellow-professionals or from the public. Jo Sandilands found her early days at Capital 'pretty lonely to start with', and both Andrea Wonfor and Verity Lambert have known what it is to have programmes apparently born under a lucky star come unstuck through the mysterious failure of the anticipated reaction.

Success, however, is not about robotic consistency, but about being right more times than wrong. If there is a secret, it is the old friendly open secret of trusting your own judgement. Jo Sandilands says that she is ready to listen to anyone: 'I enjoy arguments and I don't mind being opposed. But ultimately the decisions have to be made by me and *I will follow my own belief.*' Verity Lambert supports this wholeheartedly: 'The two things I have always put great importance on are being true to my own instinct, and not allowing myself to be intimidated by people telling me they have done the job a lot longer than I have, and therefore I should do it their way.' The responsibility to yourself is part of the responsibility of power.

The question of power is one that these women, although

200

personally disinclined to grandiose pretensions, do not shirk. For Jo Sandilands, it is where the buck stops: 'Anything you hear coming out of that box which isn't a commercial is down to me. If there's credit going I can claim it, if there's abuse I can't disclaim it.' But that is part and parcel of taking 'a job of ultimate responsibility'. Andrea Wonfor is in agreement with this:' 'Power is only of any use if it results in some beneficial effects,' she says. 'If you judge that you wouldn't really use that power to its best advantage, there's no point in seeking it.' Power in the context of these women means power to initiate, to stimulate, to set the ball rolling; Jo Sandilands has a rule that no suggestion ever receives an outright immediate no, but at least gets its chance to see the light of day, while Verity Lambert nowadays has 'huge power in setting projects into motion'. But power is also interpreted in a personal context. 'You can put your interest and expertise into operation and get proved right, and that's good,' says Verity Lambert. 'That's the most genuinely satisfying thing, pushing yourself along and adding to yourself.'

Like other top women, Verity Lambert is very conscious of the people who work with and around her.

> One of the first things that you have to accept about power is that you control and influence the people's lives around you. You have to be careful. If you lose your temper, you lose it as the head of department. It is very frightening, and you don't want to frighten people. It reverberates because of your power, not of you.

In her position, power also means the chance to reflect and comment upon contemporary themes, and with that a chance to enrich the stock of media attitudes to women. 'I'm a feminist even though I'm not allied to a special group or spouting feminist dogma,' Verity says. 'I can't relate everything I do to women's role, but I do portray women honestly and properly. I'm very drawn towards portraying women as people, not stereotypes.' What she means is illustrated by one of the prize-winning series that she has been responsible for, *Widows*, in which four women sucessfully carried out the crime left unfinished by their dead husbands – a far cry from the mother/nurse/teacher/female cop gaggle of service roles to which women are usually restricted in media portrayals.

Woman at Work

The new-found power of women to initiate projects and develop
ideas that have never been possible before is by degrees eroding
the unquestioned and unthinking assumptions of the old-time
power-holders in the media industries, men. This is not an easy
task. As Marjorie Proops, doyenne of Fleet Street's women
columnists, has commented:

> Even now, when I'm an executive of my paper, I feel I am
> always the statutory woman. It is still a struggle to exert
> influence. To give a minor example, I could not persuade my
> editor to abandon the campaign somebody dreamed up to revive
> the mini-skirt. I keep hoping men will grow out of this sort of
> attitude, but it is an uphill struggle.

As Andrea Wonfor has drily observed, the real revolution will
come when a TV company has a female head of engineering.
Media work is in many ways more open and accessible to
women than the more traditional industries. But it is also a
prime hunting-ground for some of the most competitive males
ever to go for a jugular, and a natural home for the
twenty-four-year-old killer male with no O-levels or else a double
First. And since the media industries were self-invented in the
twentieth century and operate according to its slacker and more
accommodating *mores*, its denizens will not feel governed by the
old-style rules of gentlemanly behaviour that govern the conduct
of Shell Oil, say. So Jane Deknatel reports being harassed with
dinner invitations for ten nights running by a top man in
film-making in Hollywood, who finally said, 'To hell with all this
dinner business, what I really want is just to fuck you.' Her
refusal, she thinks, cost her not only the job she then had, but
any other chances where his writ had power to run.

Anecdotes like this confirm Hollywood's reputation as a place
where a friend is someone who stabs you in the front. In a recent
assessment of women's 'careers in movieland', Ellin Stein asked
how women break into the film industry, and answered, 'It's a
bit like getting to the South Pole: slowly, and with great

difficulty, battling occasional cold feet and relying on hints from those who got there first in the absence of reliable maps.' Three things are essential for the climb to the top, Stein says: patience, persistence, and especially contacts. Tenacity, not talent, is the order of the day, as ambitious women are caught in a classic Catch 22 situation. Martha Coolidge, one of the few women feature film directors, explains: 'The director is the captain of the ship, where the buck stops. Women don't fit the role as that kind of authority figure. You can't expect producers to take you on faith. You have to have something to show.' But a woman cannot get anything to show, because none of the money men will put cash up front on an unknown quantity. Coolidge established her credibility over a long and often arid haul through self-financed, independent and marginal work. Only in 1984, hired by Paramount to direct *Joy of Sex*, could she say: 'It's my first studio picture, my first union picture, and my first picture as a member of the Directors' Guild of America. It's taken me eighteen years to get where I wanted to be.'

Despite the success of a handful of women like Sheree Lansing, much the same reasons operate to hold back women on the executive side of movie-making. 'There are shortcuts,' says Ellin Stein. 'A good one is having a father, mother or siblings in influential positions. Or you can buy the rights to a property, thus becoming the executive producer.' Every studio is a boys' club, according to one senior woman vice-president for creative development, so 'bright girls' need all the speed they can muster to run with the 'boys': 'Film school helps. A Harvard MBA really helps. It still helps to be someone's girlfriend. But you don't need creativity as much as chutzpah.' But there is still a very long road ahead: 'Some women got to be figureheads in studios, but few have as much power as their male counterparts.' This is not such bad news for women as it sounds, since the studio system is now as dead as the despots and dodos who created it. Her advice is, go independent or go it alone.

This industry is more lenient and less conservative than other industries, perhaps, but money is power, and power is not easily given up.

Mary Ledding, vice-president for business affairs
at MGM and president of the Los Angeles branch of
Women in Film

Like Jane Deknatel, other women have wearied of waiting for men to give away any of the top territory, and have struck out for their own patch. Audrey Slaughter is unique in having created two major British magazines by identifying areas of the market that were not being served and bringing her own flair and determination to fill the gap. Audrey's experience of the terrors and the rewards of holding the position of ultimate responsibility goes back to the time when as editor of *Honey*, the youngest editor of a national magazine, she turned it around from a circulation of 98,000 and falling, to a figure of almost a quarter of a million.

Audrey worked the same magic on the first of her own magazines, *Over 21*. For this shoestring production she received the professional tribute of the 1973 Magazine Editor of the Year Award, and the equally gratifying commercial accolade of 'selling it very quickly for a lot of money'. Now she has moved on to the launching of *Working Woman* to offer some kind of counterbalance to a press which can still burble in response to the appointment of a female industrialist HOUSEWIFE AND MOTHER OF THREE JOINS THE CBI. 'This one is my flowering,' Audrey says. 'This feels so good.' There can be nothing in this world to compare with the top job. To Audrey, 'editing is marvellous. You work with nice, interesting, creative people. Editing is freedom, control and power.'

As Audrey's career shows, to have the power you have to have the courage that goes with it. Few women, though, are put in the unenviable position of discovering if they have enough courage to change the course of history. That has been the extraordinary decision faced by the fortunately extraordinary Katharine Graham.

Katharine Graham has become both by inheritance and temperament the twentieth century's leading newspaper proprietor. The daughter of a banker and educated at Vassar and the University of Chicago, she was always encouraged to work at a career although her father was a millionaire who had bought up the *Washington Post* in 1933. Katharine worked as a reporter before marrying and having four children. She and her husband then bought the *Post* from her father, turned it into a successful newspaper and added *Newsweek* to the flourishing empire in 1961. When her husband died, Katharine took over as president of the company, and since 1973 has been chairman of the board, chief executive officer and publisher, a concentration of power unprecedented in the hands of a woman.

On one level, any woman is blessed by fortune who inherits such a legacy of power and the opportunities that go with it from both her father and her husband. On the other hand, any woman in this position has to work twice as hard and do twice as well to achieve respect and to live up to the departed greats. During her time at the helm Katharine Graham has substantially increased both the value and the prestige of her holdings. She controls paper mills, associated newspapers and TV companies, and her business is now a public corporation and one of Fortune's top 500 companies. Her financial acumen and commercial flair have made her widely admired throughout the business world.

Katharine Graham has, however, won even more admiration for the way in which she exercises her enormous power within the company. In a most marked contradistinction to the British press proprietor traditions (and in some cases current realities) of bad barons and moneygrubbing monomaniacs, Katharine Graham does not dictate editorial policy or use her newspapers for the purpose of personal aggrandisement. She believes in and is prepared to stand up for the freedom of the press. Her policy has been to hire the best people and then back them to the hilt, and she has frequently been praised for the responsibility she gives her editors, not to mention the high salaries.

Katharine Graham's courage in being prepared to live by her ideals, her even more unusual dedication to a precept expressed by her father that 'in the pursuit of truth, the newspaper shall be prepared to make sacrifices of its material fortunes', were put to the test in 1971. The decision of the *Post* to publish the Pentagon papers subjected Katharine Graham to political pressure and government sanction, with heavy legal fees involved in the company's defence of its right to publish. But this was not all. 'The expense of the legal fees was not the most notable of our risks,' she comments. 'We were in the process of going public but had not yet sold the stock, so we were in an especially vulnerable position. The real risk was the liability to the company.' In the event Katharine Graham's independence of mind was vindicated by the judgement in favour of the *Post* by the US Supreme Court. It was to be even more severely tried by the historic Watergate saga.

The story of Watergate illustrates the power of benign proprietorship at its height. Between 1972 and 1974 the *Post* chipped away at this complex of issues, evasions and deceptions, amid official obstruction on the one hand, and accusations of overplaying the story on the other. 'We kept the story alive while the administration was trying to hush it up and discredit and threaten us in a variety of ways,' Katharine Graham now says. The exposé involved a massive amount of checking and re-checking, over years of work, with the consequent costs in terms of reporters, money and time, to produce the 200 articles in all through which the events were finally brought out into the open. From being an insignificant and even boring story, Watergate eventually proved to be an episode with the unparalleled power to pull down a President of the United States. Katharine Graham's fearless strength and independence not only in backing her paper but in backing her own judgement has put her in that élite band of people who have been instrumental in changing the course of history.

Katharine Graham has recently addressed the subject of women and power in a speech given to the 1984 winners of the New York Women in Communication Matrix Awards. In preparation she interviewed several top women including Sandra Day O'Connor and Mary Wells Lawrence, and laid down some guidelines for women seeking such positions and the power that accompanies them. Many of the current proposals for improving women's career chances are, she feels, inadequate: 'Their flaw is that they require special accommodation to be granted by the existing, male élite.' As an essential part of obtaining power, women must get to grips with the whole concept and not be shy of its implications. 'The older generation of women I interviewed seemed to treat power like sex,' she said, 'something that should be participated in, but not discussed.' Women's willingness to share and to shake of this reluctance will be vital to their prospects of upwards movement in the future.

In facing the facts of power, women should also face up to the

206

negative connotations that it has held for women. 'Once power was a masculine attribute,' Katharine Graham commented. 'Mary Wells Lawrence said that when she rose to prominence, rumours circulated that she smoked cigars and swore like a trooper.' Enduring misunderstanding and misrepresentation are only part of the price that power-seeking demands:

> To get to the top women, like men, will simply have to put their careers and companies first for some part of their working lives. Their families and children may suffer to some degree, as may their friendships. I know mine have. But men in power have always been willing to pay this price.

In Katharine Graham's analysis, the keys to success are: a real love of your work, a workable career blueprint, the development of self-confidence, and a willingness to abandon the traditional female way of working as a detail-orientated perfectionist. With these things, there is no reason why women should not achieve as highly as men: 'Ambition and aggression are not masculine characteristics. Sensitivity and consensus-building are not female traits. Women must be willing to embrace all of these qualities – and use them – to gain power.'

Megapower

Of modern women who have followed a Graham-type formula for success, the most spectacular results have been achieved by a handful of Hollywood megastars. Women like Barbra Streisand, Meryl Streep, Goldie Hawn and Jane Fonda now achieve megastardom not because of their glamour and talent, but because they have made themselves mistresses of the machine that in the past would have made 'love goddesses' out of them.

They form in fact a new breed of media goddess, one who has her hand on the controls instead of tucked trustingly into the hairy paw of her leading man. The stunted careers and ruined lives of their predecessors, whose stories can all too often be summed up in Robyn Archer's phrase, 'A Star Is Torn', teach them not to entrust themselves to the studio bosses. Recent years have seen more and more film actresses trying to turn their cultural and commercial power into direct control, moving by degrees towards the sole artistic and financial management of their talents, their careers, their lives, their projects, their companies – their work.

Reaching for power is, in the first instance, seeking the critical control over yourself and the way you are seen. Jane Fonda's early career is a history of struggling to overcome the almost crippling legacy of the childhood trauma produced by her father's selfishness and indifference and her mother's breakdown and suicide. She wanted then not so much to make 'it' as to make somewhere, to touch base. 'Acting gave her the kind of applause she never got as a human being,' said Brooke Hayward, daughter of Henry Fonda's first wife and Jane's childhood friend. 'I've never seen ambition as naked as Jane's.' As a child Barbra Streisand too had writhed under the goad of other children calling her 'big beak', 'ant-eater' and 'hooky', a step-father who taunted her by dwelling on her plainness, and a mother who reacted to her dreams of being a star by enrolling her in typing school. As Barbra later commented: 'With my looks, I just had to be a star or nothing. I'm just too whatever I am to stay in the middle.'

The first task of Barbra's life work was to create a unity, an identity, out of her assortment of talents and distinctive appearance. At one glance she wasn't a conventional female 'juve', as the profession has it, or a romantic heroine – and that voice! 'I am an actress who sings,' Barbra announced, and stuck to that until it was accepted. Jane Fonda had to undertake the scarcely less daunting task of dismantling and remaking the assortment of identities and images within which she had been strait-jacketed, from the restrictively wholesome immaturity of 'Hank's little girl' to the vacuous, even sinister 'Barbarella' sex symbol created by Vadim.

Jane Fonda's attempts to remodel her previously acceptable image were only slightly less objectionable to the US public than her efforts to reform their political attitudes. Her emergence as a radical activist opposing the war in Vietnam during the 1970s not only earned her the rabid hatred of patriotic diehards – it seemed to shatter and desecrate the relationship between the public and their star. Branded as a 'Commie slut', 'traitor' and 'Hanoi Jane', she suffered a barrage of negative press reaction and a nosedive in popularity, illustrating the fragile nature of the 'heroine power' that she had previously enjoyed.

Yet by the end of 1976, a national poll once again showed Jane Fonda in the list of the ten most admired women in America. Since then, her various ventures, particularly in the exercise field, have consolidated her status and won her new fans. Now she takes the courses she wishes to pursue, makes the films she wants to make, has control of her life personally and professionally. After the frenzied years of casting around, she has taken hold. It has been a long haul. But possibly that is the secret of her continuing appeal. As she has said, 'People root for a survivor who sticks her neck out. Maybe I represent someone who fights back and doesn't stop and still survives.' Maybe too she has finally educated both her public and herself to take her as an adult woman, not a 'man-junkie' or kewpie doll, through being able, finally, to live her discovery that 'control is the whole issue'.

The issue of control has been one of legendary significance in the career of Barbra Streisand. At the start of her career she had refused to make the usual rounds, hustling herself to the theatrical agencies, because 'people had the power to treat you like animals'. Her earliest contracts had as much artistic control built into them as she could possibly get away with. As a performer her involvement with all aspects of the production in which she appeared was so total as to cause Walter Matthau to say of her acting in *Funny Girl* that it was 'not bad, considering it was the first film she ever directed'. Resistance by co-workers to her perfectionism ('I love detail; it's the difference between right and wrong. That's why I'm called difficult') finally led her to take over artistic as well as production control on her films.

Nothing so clearly catches up the twin issues of power and control as the making of *Yentl*. In Barbra's own account:

I never felt really discriminated against as a woman, as a singer, as an actress. It was only when I started to produce movies that I received flak, and now directing, too. It's funny, men can do these things, be polymaths, and they're admired for it. Warren Beatty did it in *Reds*. Woody Allen does it. Charlie Chaplin did it. And Orson Welles. Nobody says it's too much for them, that they're over-reaching. But when *I* do it ...

209

Despite Streisand's famed 'bankability', every major studio turned her project down before MGM finally agreed. Even then it was only under such stringent conditions that as she recalls, 'To make this movie I had to give up all my so-called power.' The studio had script approval, final say-so on actors and even on the final cut. 'And that's odd for me, because I've always controlled my work, down to the lettering on the covers of my albums.' Yet in the event, in the making of the film in which Barbra was producer, director, star, co-writer and solo singer of all nine songs, Barbra's power was total and totally unparalleled; no man has ever played so many roles on one film. 'I was frightened of so much power,' she has admitted, 'so I tried hard to appear unpowerful.'

Finally, for Barbra Streisand, power means the ability to say, 'In my work I have total control'. It means too something more. It means the challenge, the opportunity to stretch herself, to develop and to grow. She discovered that she relished the difficulty of raising the money to make the film as 'a wonderful shaker-upper', a chance to measure her power against the weight of resistance. She found in *Yentl* an irresistible metaphor for her own ambition to take on a role hitherto reserved for males, and so crack open the enclosed world of male knowledge and mastery. Against all opposition, against all odds, she did it.

Even before the successful completion of *Yentl*, Barbra Streisand had been accustomed to the kind of power that gave her total control over the direction, lighting, camerawork, writing, sets, even hairdressing, on all her shows. She had attained a pinnacle of professional eminence never before achieved by winning all the entertainment industry's major awards, a Tony for theatre, a Grammy for records, an Emmy for television and an Oscar for films – and all by the age of twenty-seven. Yet as she herself has said, 'Women now are only just beginning to assert themselves,' and in a very real sense *Yentl* is her first movie. It is impossible in these circumstances to resist the dry summary of her biographers Donald Zec and Anthony Fowles: 'Incredible though it may seem, the interim verdict on Barbra Streisand must be that given her talent, her will, her intelligence, her stamina, she is to date, like Woody Allen's God, an under-achiever.' If she can continue to use her power as she did in *Yentl*, this beginner may go far.

210

Someone else's words but my reason for doing *Yentl*: 'If I do not rouse my soul to higher things, who will rouse it?' – Maimonides. Best wishes, Barbra.

telegram to Rabbi Chaim Potok

CHAPTER 10

All Stars

Whatever name we give it, we shall always find in human beings this great line of activity – this struggle to rise from an inferior to a superior position, from defeat to victory, from below to above.

Alfred Adler

Power for most women remains as yet an imaginary garden in which only the toads are real. If I ruled the world ... While some women are pushing forward to explore all the dimensions of power, others are trapped in wish-fulfilment fantasies of the all-powerful woman like that created by Judith Krantz, where 'Scruples' is only the name over Billie Ikehorn's shop, and no brake upon her achieving her every desire. But many women now are making it in reality, not fiction. Why shouldn't you? So much talent is being lost to the world for the want of a little courage and cunning. How can you translate your latent energy into power?

It is vital that every woman should realise that this is a 'how can I?' not a 'should I?' issue. Women need to ask themselves all the key questions of power, like 'how much?', 'how soon?' and 'what would it mean for me?' But the fundamental election for every woman is simply for or against. Either you determine to move forward in a spirit of discovery and self-discovery, to maximise your own potency and personal skills, seeing how far the road will take you, or you condemn yourself to the half-life of birth-strangled hopes and unanswered needs that so many women live.

Many women do not make the election for power in their lives, either personal or professional. Even more do not grasp the fact that there is an election, and that by evading responsibility, dodging decisions and hiding behind others they are signing away their single most precious possession, power over their own lives. But the price of non-power is a terrible one, and no woman realises that she has paid it until too late. Then comes in the harvest of bitterness, rage and despair, possibly even marriage break-up or personal breakdown; for as Elinor Guggenheimer says, '*Nobody can live without some sense of power in their lives.*'

The price of powerlessness is fear and weakness, in even greater degree than that which holds women back from achieving their full potential in the first place. Part of the fear, perhaps the most crippling part, is of being so very ordinary and insignificant – who are you anyway and why should anyone bother? Meanwhile, women who have made it seem so achieved, so extraordinary, so exceptional in comparison. The myth of the exceptional woman has provided a very good excuse for men not to promote women. It has also, equally damagingly, provided an all-too-convenient evasion for women in the suggestion that it would be a waste of time to try for the top – they would not stand a chance because they are not 'exceptional'.

Women both look and become the exception not the norm when they rise to power. But none of them started out this way. They do not have a specific vision of 'my brilliant career', nor do they have the experience of soaring upwards unimpeded to dazzle the multitudes from on high. So far from being always out ahead of the others, often they are not even in step, but experience the sensation of being 'out of phase'. As round-the-world yachtswoman Clare Francis told reporter Penny Perrick, she had reached the age of twenty-six before she decided she had to '*do something*':

> At that age, most people are thinking of settling down and mortgages, but I was such a late developer that at heart I was only eighteen. Someone said to me that it was a shame I wasn't good enough to enter the single-handed race, so I thought right, that's it – I'll do it. Looking back, I wonder how I ever managed to.

213

Beset by the masculine notion of the steady upward spiral, women lose heart and decide that they have not got what it takes, or that they've missed the boat. But 'You don't have to go for a big career,' says Ambassador Jeane Kirkpatrick. 'Go for what you care for and can do well, and the rest will take care of itself.' It is important, too, for women to recognise and value the totality of their experience and skills, not defining too narrowly what they take to be the requirements of high achievement. The ambassador explains:

> Of all the roles that I have occupied that have been most relevant to my political role in government and my public role as chief of this mission, the most relevant has been that of mother. The problems most relevant were those in dealing with my sons, which could be contentious, complicated and difficult, often. Traditional women's roles have in normal contemporary families more power attached than is often recognised. The arena is different but the processes are the same in managing and persuading, cajoling, low-level intimidation. These skills are very similar to the exercise of bureaucratic power. A lot of women are equipped *right now* to move into public life!

Looking at an array of brilliant and high-achieving women can often raise the disheartening question of how they are so successful and inspirational. By the time they reach this point, however, there is little concentration upon their early beginnings, faltering approaches or wrong turnings. The glamour of the top job wipes out the approach to it – nobody now thinks of the elections Margaret Thatcher *lost*. But they managed it as every human being does, step by step. The point is, though, that they *took* each step and did not refuse any opportunity that came, but rose to the challenge and found themselves good. This then formed the basis of the necessary confidence and experience for the next step, and the next.

The women who achieve power and become personally powerful, in a related and interlocking process, are not geniuses, goddesses, or favoured in the cradle with a magic secret that was withheld from 'ordinary' females. They are not stronger by nature – they become strong by behaving as if they are. They do not know that they can succeed, but they believe that it is a possibility, and they are prepared to take the risks involved in

214

finding out. They know that more women fail through fear of trying than through overreaching. They know that you regret the things you don't do far more than the things you do. They know that you learn from your failure and mistakes, that nothing is wasted, and that getting power need not cut you off as a woman from everything you hold dear. But they do not know anything that you don't know. All that they have, and all you need, are a positive self-evaluation and strong sense of self-worth which can be realised as vision, purpose, application and forward drive. How does the individual woman achieve this realisation?

Working At It

Ambitious young people of both sexes are always piously advised to 'work hard' without being told how or why. The purpose of work is to make yourself good (or at least to look good), to turn yourself from a know-nothing to a learned-something, and to raise your abilities and usefulness notch by notch. Nobody ever gave a woman a job because she wanted it, but because they wanted her. You work to make yourself wantable. You also work to build up your ability to work, as athletes train to increase endurance. For nobody ever spells out quite how hard the people work at the top, and the very hard work *en route* is not only the qualification but the preparation for more of the same.

Many top women give accounts of the kind of work that any society for the protection of human beings would take action against. At one stage of her career Janet Mead worked from 8 a.m. to 6 p.m. translating telexes, then went on to an evening class from 7–9 p.m. five nights a week and Saturday mornings, to get her translating diploma. In her early days in business Anne Joy once turned out 10,000 hand-outs on a hand-cranked copier, and also worked in a couturier house modelling designer gowns to assist the cash flow: 'A couple of hours' twirling on a Friday afternoon would pay someone's salary.' Margaret Pereira studied for five years, four nights a week, while working full-time and travelling all over London to do it; the other evening students called her group 'the grey ghosts' because they looked so ill. Even this level of dedication is excelled by Judge Jean Graham Hall, who worked full-time in the day and kept up evening classes, first as a student and then as a lecturer, for thirteen years.

These hours, although heavy, are not beyond the capacity of most women. Ours indeed is the sex that although nominally 'the weaker', as long as that suited masculine convenience, has also always been stuck with the punishing formula, 'a woman's work is never done'. Those women today who are carrying the unfair double load of doing a full-time job, and then coming home to start on 'the other eight hours', are not working less hard than a top-flight professional woman committed to her job. Yet although shrill warnings are sounded by male power-holders of the dangers to women of taking on a top person's work load, no one ever worries about their desperately overloaded but unnoticed sisters in the 'working' class. There is all the difference in the world between such grinding labour and the varied, stimulating work enjoyed by women in positions of power, which clearly they thrive upon. Of the women surveyed for this study, 69 per cent had by choice less than seven hours sleep a night, and a high proportion managed on five or six.

But sleeping less and working harder is not the key to power for women, although we always used to believe that it was (this is the 'discovery myth': that if you do your work conscientiously and well, your boss will *notice* you). Women are now learning and applying what men have always known, that you have to work at your career as well as your work. Ground rules for women, however, are necessarily quite distinct from the boys' set, which begin, 'Join the Golf Club/Freemasons/Conservative Association', and may get even bluer, depending on where the good ol' boys hang out. How should 'the girls' do it?

If you are a woman ambitious for power, you must first grasp the terms and conditions on which it works before you can understand how it may be made to work for you. All power groups are enclosed and self-regulating élites dedicating a high proportion of their time and energy to resisting the encroachments of the out-groups. Women have been and remain the largest out-group in human society. The woman power-seeker must therefore acknowledge at the outset that women only ever achieve in-group status on three conditions:

(1) **They succeed in locating themselves within the pool of eligibles from which recruits to the élite are drawn.** This means at its simplest that, if you want to become a High Court judge, you have to be able to get into law school. The problems for women have been, first, the difficulty of getting into higher education on equal terms with men (a century has passed since the first woman doctor and accountant and we are still nowhere near equal numbers in recruits to those professions); second, the problem of discovering *where* the pool is and *how* recruits are recruited (how many women know how you get into the movie business? the EEC? the diplomatic service?). Certain professions, such as business or elected public office, have no clear or single method of entry. In all these cases, the strategy for women is to gain as much in the way of particular qualifications and of general experience as is humanly possible. Both work together to make up women's *lack of social capital*, which is the factor militating against us rather than any one specific deficiency.

(2) **They are not perceived as threatening to the power-holders, as a source of competition or as alternative to them.** A number of critical points here. Only weak men fear able women, says publisher Marion Boyars; but there seem to be a lot of both of these about. Women must realise that men are very easily threatened (or like to think they are), even those who should be safe and sound at the top of the tree. On a specific level, then, be very careful with the sexual signals. Don't go to one extreme and come on like a man; they have enough of those already, and it only confuses them. Don't go to the other extreme and come on like a hot number; they *don't* have enough of those, and it only confuses them. Find a comfortable middle path and concentrate on realising your potency via your total personality, not just your sexuality – that so often leads to the *cul-de-sack*, even for executive women.

More generally, it also makes good survival sense for women in what are still predominantly men's institutions to avoid blatantly competitive or alternative behaviour. Lynda Chalker, Minister of State for Transport in

217

Margaret Thatcher's government, sees such basic diplomacy as one of the key skills of power. 'You have to be very disciplined about not getting idiosyncratic,' she says. 'You have to carry people with you and remember no man is an island.' It is easy for women to make critical errors by pushing ahead regardless of others, and you are no use to yourself or anyone else out on a limb. Women also need to show sense and discretion in pursuing their own advancement, as Lynda Chalker explains:

> Women have got to be very careful not to set additional hurdles by being over-ambitious. You have to win on merits. Never expect anything to go your way, you have to win it. There's one woman in the House I remember who has put all the men's backs up. If you alienate all our male colleagues you're a liability to the rest of us. Have ambition by all means, but don't ram it down people's throats!

(3) **They suggest some positive gain for the élite in accepting them.** All too often the only positive gain that men can see in appointing or promoting a woman is that she will be able to supply the 'woman's touch'. This is the root cause of tokenism, since once they have filled this gap with 'their' woman, there is no need to have another. A woman therefore has to be able to offer something else, and more than a man would; this is why a woman has to be twice as well qualified as a man for a given job, because otherwise there would be no *positive* gain in taking her over an equal man. The strategy here is to develop and play up your separate and unique experience; work or study abroad, pursue an unusual specialism, master an unpopular work area. The 'positive extra' need not necessarily be of a professional nature – one female accountant owes her selection by a very good firm from a ruck of applicants to the fact that she had climbed the north face of the Eiger. None of the male accountants has ever done anything like that, and it makes a wonderful talking point when clients come in.

Along with an understanding of the theoretical structure and the strategies to handle it, women need to give attention to the

218

on-the-ground tactics of the work-place. The failure to play politics, the refusal either to see this aspect of working life or to accept its importance, accounts for women's lack of success more than any other single factor. As one very senior woman explained:

> Women get so involved with their work, they think, 'Oh, I can't play those games, I won't be bothered with that, I have to concentrate on my work.' But they don't realise that the politics are another important way of proving yourself in addition to work, and often actually *instead of it*. It's men's way of making things easier on themselves!

A woman can make it easier on herself, therefore, if she makes it her chief objective not only to work with, but *through* people, learning *how* those people work and *with whom*. A woman on the way up must learn how to perform on task, team and individual levels, knowing on each of those who are the key functionaries, and where to apply pressure at the point of leverage. But it won't all be onwards and upwards. Train yourself to be able to do, and to accept, disagreeable things. Work on your weaknesses. Women are often very bad at taking criticism *positively*, feeling so identified with their work that adverse comments are received as a judgement of total worthlessness. Orna Ni Chionna advises:

> Don't ever expect men in the work-place to treat you as if you were in a social setting. Remember that men kick each other on the shins in rugby, then go off for a drink together afterwards all pals. Women need to think as if they were on the hockey pitch – you don't expect anyone to be chivalrous to you there!

From the beginning a woman must be constantly training herself to behave towards men in a professional, not a personal and emotional mode. This causes difficulties in relation to men, who can be enough of a difficulty in themselves. Orna again:

> Ask yourself, how would I relate to him if he were a woman? Would I let a woman colleague push me around for fear of hurting her ego – or would I expect her to be constantly telling

my boss how terrific I am? Don't pussyfoot around worrying how to handle a man. *Treat him as if he were your sister!*

Relative Values

The men problem does not end for upwardly mobile women when they close their office door and go home. That in fact is where it begins. Of all the 'how to' handbooks giving advice to women on career management, few even recognise what one top woman called 'the biggy, the sixty-four thousand dollar question' of how you integrate a high-level job with a husband and children. Over the last ten or fifteen years women have been strongly encouraged to go all out for work fulfilment, for a 'proper' career, for the professions, for promotion. But no one has even begun to tackle the question of what happens to all that other work, both emotional and physical, that used to be women's full-time occupation before freedom was invented.

What no one has been brutal enough to spell out is that having a man in your life is *work*; having children, unimaginably *more* work. 'Problems increase for a businesswoman many times over just by getting married,' says Barbara Thomas, 'and they increase again when you have a baby. That changes the whole problem.' Add all this new work to your work-work, and no matter what plucky little creatures we women are, it is easy to suffer overload. What many successful women have grasped is that 'man' does not necessarily equal husband, nor does husband equal children. They take apart the apparently seamless web in which most women's lives are invisibly and irrevocably stitched up. They separate out the elements and take as much or as little at each stage as they need or can handle.

'A man should be fun to be with,' says Janet Mead, 'and from what I've seen, that isn't often the case with husbands. A relationship with a man should be just one aspect of life, not the fulcrum on which everything else has to pivot.' Other top women too agreed that what they did *not* need was a live-in lover or husband. On her own, a woman can create a living environment perfectly tailored to her needs; this can be awkward, when service engineers have to call at home in working hours, but no big deal. With a man in the frame, however, it somehow escalates into a *household*. Shopping, cooking, washing, cleaning all are doubled overnight and *men will not accept their share in or responsibility for this*. Research studies invariably show that males both underestimate the amount of domestic work and overestimate their contribution to it. One major 1984 survey by Gallup showed that women working full-time still perform 75 per cent of all household tasks, and that males reserve the right to do the clean and pleasant jobs rather than the boring or distasteful numbers like ironing or cleaning the lavatory.

Even when women achieve the level at which it makes sense, in terms of time and money, to pay someone else to do this work, they still find that it is 'their' job to organise it all. Running the home becomes another and not the least of their management responsibilities. One woman director was in the process of leaving the man she had been living with for eight years because of what she described as his 'you handle it' attitude. 'He wants me to be a five-figure woman *and* a housekeeper,' she commented bitterly. Another stressed the positive side of single life: 'I sometimes feel peeved that I haven't got a wife as men have, but then I think, I could have a husband!'

Having a family naturally increases enormously not only a woman's physical work, but her emotional work too. No matter how good she is, the nanny goes off at 5.30 p.m. and you are left holding the baby or walking the floor at 3 a.m. with a vital meeting next day. And children's demands change rather than recede as they get older. It is considerably more difficult and time-consuming to resolve with a teenager the mystery of life and the problem of their future than it is to comfort a toddler who has grazed her knee. Again, top women handle this one by eliminating or restricting motherhood. Remaining childless, or having one child only, keeps this part of their lives within manageable boundaries.

All this is not to say that ambitious women should not have lovers, husbands or children. That smacks of the punitive rhetoric of the past, when women were forced to trade off their womanhood and hopes of personal fulfilment for a chance in the 'man's world'. It is simply to state that the current ideology offered to women of 'having it all' can contain a recipe for self-sacrifice every bit as pernicious as the one that it has replaced. A woman simply cannot, in practice, go all out for top jobs on equal terms with men, and simultaneously run a husband, family and home by herself according to the traditional conventional pattern. This is a formula for martyrdom or madness. Something has to give, and it should not be you. *Having it all must not mean doing it all.*

What it means is that women are now in a position to make choices as never before; but choice equals responsibility. It is the responsibility of each woman to think very clearly and *in advance* how she sees her own life shaping up amid these conflicting demands. For they are in conflict, often nakedly so. One now-successful woman in London publishing described how her live-in lover had 'thrown a dying swan' at her, coming up with 'flu' on the weekend of a major conference, her first as a young executive. Plagued by guilt, she stayed home to look after him and 'lost all credibility there', so much so that she eventually had to go to a new job to regain it. For credibility is like virginity, as Robert Maxwell has remarked – you can only lose it once. Another woman who described herself as 'just on the cusp' of success declared that her current career strategy focused on one issue only, '*murder or divorce!*' So often the menfolk of rising young women are seen by them as 57 varieties of problem, rather than as a potential partner either in their career management or domestic work-load. It makes the only kind of sense for both your career and your life to anticipate this, and plan accordingly.

Make your personal election for lovers, husbands or children (how few/many, how soon/late) in the knowledge that limitation is not deprivation. The common assumption is that women who do not marry or have children are 'paying the price' for success in loss or self-denial. This is in part the grimly puritanical belief that fortune never comes with both hands full, that if you get anything good you have to pay for it. It is also related to the central myth of womanhood, that females can only find 'true' fulfilment through emotional relationships and motherhood in particular. But women who are privileged to experience professional fulfilment have a glow, a confidence and serenity that you may look for in vain on the face of a housewife or mother. 'I've had a very happy life, a very happy life,' said Judge

Jean Graham Hall, rosy with contentment. In the course of preparation for this book, I saw again and again on the faces of these women what Blake called 'the lineaments of gratified desire'. 'My work is the great love of my life,' said one classic high achiever. 'When a job really gets into your blood, it's hard to find a man who comes up to that.' 'The hand that rocks the cradle, rocks the cradle,' said another. '*Get out and rule the world.*'

> I ask no favours for my sex. All I ask is that men take their feet from off our necks.
>
> Sarah Grimke, US abolitionist and feminist

Working the System

Women desirous of ruling the world, or at least of giving it a try, have to work at it in the recognition that it is still a world top-heavy with men. Women's increased participation in the work force and rapidly rising share of its high honours has dented rather than destroyed the habit of male supremacy that has been with us for so long. Deep in the heart of the fortress the power-holders yielded the central citadel when they abandoned the concept that only males can rule. But it is nevertheless taking time for women to bring up troops in numbers, and meanwhile there are plenty of vigorous skirmishes still to be faced on the outer walls. As with the crucial question of the integration of private and professional life, women have to recognise that this is a strongly determining factor on their personal situation, and a main context within which they are constrained to work.

One problem for high-achieving women that is diminishing but by no means dead is that of isolation. While female incomers to all the professions have risen dramatically in the last five years, the top ranges are still manned by those who set out twenty, forty, fifty years ago with never a woman in sight. Any cursory breakdown of the available statistics in Britain makes this clear:

* in the civil service, of the 986 top jobs, only 13 are held by women.
* in the universities, only 15 per cent of all staffs are women;

only 3 per cent of university professors are women (9 per cent in America); and Britain does not have a single woman in a chief administrative post like that of vice-chancellor
* of bank managers, 97 per cent are men
* of company directors, only 2 in 10 are women
* in the law, of 100 Lords of Appeal, Judges in Chancery, Queen's Bench and Family Divisions, only 3 are female; of 333 circuit judges, only 10 are women
* on public bodies, women make up only 30 per cent of appointments at the highest, sinking to 3 per cent on bodies responsible to the Treasury
* in medicine, of 13,631 consultants, only 1632 are women; of 3235 senior registrars, only 756. Of the women consultants, a 1982 survey showed that only 15 per cent hold one of the lucrative 'merit' or 'distinction' awards, which was described by the pressure group Women in Medicine as 'an overt manifestation of the Old Boys' network which excludes women at every level in medicine'.

As this shows, the difficulties of women in rising to power are still connected, dominated even, by the fundamental difficulty of access. With the first women professionals, doctors, accountants, academics and entrepreneurs storming the barricades in the 1880s, women may well feel that a century of knocking at the doors is long enough for anyone. But the older a profession, the older its traditions of anti-feminism, and the longer and stronger its will to resistance. This has taken two forms, the simple opposition to women's entry via devices like quotas for women's entry to medical school, for instance, and the refusal to allow women membership of professional organisations. More complex, and more difficult to fight, is the strenuous symbolic rejection of women as power-holders. This has expressed itself as a heavy and continued stress on the 'negative' aspects (often mythical) of women's power-holding.

Perhaps the most powerful of the ideas which are put about to discourage women from power-seeking is the implication that to do so is to lose your 'femininity'. This is the ball-breaker 'bitch as goddess' myth, carrying the message that to succeed you have to be *tough*, and to be tough makes you unfeminine. Media hostility to women's achievement finds its vent worldwide in such matters as 'THE QUESTION-MARK OVER THE WOMANHOOD OF BILLIE JEAN KING', or the focus upon Mrs Gandhi as 'Kali', the goddess of death and destruction. High-achieving women even today are placed in the double-bind of having to live *up* to their personal, intellectual and professional abilities, and to live *down* the negative aspects of all these. The paranoid fantasy and terror tactic of stigmatising top woman as *vagina dentata* dies very hard, and if there's nothing as powerful as an idea whose time has come, there can be few things so tiresome as an idea whose time has gone but which *won't go*.

The fight is still on for women in other ways, too. As women claim their rights, including the right to power, the 'natural' pattern of dominance and subordination is giving way to an increase in the competitive mode. Men who take it for granted that they will compete with other men feel subtly outraged at having to compete with women. Patterns of male paternalism and voluntary subservience on women's part are fractured by the success of any one woman who does without the paternalistic protection/repression syndrome and volunteers herself out of inferiority. As women learn habits of power, including the desires to obtain, secure and enjoy it, male patterns of power will not necessarily change to accommodate this. They may simply go underground, become more covert and impenetrable, re-group and firm up, in fact. 'Remember that all men would be tyrants if they could,' wrote Abigail Adams. While it may be difficult to apply this to dear old John in finance, it is still advisable for every woman to bear in mind that the age-old struggle for women to be accepted as people, let alone as serious professionals, is still far from over, and that none of us as yet occupies a place of power *by right* in the eyes of the power-holders. Although the rare man has conceded gracefully, cheerfully and enthusiastically even, and a number have subsided into grumbling acquiescence, the tyrants and terrorists are still about. So walk carefully, and stay alert. There is a long road ahead before the dominant male will be genuinely ready to accept that a woman not only can be but *is* equal to him.

Men, their rights and nothing more. Women, their rights and nothing less.

Susan B. Anthony

As significant as the opposition of men may be to a woman's achievement, even more dangerous may be the obstructions inside your own head. Many women are still intensely uneasy with the experience of competition, hopelessly conflicted between feelings of crippling inferiority if they lose and paralysing guilt and empathy with the loser if they win. They fear to strike out ahead of other females and claim for themselves the right to personal success and the applause that goes with it. And research has shown that where men interpret the word 'risk' as meaning 'excitement' or 'adventure', women take it in the darker and more negative meaning of 'danger' or 'disaster'. Men see risk as a chance you take to secure some future gain; women see it as hazarding all that they have painfully won. Women who succeed do so by training themselves not only to accept risk, but to accept losing as simply one of the things that happens in a working life, rather than as a public confirmation of hopeless inadequacy. 'Learn to forgive yourself,' says Barbara Hosking.

Many top women identify women's own internalised sense of inferiority as a major block to their achievement. Elizabeth Crowther, director of social services for the City of London, explains:

> Going into social work, it never occurred to me that I didn't stand as good a chance as anyone else. Then, it was a woman's field. But at the top in local government you see it in a wider context and only at that stage was I conscious of being in a minority. Very few women aspire to or even apply for most senior positions. Women tend to be more conscientious. They are reluctant to take responsibility for difficult and demanding jobs and they are not satisfied with performing less well than they know is required.

Professor Marian Hicks agrees that women can be their own worst enemy:

> At the crucial stage in the late twenties and early thirties, when men are very focused, very ambitious and competitive, women suffer a fatal ambivalence. They think, 'Shall I take this job, it'll be very demanding, or go for something less?' and *at that point*

they are off the inside track and going into something less high-achieving.

These and other comments fully supported the rueful summary of US psychologist Morton Hunt: 'The mechanism of modern woman has many outmoded and archaic parts and runs haltingly towards its future. A major difficulty is woman's – and her employers' – poor opinion of her capacity.' If this is your situation, there is no substitute for a sustained overhaul and systematic replacement of all the 'archaic parts' that are holding you back. It is hard and painful work, and it takes a long time. But you have time. You have a whole lifeful ahead, and it can be done. Every woman her own Svengali!

The Promised Land

Those women who have successfully made the journey, both personal and professional, to the top, are in no doubt that it has all been worth it. Certainly to one who has been exploring and observing the achievements of these women on both sides of the Atlantic, the rewards are obvious. These are not merely the luxurious offices, the company cars or chauffeur-driven limousines, the expense account dinners and amiable well-trained assistants, although these are very pleasurable in themselves. It is rather that at this level of comfort and care, relieved of the mundane tasks that take up so much time and energy, women are freed to focus entirely on their work, and to give it their best endeavours. Again and again, their enthusiasm and commitment were a reminder that the work is the reward, not material manifestations of success.

Work is dignity, said Scott Fitzgerald. This is clearly borne out not only by the tremendous personal authority of these women, but also by a number of research studies. Barnett and Baruch for instance, showed in a 1979 study that working increases a woman's sense of well-being, and the higher the work, the greater the level of confidence, competence and control. Certainly on the evidence of the women in this study, high achievement is very good for you. All are in their different ways extremely attractive, with that compelling blend of radiant vitality and the security of fulfilment. They enjoy their lives, and they enjoy the charismatic buzz produced by the nexus of fame, success, money and fun that is power. Then, too, there is more room at the top to be gracious and generous, as they frequently are in both their private and professional lives, involved with charity work, fund-raising organisations, or over and over again, the countless nameless acts of kindness and assistance to others, especially other women; for them, power most often seems to mean the power to reward others, not yourself.

When a woman gets such a rewarding job, she does not simply make a good living, but a good life. For in that world, you can keep good company. Instead of sitting around bewailing your failure with a bunch of depressives, or looking in a mirror counting grey hairs or spots, they mix with others as interesting as they are, and as interested. Whether they are jetting off to Australia or Abu Dhabi, or furiously sewing up a deal on the short-haul hop between New York and Washington, they touch down anywhere into the freemasonry of the select group who know and care about the same things as they do. 'And that's fun,' says Jane Deknatel, who has now joined the élite club of those who fly so often, so far, that they finally get VIP status, and flights for free. 'I *like* bankers,' concluded Barbara Thomas. 'I like lawyers and bankers and businessmen. And I don't have the ladies withdraw after dinner in my house either!'

As the careers of these two women show, women are getting there, reaching the promised land at last, instead of being left out in the desert with the camels. The achievement is not solely in the ascent of individuals, heartening though that is. The success is rather to have got this whole question firmly onto every agenda. Power for women is now a topic in banks and business corporations, in government institutions, schools and colleges, even in choirs and places where they sing. By precept and action women worldwide are electing themselves to be members of the governing bodies of the human race, in open rejection of the hallowed female role of the supportive non-élite. Few now can claim to be ignorant or unaware of women's historic exclusion from the world of work and achievement; many are expecting the long-overdue redress. 'I am a feminist, I must be,' said Dame Josephine Barnes. 'Women who want a career should have the opportunity to achieve one.'

A sense of things changing, of dams bursting and the river of female talent at last being allowed to flow unchecked is passing between women today as a sense of strong excitement. While still soberly aware that it will take time before the river becomes a torrent and the torrent meets the sea, they are so strongly encouraged by recent developments as to look ahead with the highest hopes. 'The prospects for women are dazzling,' says Donna Shalala. 'It's limitless. We shall have a woman running for President of the US in 1988.' Judith Hope agrees: 'Women now are coming into their own in every field. We can have an unlimited horizon!' Many comments from British women also hail the rising of the sort of dawn that it is bliss to be alive in, when to be young in power, as all women are, is very heaven. 'You can do anything if you really want to!' is Barbara Hosking's view, and Jean Denton concurs: 'There's nothing now that you can't do if you want to do it. If the doors don't open, we aren't kicking hard enough. Go on, keep at it – do it!'

Do It

Do it, and you may become president of a multinational corporation. Do it, and you may not. But do it anyway. Women now have it within their power not simply to move forward as individuals, but to bring to government, business and industry a set of experiences and perspectives totally different from those which at present control them. In the classic analysis of the economist Pareto, men rule as lions or foxes, some choosing to dominate by force, others by cunning; but power, to all of them, is a relationship in which somebody has to *lose*. With their vastly superior affiliative skills, women can bring to these cold and echoing corridors their skills of power-sharing, and make them work.

Women will not be able to do this alone. The positive contribution of men is vital. Referring to 'the sustained effort to achieve equality of treatment for women in which we are all engaged', Dr Patrick Hillery, vice-president of the EEC, made these demands as long ago as 1976: 'An increasing male commitment to our work is essential. Although it is male attitudes that are most in need of change, today's reality is that men control the means of change.' Or as Andrea Wonfor has observed, 'It's a matter of women being brave enough to grasp opportunities, but also of men being courageous enough to offer those opportunities.' A strong appeal can be made to men on the lines of enlightened self-interest. All men will benefit from the diversification and humanisation of the work-place that will follow with the increasing numbers of women entrants. But willy-nilly, the demand has gone out: 'The second stage has to transcend the battle for equal power in institutions. The second stage will restructure institutions and transform the nature of power itself.' Or to rephrase this prophecy of Betty Friedan in human and personal terms: here are the new women – *where are the new men*?

Finally, however, every woman must do it for herself. In its ultimate reduction, power, *pouvoir, potentia*, in any language, is *what you are able to do*. In that sense, no one exerts their power to the full. The sad, unspoken lives of so many women, whose only history is a blank, testify with particular poignance to this litany of underachievement. By contrast happiness, as John F. Kennedy was fond of saying in paraphrase of Aristotle, is the full use of individual faculties along lines of excellence. Neither of them ever said that only men could play.

Many women do not seek and would not wish to have great power with its corollaries of public accountability and responsibility. But look around – who is already running your local social service, PTA, Citizens' Advice Bureau or Law Centre? She is likely to be what we all think of as an ordinary woman. Think too of the increasing numbers of very powerful women who choose to remain invisible and not to become household names. They too are ordinary women, only more so, and they are all out there to help any woman who wants to join them.

No woman knows her power until she tries the extent of it. And this, as Ambassador Kirkpatrick said of her UN post, is 'too important a job not to do'. After all the high achievements of today's top women have been given their due, the ultimate model remains the almost unknown Rosa Parks, who, as a poor black woman going home laden with shopping just before Christmas in 1955, refused to give up her seat and go to the back of the bus when ordered to do so by a white man. Her action sparked the wave of civil rights reforms and caused Martin Luther King to say, 'A miracle has taken place'. That miracle takes place again every time a woman becomes herself, exercising her personal potency to become a positive force. The prize of being and believing in yourself is the fulfilment of emotional, intellectual and human potential. All women are implicitly women of power. Today's top female leaders are pioneering on behalf of us all, leading the way forward to a future in which all women will more and more claim not only their rights, but their own souls.

Only power can place people in a position where they may be noble.

Alfred Kazin

Acknowledgements

My thanks are due to the following for their help in the writing of this book:

Leslie Abdela
Founder
The 300 Group
London

Mary Baker MA
Former Chairman, London Tourist Board
Director, Thames Television
Director, Barclays Bank UK Ltd
London

Dame Josephine Barnes DBE, DM, FRCOG
Former President
British Medical Association
London

Olive Barnett OBE
Head of Training
The Savoy Group
London

Dr John Bland
Chairman
Warwickshire County Council
Warwick

Carmen Callil
Managing Director
Chatto & Windus Ltd
London

Barbara Cannon BSc, FCCA
Director
The Jordan Group
London

Mary Lou Carrington BSc, MBA
Associate Director
First Chicago International Capital Markets Group
London

Lynda Chalker MP
Minister of State for Transport
London

Chief Executive Magazine
London

Orna Ni Chionna BE, M Eng Sc, MBA
Management Consultant
McKinsey and Co Inc.
London

Jennifer Coutts Clay BA, MA, LTCL, MCIT, M Inst Dir
Controller, Corporate Identity
British Airways
London

Julia Cleverdon MA (Cantab)
Director of Education
The Industrial Society
London

Ann Clwyd MP
Cynon Valley
Wales

Mike Colley
North Warwickshire Area Health Authority
Nuneaton

Elizabeth Crowther MA, Dip Soc Sci, AAPSW
Director of Social Services
City of London

Jill Currie
Commercial Director
Bass Mitchells and Butlers Ltd
Birmingham

Judith Davenport
Financial Director
Channel Foods Ltd
Cornwall

Jane Deknatel
Film Producer
Film Partners International
Los Angeles

Jean Denton BSc (Econ), FIMI, F Inst Mktg
Managing Director, Herondrive
Governor, The London School of Economics
Vice-President, NOWME
Secretary/Treasurer, Marketing Group of Great Britain

Mr Dimant
The Cabinet Office Library
Management and Personnel Office
The Civil Service
London

Mme Tinou Dutry
President
Les Femmes Chefs D'Entreprises Mondiales
Brussels

Jack Eldridge
The Office of Population, Censuses and Surveys
Government Statistical Service
London

The Information Service
The Equal Opportunities Commission
Manchester

Katherine Graham
Chairman, the Washington Post Company
Washington DC

Elinor Guggenheimer BA
President and Executive Director
Child Care Action Campaign
New York

Her Honour Judge Jean Graham Hall LLM
London

Dr Leah Hertz LLB, PhD, FBIM
Lecturer in Business Studies
London

Stephanie von Hirschberg
Doubleday and Company
New York

Judith Hope JD
Attorney-at-Law
Washington DC

Barbara Hosking
Controller of Information Services
Independent Broadcasting Authority
London

Suzanne Hunter B Eng, MSc
Engineering and Production Manager
British Oxygen Special Gases
London

Margery Hurst
Founder and Chairman
The Brook Street Bureau
London

Anne Joy
Managing Director
Challoners Ltd Recruitment Consultants
London

Nicky Joyce
President, British Association of Women Executives
Secretary-General, Les Femmes Chefs D'Entreprises Mondiales
London

Petra Kelly
Member of Bundestag
Founder and spokeswoman of Die Grünen
Bonn

David Kidner LLB
Secretary to the Magistrates' Association
Clerk to the Justices
City of Coventry

Dr Jeane Kirkpatrick
US Ambassador to the United Nations
New York

Verity Lambert
Production Director
Thorn EMI Screen Entertainment
London

Faith Leigh F Inst D, M Inst SP, M Inst M, M Inst Mktg M (Hon)
Secretary-General
Institute of Sales Promotion
London

Gill Lewis BA (Oxon)
Director and part-owner
Fisher Dillistone and Associates Ltd
London

Dr Anna Mann
Managing Director
Whitehead Mann Executive Search
London

Helen Matthews BSc, MBA
Investment Banker
City of London

Janet Mead Dip D'Etudes Francaises, Alliance Francaise Translators'
    Diploma, Dip Cam PR, Advertising and Marketing
Managing Director
Associated Research Ltd
London

Debbie Moore
Chairman and Managing Director
Pineapple Dance Studios
London

Mary Moore MA (Oxon)
Principal, St Hilda's College
Oxford

Anne Mueller CB, MA (Oxon)
Second Permanent Secretary
Cabinet Office
Management and Personnel Office
The Civil Service
London

Sheila Needham
Founder and Managing Director
Needham Printers Ltd
London

Alison Newell
Managing Director, F International
President, Computing Services Association
London

Detta O'Cathain OBE, BA
Director and General Manager
Milk Marketing Board
London

Judge Sandra Day O'Connor
Justice of the Supreme Court of the USA
Washington DC

Margaret Pereira BSc, FI Biol
Controller of Forensic Science Services
Home Office
London

Lady Porter
Leader, Westminster City Council
London

Rasty Rasmussen
Australian Information Service
London

Nancy Clark Reynolds
President
Wexler, Reynolds, Harrison and Schule Inc.
Washington DC

Joan Ruddock
Chairman
Campaign for Nuclear Disarmament
London

Jo Sandilands
Programme Director
Capital Radio
London

Donna E. Shalala
President
Hunter College
City University of New York
New York

Audrey Slaughter
Editor
Working Woman
London

Patricia B. Soliman
Associate Publisher and Vice-President
Simon and Schuster Inc.
New York

The Lady Taylor of Hadfield
Director
Taylor Woodrow PLC
London

Barbara S. Thomas BA *cum laude, JD cum laude*
Former Commissioner, Securities and Exchange Commission of the USA
Executive Director, Samuel Montagu Ltd
President, Samuel Montagu Holdings
London

Sian Vickers
Creative Director
Young & Rubican
London

Julia M. Walsh BBA
Chairman, Julia Walsh and Sons Inc.
Managing Director, Tucker, Anthony and R.L. Day Inc.
Washington DC

Baroness Warnock
Chairman, Warnock Committee
Mistress of Girton College
Cambridge

Anne Wexler
Chairman
Wexler, Reynolds, Harrison and Schule Inc.
Washington DC

Dr Richard Whittington
HM Coroner for the District of Birmingham
West Midlands

Elizabeth Willis BA
Head of the Pepperell Unit
The Industrial Society
London

Andrea Wonfor BA (Cantab)
Director of Programmes
Tyne Tees Television
Newcastle-upon-Tyne

The Right Hon. the Baroness Young
Minister of State in the Foreign and Commonwealth Office
Deputy to the Foreign Secretary
London

References

Almquist, E.M. and Angrist, S.S., 'Career salience and atypicality of occupational choice among college women', *Journal of Marriage and the Family* (1970), 32, 242-9

—, 'Role model influences on college women's career aspirations', *Merrill-Palmer Quarterly* (1971), 17, 263-79

Barnett, R.C. and Baruch, G., 'Career competence and well-being of adult women', *in* B. Gutek (ed), *New Directions for Education, Work and Careers: enhancing women's career development* (Jossey-Bass, San Francisco, 1979)

Baruch, G.K., 'Maternal influences upon college women's attitudes towards women and work', *Developmental Psychology* (1972), 6, 1, 32-7

Baruch, R., 'The achievement motivation in women: implications for career development', *Journal of Personality and Social Psychology* (1967), 5, 260-7

Carter, Rosalynn, *First Lady From Plains* (Houghton Mifflin, Boston, 1984)

Cunningham, Mary, *Powerplay: what really happened at Bendix* (Simon and Schuster, New York, 1984)

Deaux, K., *The Behavior of Women and Men* (Brooks/Cole, Monterey, California, 1976)

Friedan, Betty, *It Changed My Life* (Victor Gollancz, London, 1977)

—, *The Second Stage* (Michael Joseph, London, 1982)

Gould, Lois, 'Who is Eva Peron and why has she come back singing?', *MS* magazine, September 1979

Harragan, Betty Lee, *Games Mother Never Taught You* (Rawson Associates, New York, 1977)

Hitchfield, Elizabeth, *In Search of Promise* (Longmans, London, 1973)

Hurst, Margery, *No Glass Slipper* (Arlington Books, London, 1967)

Kanter, R.M., *Men and Women of the Corporation* (Basic Books, New York, 1977)

Kanter, R.M., 'Some effects of proportions and group life: skewed sex ratios and responses to token women', *American Journal of Sociology* (1977), 82, 5, 965-990

Lainson, Suzanne, *The Instant MBA* (Putnam, New York, 1985)

McGregor, Douglas, *The Professional Manager* (McGraw Hill, New York, 1967)

Margach, J., *The Anatomy of Power* (W.H. Allen, London, 1979)

Roosevelt, Eleanor, *On My Own* (Hutchinson, London, 1959)

Sampson, A., *The Changing Anatomy of Britain* (Hodder and Stoughton, London, 1982)

Stanworth, M., *Gender and Schooling* (Hutchinson, London, 1983)

Tangri, S., 'Determinants of occupational role innovation among college women', *Journal of Social Issues* (1972), 28, 177-99

Terman, L.M. and Oden, M.H., Genetic Studies of Genius: V: *The Gifted Groups at Mid-Life: 35 Years' Follow-Up of the Superior Child* (Stanford University Press, Stanford, California, 1959)

Tiger, L., *Men in Groups* (Random House, New York, 1972)

White, Martha S., 'Psychological and social barriers to women in science', *Science*, October 23, 1970, p. 414

Wilson, Harold, *The Governance of Britain* (Weidenfeld and Nicholson, London, 1976)